CIVILISING GLOBALISATION
Human rights and the global economy

CIVILISING GLOBALISATION

Human rights and the global economy

DAVID KINLEY

CAMBRIDGE
UNIVERSITY PRESS

ahsoc

WISSER MEMORIAL LIBRARY

JC 571
.K534
2009
c. 1

CAMBRIDGE UNIVERSITY PRESS

Cambridge, New York, Melbourne, Madrid, Cape Town, Singapore, São Paulo,
Delhi, Dubai, Tokyo

Cambridge University Press
The Edinburgh Building, Cambridge CB2 8RU, UK

Published in the United States of America by Cambridge University Press, New York

www.cambridge.org
Information on this title: www.cambridge.org/9780521716246

© David Kinley 2009

This publication is in copyright. Subject to statutory exception
and to the provisions of relevant collective licensing agreements,
no reproduction of any part may take place without
the written permission of Cambridge University Press.

First published 2009
Reprinted 2010

Printed in the United Kingdom at the University Press, Cambridge

A catalogue record for this publication is available from the British Library

Library of Congress Cataloguing in Publication data
Kinley, David, lecturer in law.
Civilising globalisation : human rights and the global economy / David Kinley.
p.   cm.
Includes index.
ISBN 978-0-521-88781-6 (alk. paper)
1. Human rights.   2. Human rights – Economic aspects.   3. International economic
relations – Social aspects.   4. International trade – Social aspects.   5. Globalization – Economic
aspects.   6. Globalization – Social aspects.   I. Title.
JC571.K534   2009
323 – dc22   2009015014

ISBN 978-0-521-88781-6 hardback
ISBN 978-0-521-71624-6 paperback

Cambridge University Press has no responsibility for the persistence or
accuracy of URLs for external or third-party internet websites referred to
in this publication, and does not guarantee that any content on such
websites is, or will remain, accurate or appropriate.

For
Finn, Jacques and Louis,
whose civilisation we await.

CONTENTS

ILLUSTRATIONS

x

PREFACE

A plethora of influences, inspirations, experiences and encounters prompted me to write this book. But if I was to nominate the seminal moment in its evolution, then it would have to be one morning in the middle of September 2003, when I met with a senior economist in his office at the World Bank on H Street in Washington DC to talk about the place of human rights within the work of the Bank. I was doing some preliminary research for a Senior Fulbright Scholarship project that I was to take up in 2004 on that same subject. My host was and is a highly respected economist and strategic thinker both inside and outside the Bank. He was most hospitable, not least for honouring the meeting in the first place given the deluge of work that was pouring into his in-tray following the collapse of the Cancún ministerial trade talks barely twenty-four hours earlier. I enjoyed the encounter and I learnt a lot. During the meeting he said one thing in particular that struck me then and stayed with me thereafter. We were discussing the nature of human rights, and from that building a picture of what impact Bank operations had on them, and they on the Bank. We agreed that the Bank's impact on matters of people's economic and social welfare was profound, as indeed one would expect given the Bank's goals to alleviate poverty and bolster standards of living. However, its impact on people's and governments' civil and political circumstances was, at least in terms of direct action, much less significant (though not immaterial). My host believed that only the latter category of issues constituted the proper concern of human rights, and the former did not. Desirable though the advancement of people's economic and social circumstances clearly may be, these were policy goals, in his view, not enforceable obligations. As such, the answer to the question of the Bank's impact on human rights was that it was minimal, and did not and should not therefore bear significantly on the strategic thinking and operations of the Bank.

This is not an uncommon line of argument in debates over the ontology of human rights more generally. However, within the context of its delivery, it crystallised for me the idea that there are today two major, and often competing, globalising forces that strut the global stage. These are the universalisation of human rights on the one hand, and economic globalisation on the other. While it may be said that they occupy the same global space, they often appear to conduct their affairs separately, and when they do intersect it is more usually in collision rather than collusion. This is an impression that has been reiterated for me over the years in dealings with those from both sides of the debate, be they corporations, human rights activists, governments, academics, students, or officials from international organisations. In fact, an early working title for this book was 'Two Globalisations'. But as my research and thinking developed, I understood that it was in fact too simple a representation of the whole scene. Certainly, it is an important point to make in order to appreciate the history and sentiments of the two fields that persist even today, but as a depiction of the totality of interrelations between the global economy and human rights the title was incomplete. Across the board, the intersections are numerous, subtle and inexorable, and as such I plumped for 'Civilising Globalisation' for the book's title, with its connotations of globalisation being both a civilising force and a force that must be civilised. This *double entendre* constitutes the book's abiding theme. It also reflects the positioning of the book within the broader imperative of needing to curb capitalism's excesses, so graphically illustrated by the monumental interventions being made by governments in the global capital markets at the time I write these words in late 2008, and the mounting calls for the tightening of the regulatory frameworks within which financial institutions operate.

ACKNOWLEDGEMENTS

This book has been rolling around in my head for nearly ten years. Emanations of its thesis have made appearances in other books, articles, reports, talks, conference papers and seven years of university courses and workshops in Australia, the United States, Europe and South East Asia. The research upon which it is based has been enabled by two grants from the Australian Research Council (one covering corporations and human rights, and the other covering trade and human rights) and one from the US Fulbright Commission (for work on the human rights dimensions of World Bank and IMF operations). My coalface experiences of human rights and the global economy in action have mainly come through work undertaken with AusAID, the United Nation's Office of the High Commissioner for Human Rights, the World Bank, and a number of transnational corporations and law firms, as well as state and non-state agencies in and from developing countries, including China, Indonesia, Iraq, Laos, Myanmar, Nepal, South Africa and Vietnam.

I have benefited enormously from many discussions with numerous officials, from national governments, international organisations (such as those institutions mentioned above, as well as the Asian Development Bank, the European Commission, the UN Development Fund, the UN Children's Fund (UNICEF), the UN Conference on Trade and Development, and various UN human rights treaty bodies, special rapporteurs and special representatives), international non-governmental organisations (especially Amnesty International, Human Rights Watch, Oxfam, World Vision, Human Rights First, the International Commission of Jurists and the Human Rights Council of Australia), and transnational corporations, in both the northern and southern hemispheres. Scores of colleagues, students, friends, family and foes have commented on, criticised or concurred with my ideas, logic and delivery, and to them I owe a debt of which they are as unaware as it is great.

Of particular note are those kind and thoughtful souls who undertook not only to read various drafts, but also to allow me to profit from their many and various comments – namely, Philip Alston, Chris Avery, Lorand Bartels, Ross Buckley, Karin Buhmann, Tom Campbell, Mac Darrow, Tom Davis, Brice Dickson, David Feldman, Conor Gearty, Catherine Giraud-Kinley, Andrew Lang, Verity Lomax, Siobhan McInerney-Lankford, Sabine Michalowski, Gig Moon, Justine Nolan, John Pace, Annika Rosenblatt, John Ruggie, Hélène Ruiz Fabri, Jeffrey Sachs, Ben Saul, Andrea Shemberg, Chris Sidoti and Sune Thorsen. Though, privately, each of them knows how much I appreciate their contributions, let me here register the fact publicly.

I am also very grateful to the staff at Cambridge University Press for their efforts in bringing the book into existence, and especially Frances Brown, Daniel Dunlavey and Richard Woodham for their careful editorial ministrations, and Finola O'Sullivan for her support of the idea of the book from the outset.

Finally, special thanks are due to Nikki Goldstein, who read the manuscript in full and who was unfailingly supportive in her comments and generous in her counsel; and to Odette Murray, who assisted enormously in tracking down source materials, acting as a sounding-board for ideas, and subjecting the text to an eagle-eyed edit. To both of them I am profoundly grateful.

The writing of the book was almost wholly undertaken between January and September 2008, with emendations and updates made in the five months thereafter. It was a peripatetic affair, starting and ending in Sydney, with significant encampments in between, in England (Cambridge and London), France (Estensan and Paris) and Northern Ireland (Belfast and Island Magee), roughly in that order. The space and opportunity to commit thoughts and deeds to paper was made possible by the Sydney University Law School, which freed me from the delights of teaching and the scourge of administration for the first half of 2008, and by the Law Faculty at Cambridge University, which generously bestowed on me a Herbert Smith Visiting Fellowship, and provided me, through the Lauterpacht Centre for International Law, with a most convivial and intellectually stimulating base during my stay in Cambridge.

Economic globalisation and universal human rights

Overview of the relationship

The phenomena of human rights and the global economy are two of the most prominent and influential features of international relations. Like star actors sharing the same scene, they jostle for attention, try to pull rank and sometimes undermine each other, all the while knowing – if they are wise – that their best prospects for individual success lie with ensuring that the other succeeds too. Certainly, human rights and the global economy might appear at first, and even later, to be a rather odd couple, destined to disagree and diverge, with one concerned with human well-being, the other with economic well-being. But the two intersect often and increasingly so in terms of their goals, their operations and their institutions. This book focuses on these points of intersection from the particular perspective of advancing the aims of human rights, by asking: in what ways does, can and should the global economy support and assist human rights, and in what ways do, can and should human rights instruct the global economy? The ambiguity in the use of 'civilising' in the book's title is meant to convey both of these perspectives – that is, the civilising influence of globalisation itself (it can provide the means for individuals to live better lives), and the civilising influence of human rights that can temper the inequities (or 'market failures' as they are euphemistically called) that unbridled globalisation would otherwise produce.

This avowedly human rights perspective is adopted not just because of my professional predilection, though that is certainly a factor, and despite the fact that my intended light dips into the waters of economic theory and practice ended up more sobering dunks. Rather, more significantly, it is because human rights represent more ends than means, whereas with the economy it is the other way around. At their barest minimum human rights are the features of an individual's life lived with irreducible levels of safety, comfort, freedom, dignity and respect. And beyond the individual, collectively they constitute integral components of the health, order and good governance of whole communities and states, and indeed of the entire globe – being 'the foundation', as the Universal Declaration of Human Rights (UDHR) puts it, 'of freedom, justice and peace in the world'.

The various goals of the global economy on the other hand are pursued not for their own ends, but rather as means – almost invariably, essential means – to achieve broad social and personal ends, including such self-actualising ends as human rights prescribe. This is, of course, a view that one would expect to hear from human rights advocates and globalisation sceptics, but importantly it is also how many economists and other key players in the global economy perceive the circumstances. The deepening and widening of the global economy are not ends in themselves; rather they are teleological activities that serve other, broader ends. The provision of economic aid, the expansion of global trade and the establishment and development of commercially robust economics are, or can be, mechanisms for stimulating chain reactions that increase individual and aggregate wealth, alleviate poverty, promote opportunities and freedoms, and strengthen governance. Therein and thereby the objectives of human rights are served. Authoritative statements on the functions of the global economy to this effect are readily made. Thus, for example, in respect of trade, Dani Rodrik argues that it 'is useful only insofar as it serves broader developmental and social goals';[1] in respect of aid, Roberto Dañino, the former General Counsel of the World Bank, proclaims that as 'the Bank's mission is the alleviation of poverty through economic and social growth', so he sees this conception as having 'an especially strong human rights dimension';[2] and of free market capitalism, Milton Friedman maintained that 'economic freedom is . . . an indispensable means toward the achievement of political freedom'.[3]

In this quest, however, I am also concerned not to court extremes. Thus, on the one hand, I maintain that too much must not be demanded of the economy. That is, I will point out the limits of what the economy can and must do for human rights, and argue for curtailing the tendency within human rights advocacy to over-reach both what human rights can

1 Dani Rodrik, *The Global Governance of Trade: As If Development Really Mattered* (New York: UNDP, October 2001), p. 29.
2 Roberto Dañino, 'Legal Aspects of the World Bank's Work on Human Rights: Some Preliminary Thoughts', in Philip Alston and Mary Robinson (eds.), *Human Rights and Development: Towards Mutual Reinforcement* (Oxford and New York: Oxford University Press, 2005), p. 514.
3 Milton Friedman, *Capitalism and Freedom* (Chicago: University of Chicago Press, 1982), p. 8.

legitimately claim and what the global economy can sustainably deliver. The quest is to civilise the economy, not obliterate it. On the other hand, keen as I am to seek out what the economy can do for human rights, I do not want to deny that human rights can and do usefully aid economic ends. Amartya Sen's seminal work on the two-way relationship between (economic) development and (political) freedom eloquently and convincingly argues the case for just such instrumentalism.[4] The point that I am making is that even in this case when, for example, freedom of information, or the wider provision of education or health services, or the securing of an independent judiciary can be seen directly to impact on the well-being of the economy, that impact typically registers in ways that reinforce the very human rights used at the outset – that is rights to free speech, education, health and a fair trial. Fundamentally, the economy must be seen as a vehicle, not the destination.

Complexity

Working out whether and how the dimensions of the global economy affect human rights is conceptually complicated and practically challenging. Alongside the vital role of states, the institutions of the global economy with which this book is primarily concerned – such as the World Bank and the International Monetary Fund (IMF), the World Trade Organization (WTO), and transnational corporations (TNCs) – all clearly make strategic interventions in society. The crucial question is, as Sally Wheeler puts it, 'whether the strategic intervention is a desirable one or not'.[5] In the present context, I am concerned with assessing this desirability in terms of human rights, accepting the manifest difficulties of the task.

An instructive example of the complexity of the problem, but one that also demonstrates the need to understand better the relations between human rights and the global economy, can be found in burgeoning levels of Chinese economic investment in and support of such failed, pariah or authoritarian states as Myanmar, North Korea, Sudan and Zimbabwe, where human rights abuses are brazen and rampant. China's economic relations with Myanmar illustrate the point well.

China is now by far the largest provider of aid to Myanmar. Since the 1980s, Western aid has shrunk dramatically following the Junta's

---

4 Amartya Sen, *Development as Freedom* (New York and Oxford: Oxford University Press, 1999), chapter 2.
5 Sally Wheeler, *Corporations and the Third Way* (Oxford and Portland, OR: Hart Publishing, 2002), p. 45.

tyrannical suppression of the country's democracy movement in 1989, and now even Japanese aid has dried up since 2003 (save emergency support) following the re-arrest of the opposition leader Daw Aung San Suu Kyi and the brutal treatment of her supporters. It has been reported that China's aid contribution of $100 million in 2005 accounted for roughly 75 per cent of all aid received that year by Myanmar, and unofficially it has been estimated that, in the decade to 2007, Beijing's assistance to Yangon[6] amounted to more than $1 billion.[7] China is also the greatest source of Myanmar's imports, accounting for 34 per cent of total imports in 2006, nearly all of it across their 1,384 mile shared border. Foreign direct investment by Chinese businesses is also significant; indeed it is dominant in infrastructure projects, with, for example, many major road, river, port, dam and oil pipeline construction projects having been awarded to Chinese corporations, and the current construction of nearly all hydro-electric power plants in Myanmar is being undertaken by Chinese firms.[8] The relative absence of Western corporations due to trade and investment embargoes has left the field open to China. The overall result has been that the traditional linkages between China and Myanmar have strengthened considerably since the early 1990s, largely on the back of these economic ties, as well as, importantly, enhanced military cooperation.

The types of human rights questions that these economic circumstances raise are intricate and multilayered and relate to all three aspects of the global economy with which this book is concerned – namely, trade, aid and commerce (herein chapters 2, 3 and 4, respectively). The Myanmar military government's long-standing record of abuse of human rights is both brutal and systematic regarding political freedoms in particular, but also, crucially, in respect of the failure to provide basic economic and social rights through appalling economic mismanagement as much as oppression and malign discrimination.[9] In such circumstances, can we

---

6 Though, in further illustration of the warped thinking of the Junta, the capital was in fact officially and suddenly moved in 2005 from Yangon to Pyinmana, a jungle town 320 kilometres to the north, for reasons that were never properly articulated.

7 Reuters, 'RPT – Factbox – Trade, Aid, Heroin: Myanmar's Links to the Outside', 29 September 2007, at www.reuters.com/article/asiaCrisis/idUSBKK302022.

8 Toshihiro Kudo, *Myanmar's Economic Relations with China: Can China Support the Myanmar Economy?* Discussion Paper 66 (2006), Institute of Developing Economies (Japan), pp. 13–15; and Earth Rights International, 'China in Burma: The Increasing Investment of Chinese Multinational Corporations in Burma's Hydropower, Oil & Gas, and Mining Sectors' (September 2007), at www.earthrights.org/files/Reports/BACKGROUNDER%20China%20in%20Burma.pdf.

9 See the Reports to the UN Human Rights Council of the UN Special Rapporteur on the situation of human rights in Myanmar, Paulo Sérgio Pinheiro, of February

see China's substantial economic engagement being anything other than supportive of the military regime's human rights abuses; indeed, might we see it as complicit in such abuse? After all, China's trade relations with Myanmar, its corporate investments and its provision of aid are all conducted without any reference to, let alone criticism of, the Junta's human rights record,[10] even after the most recent crackdown on Buddhist monks in October 2007, and the Junta's abject neglect of the plight of millions of people following the devastation of cyclone Nargis in May 2008, both of which attracted unprecedented international condemnation.[11] Alternatively, can it not be argued that there are human rights benefits that flow from these Chinese investments, at least in terms of their capacity to secure basic economic and social rights?

In contrast to China, the prevailing attitude of the West to Myanmar has been one of censure and ostracisation. But do the economic sanctions imposed by Europe and the United States, for example, better serve the protection and promotion of human rights in Myanmar? Undoubtedly a critical message is delivered through the combination of: (i) nearly all Western nations severing nearly all economic ties (ii) few Western corporations remaining in the country (the oil giants Total and Chevron being notable exceptions), and (iii) the World Bank and IMF having suspended their operations in the country. But has that message led to an improvement in human rights in the country itself? Some argue that it has not, and that what is needed is more not less investment in the ailing economy;[12] others say that it has, or at least that the importance of the message and the pressure it exerts is worth any added hardships. Certainly my own experiences of working on human rights programmes in the country between 2000 and 2003 do not provide me with any clear

---

2007 (A/HRC/4/14) and March 2008 (A/HRC/7/18), available at www.ohchr.org/EN/Countries/AsiaRegion/Pages/MMIndex.aspx.

10 For example, China (together with Russia) vetoed a Security Council resolution on Myanmar in January 2007 (draft resolution S/2007/14), which reiterated 'deep concern at large-scale human rights violations in Myanmar' and called on 'the Government of Myanmar to cease military attacks against civilians in ethnic minority regions'; at http://daccessdds.un.org/doc/UNDOC/GEN/N07/208/48/PDF/N0720848. pdf?OpenElement.

11 Notably, at the very same time as the 2007 crackdown China secured the exploration rights to three more offshore gas fields belonging to Myanmar; see 'Our Friends in the North', *The Economist*, 9 February 2008, p. 29.

12 This was at least part of the thinking behind the US Congress deciding to ditch planned legislation that would have imposed sanctions on Chevron on account of its continued commercial interests in the country; see AFP, 'US Lawmakers Ease Pressure on Chevron in Myanmar', 15 July 2008; at http://afp.google.com/article/ALeqM5gIfBA1VguKfnTN_CqHMP0JzFIvhg.

idea of which path will surely lead to improvement in the human rights situation there and which not.[13]

Of course the number and variety of circumstances in which human rights intersect with the global economy – for good and ill – are beyond counting. My purpose in choosing this particular China/Myanmar example is simply to illustrate the potential depth and breadth of such relations, and the fact that their complexity can be such that there are no necessarily easy answers. The inherent difficulties in charting clear ways forward are the principal reason why a book like this is needed in the first place, and it is a theme that I return to repeatedly throughout its pages. That said, however, I endeavour in the following chapters not just to examine and explain the nature and format of the relationship, but also to draw out conclusions, arguments and pointers towards how the best of the relationship can be retained, and the worst removed, or at least curtailed.

Shared histories, separate paths

Since the time when human society developed sufficiently for systematic interactions between peoples, communities and continents to occur, the dominant themes, aside from war, have been trade (including exchange and bartering) and diplomacy, widely defined as political, interpersonal and cultural relations. Together, these two themes constitute the bedrocks of the global economy and universal human rights.

Law, politics and philosophy have long shared interests in the purpose and form of the essentially private mercantile relations between citizens, as well as the public relations between states and their citizens. The common ground between the two orbits has traditionally not been seen as substantial or significant, although certainly it can be said that from its earliest incarnations *lex mercatoria* has been concerned with order and fairness (in commercial relations),[14] and to that extent it mirrors certain essential aspects of *lex publica* (constitutional, administrative and criminal law). There do exist examples of very specific and practical instances of overlap. For example, the precursors to today's ubiquitous notion of

---

13 See David Kinley and Trevor Wilson, 'Engaging a Pariah: Human Rights Training in Burma/ Myanmar' (2007) 29(2) *Human Rights Quarterly* 368.
14 Gunther Teubner, 'Global Bukowina: Legal Pluralism in the World Society', in Teubner (ed.), *Global Law Without a State* (Aldershot and Brookfield, VT: Dartmouth, 1997), pp. 5–6; and David Kinley, 'Human Rights, Globalization and the Rule of Law: Friends, Foes or Family?' (2002–3) 7(2) *University of California, Los Angeles, Journal of International Law and Foreign Affairs* 239.

corporate social responsibility (CSR) can be found in the practices of the Quaker industrialists in the North of England during the late nineteenth century. Iconic Victorians such as Titus Salt, Joseph Rowntree and John Cadbury all took particular, if somewhat puritanical, care for the health, welfare and education of their workers both inside and outside their factories, far beyond the commercial norms of that time. At the same time and with much the same intentions and ends, Jamsetji Tata was constructing his industrial empire in Bombay, India, based on Parsi-inspired, humanist ideals that yielded the same concerns about the welfare of workers.

Furthermore, as my colleague Justine Nolan and I have written elsewhere, throughout the late twentieth and early twenty-first centuries, the growth of both global economic intercourse and universal human rights standards has been materially aided by three common phenomena of the times:

> The first of these is de-colonisation, especially during the immediate postwar years up until the mid-1970s. The subsequent attainment of independent statehood by many former colonies provided their peoples with the opportunity not only to realise the key human right of self-determination, but also to engage in international relations in their own right. The second important phenomenon has been the rapid growth of international organisations and international regimes covering a vast array of subject areas. These legal regimes and the international institutions they gave birth to have certainly hastened the spread of global interrelations in all these fields. Conspicuous and variously powerful intergovernmental organisations (IGOs), such as the United Nations, the ILO, the OECD, the IMF, the World Bank and regional development banks, as well as the WTO and regional trading blocs, have a pervasive impact – both ways – on the protection and promotion of human rights within the global economy. Third, the enormous advances in speed and capacity in technology, especially as regards travel, telecommunications, and technology transfer over the last twenty years or so, have facilitated ever-expanding means by which we interconnect with each other across countries, continents and cultures.[15]

Intriguingly, however, there is one philosophical phenomenon of particular significance which, though important to the ultimate flourishing of both the global economy and human rights, has not been seen as necessarily linking the two through a common conceptual heritage. I refer here to the emergence of liberalism out of the crucible of the Enlightenment, and its promotion of the ideals of rationality, liberty, rights, and government

---

15 David Kinley and Justine Nolan, 'Trading and Aiding Human Rights: Corporations in the Global Economy' (2007) 25(4) *Nordic Journal of Human Rights* 353, at 355–6.

under social contract, rather than by divine or aristocratic right. Both human rights and the global economy 'appeal to the sacred principles of liberty', as Bertrand Russell put it, but the appeal made by capitalism (the global economy), as he continued, acidly, is reducible to the maxim that 'the fortunate must not be restrained in the exercise of tyranny over the unfortunate'.[16] At its outset, capitalism was selective about the rights it embraced. From the body of individual rights and freedoms that evolved out of the political theory of human rights of Locke and other Enlightenment thinkers, capitalism elevated property rights above all others. As property rights were not evenly distributed – indeed, not held at all by the vast majority of people – so capitalism, at least from the Industrial Revolution until the Second World War, entrenched inequality and disadvantage. So, Michael Freeman points out, one of the 'common criticisms' of human rights theory is that it:

> begins by proclaiming universal equal rights, but, by endorsing capitalist relations of production, ends by justifying, not only unequal property rights, but also unequal enjoyment of *all* human rights.[17]

Freeman does not subscribe to this view, which he rightly notes is at the core of the Marxist critique of individual rights. But he does see the consequentialist problems for human rights caused by the pre-eminence of property rights in capitalist thinking. The decoupling of property rights from social responsibility that was a central tenet of Adam Smith's belief in the power of the free market, Freeman argues, necessarily further disadvantages the poorest in any such economic order. 'The completely free market and an unconstrained right to property is therefore incompatible with the right to subsistence',[18] Freeman maintains.

That said, many, including Freeman, have noted that Adam Smith's free market ideology was, in fact, more nuanced than this. A member of the Enlightenment himself, Smith was driven by the concern to develop a theory of social justice that would ultimately aid the poor. This meant, first, maximising productive capacity that would provide the means to do so. This, for Smith, was best secured by allowing the invisible hand of a free market of competitive self-interest to direct the economy (this is the theme of his iconic treatise, *The Wealth of Nations*). And second,

---

16 Bertrand Russell, *Sceptical Essays* (Allen & Unwin, 1977), p. 132.
17 Michael Freeman, 'Beyond Capitalism and Socialism', in Janet Dine and Andrew Fagan (eds.), *Human Rights and Capitalism: A Multidisciplinary Perspective on Globalisation* (Gloucester: Edward Elgar, 2006), p. 13.
18 *Ibid.* p. 21.

not being able to rely on the 'soft power of humanity' alone to curtail naked self-interest, there was a need for 'reason, principle, conscience'[19] to be employed to ensure the wider dispersal of wealth that the relative few have been able to extract from the market.

The free market economists who have inherited Smith's mantle – be they in lecture halls, think-tanks, Treasury departments, or the secretariats of multilateral trade or aid agencies – do not always do justice to their patron's sentiments. Thus, as Peter Dougherty argues in his accessibly insightful *Who's Afraid of Adam Smith*, Smith would *not* endorse the prevailing attitude of economists today who 'have a hard time accepting the idea that the social capital has anything meaningful to do with the thrust of economic activity'.[20] When observing such propositions being put to economists, Dougherty comments that

> [t]he image that invariably comes to my mind in these exchanges is that of the movie archaeologist Indiana Jones (in this case, the economist) confronting the sabre-wielding swordsman (the social philosopher). Jones is momentarily dazzled by the swordman's display of saberly showmanship, and then remembers that he has a revolver, casually draws it, and blows the shrouded avenger away with cool efficiency.[21]

For Dougherty, this reflects an unfounded overreaction on the part of economists. The overlooked social dimension of the market, as Adam Smith saw it, is of crucial importance to this book's concern with the intersection of the global economy and human rights, if – as I argue – human rights must embrace the power of the global economy, while insisting that its power is harnessed so as to promote the overarching goals of human rights.

Modern development of human rights

In establishing what is meant by human rights in terms of this book I focus on the modern era of human rights development which dates from 1945. In so doing I do not of course deny the importance of the antecedent ancient (especially Greek, Roman and theocratic), Renaissance

---

19 Adam Smith, *The Theory of Moral Sentiments* (1759), Part III, chapter III. Written nearly twenty years before *The Wealth of Nations* (1776), the former essentially established the moral philosophical base for the building of his theory of political economy in the latter. As Peter Dougherty so neatly puts it: Smith 'puzzled out a progressive concept of society and retrofitted it with the incentive structures necessary to achieve a broadly humane vision', *Who's Afraid of Adam Smith?* (New York: J. Wiley, 2002), p. xiii.
20 *Ibid.* p. 44.   21 *Ibid.*

and Enlightenment eras, for it is their various legacies of citizenship, visionary enterprise, individualism and rationality that underpin the capacity and claims of human rights today.[22] It is upon these bases that I do indeed draw at times throughout the book. But it is the twin proclamations of the modern development of human rights – that they are universally applicable, and that they are expressed in law as such – that really makes their intersection with the global economy so pertinent. It has been in the period since the Second World War that the promotion of the idea and practice of human rights has become inextricably associated with international laws and institutions, even more than with domestic regimes, especially as the latter are very often themselves direct responses to international obligations and pressures. Indeed, as Steiner, Alston and Goodman unequivocally put it, the human rights movement's 'aspirations to universal validity' have now come to be seen as necessarily rooted in international law.[23]

   This combination of human rights globalisation by way of international legal instruments has had the effect not only of consolidating, but also of expanding, the scope, objects and format of human rights. Iconic legal representations of human rights had of course already been formulated – the French *Déclaration des droits de l'homme et du citoyen* in 1789, the US Constitutional Bill of Rights in 1791 and even the English Bill of Rights in 1689 before them. But all of these were jurisdictionally restricted, domestic statutes, rather than international treaties with avowedly global scope. Claims as to the universality of human rights had also been long established. Natural law theorists of various hues, from John Locke through Immanuel Kant to Tom Paine and John Stuart Mill, variously considered them to be inalienable, transcendental and inherent in all human beings. However, to the extent that these Enlightenment philosophers intended the 'rights of man' to apply to *all* mankind (and there is a strong case to be made that their thinking was that groups such as slaves, criminals, non-citizens, women, children and the disabled were not to be covered), their arguments emanated from a peculiarly European cultural context at a singular moment in European domestic and colonial history. Such rights were not, as a matter of practice, applied at the time outside certain European nations and the United States.

---

22 See Micheline Ishay, *The History of Human Rights from Ancient Times to the Globalization Era* (Berkeley: University of California Press, 2004), chapters 1 and 2.
23 Henry Steiner, Philip Alston and Ryan Goodman (eds.), *International Human Rights in Context: Law, Politics, Morals* (Oxford and New York: Oxford University Press, 3rd edn 2008), p. 59.

What the immediate post-1945 consensus did for international comity and human rights was to provide the missing pieces to this picture. At this time, the broadly similar human rights projects of the Council of Europe (the European Convention on Human Rights 1950 (ECHR)), the Organisation of American States (the American Declaration on Human Rights 1948 (ADHR)) and, particularly, the United Nations (the 1948 UDHR) were setting about making universal claims as to the application of human rights (to 'everyone' and 'all human beings'), framed in international legal instruments that obliged signatory states to 'secure to everyone within their jurisdiction' these rights.[24] Certainly, at the time, it was believed and hoped in equal measure that these universalised legal proclamations represented local circumstances or, more accurately, aspirations. Many years later, as the cross-cultural theorist Abdullahi An-Na'im trenchantly argued, 'human rights cannot be protected in an effective and sustainable manner without developing an *internal* popular human rights culture and *local* human and material infrastructures'.[25] Persistent conceptual and practical debate within and without human rights circles has revolved around the dilemma that this poses – how to make the global local enough to matter in one place, and still be relevant elsewhere.

During this brief period of the few years between the end of the appalling conflagration of the Second World War and the poisoned posturing of the Cold War that followed, the ideal of universal human rights found some legal purchase in such communal sentiments and hopes as were expressed in the 1945 UN Charter, that

> to save succeeding generations from the scourge of war, which twice in our lifetime has brought untold sorrow to mankind, and to reaffirm faith in fundamental human rights, in the dignity and worth of the human person, in the equal rights of men and women and of nations large and small, and to establish conditions under which justice and respect for the obligations arising from treaties and other sources of international law can be maintained and to promote social progress and better standards of life in larger freedom.[26]

---

24 These are the words used in the ECHR (Art. 1), and are similar to the terms used in the binding legal instruments that followed the ADHR (i.e. the American Convention on Human Rights 1969, see Art. 1) and the UDHR (i.e. the *International Covenant on Civil and Political Rights* 1966 and the *International Covenant on Economic, Social and Cultural Rights* 1966, see Art. 2(1) in each).

25 Abdullahi An-Na'im, 'Human Rights in the Arab World: A Regional Perspective' (2001) 23 *Human Rights Quarterly* 710, at 720.

26 Charter of the United Nations 1945, *Preamble*.

It was in this context and by these means that the international community refined the definition of human rights to focus on the respect for the dignity of the individual as built on the twin pillars of equality and liberty, and began, thereby, to establish the regime of international legal instruments that today prescribe what this means in terms of specific rights across a wide array of circumstances. The General Assembly's adoption of the UDHR that followed three years thereafter was also instrumental. In her book tracing the 'invention' of human rights from the domestic laws of the late eighteenth century to the international instruments of the present day, Lynn Hunt says of the UDHR that, by 'crystallis[ing] 150 years of struggle for rights', it initiated the process through which 'an international consensus about the importance of defending human rights took shape', albeit, she adds, 'by fits and starts'.[27] Today, the range of human rights instruments is indeed impressive, stretching across broad categories of rights applicable to all individuals (economic, social and cultural, as well as civil and political), different types of rights abuse (torture, apartheid, racial discrimination, genocide and war crimes), and particular groupings of rights-holders (women, children, the disabled, refugees, migrant workers, prisoners, human rights defenders, victims of conflict and indigenous peoples).

Those charged with the responsibility at international law to respect, protect and promote human rights have traditionally been solely the states parties. Thus, by ratifying human rights treaties, states bind themselves to 'undertake to respect and to ensure to all individuals ... the rights recognized in the present Covenant', as the International Covenant on Civil and Political Rights provides,[28] or, as stipulated in the International Covenant on Economic, Social and Cultural Rights' alternative formulation, to 'undertake to take steps to the maximum of [their] available resources, with a view to achieving progressively the full realization of the rights recognized in the present Covenant'.[29] However, since the UN Charter expressly stated that such responsibilities also lie with the UN itself (in Art. 55(c)),[30] a case can be made for including intergovernmental organisations (IGOs) on the list where their activities encroach on matters of human rights concern, or, more directly, where they have agency

---

27 Lynn Hunt, *Inventing Human Rights: A History* (New York and London: W. W. Norton & Co., 2007), pp. 205, 207.

28 ICCPR, Art. 2(1).   29 ICESCR, Art. 2(1).

30 As further entrenched by the iteration of the recognisable legal personality of such organisations by the International Court of Justice in the *Reparations Case: Reparation for Injuries Suffered in the Service of the United Nations (Advisory Opinion)* [1949] ICJ Reports 174.

agreements with the UN. Individuals too can be held responsible for human rights abuses in the specific circumstances of international criminal law, especially during times of conflict. The relatively recent establishment of the permanent International Criminal Court in 1998, which began operating in 2002, has a long history before it of ad hoc tribunals attributing guilt to individuals, from Nuremberg and Tokyo, through Rwanda and the Former Republic of Yugoslavia to, most recently, Sierra Leone and Cambodia. But in terms of human rights abuses in non-conflict situations, the responsibilities of individuals and other legal persons, such as corporations, are regulated by domestic laws – either as independently instituted by state law-makers, or in fulfilment of international treaty obligations of states to implement measures to protect human rights at home.

Especially since the mid 1990s, the place of non-state actors (typically, IGOs, individuals, and national and transnational corporations, as well as insurrectionist or rebel groups) within international law has attracted much attention. What is of particular relevance to this book is the concern to concretise the nature and extent of international human rights responsibilities that might be properly and viably ascribed to economic non-state bodies such as the World Bank, regional development banks, the IMF and the WTO, and TNCs. The rise of such a concern has correlated with the rise of globalisation itself, as it is widely viewed not as a state-driven phenomenon, but rather, as Andrew Clapham writes, 'one driven by non-state actors outside the control of individual states'.[31] Clearly, this presents a problem for international law given its elemental focus on the regulation of inter-state relations. In practical terms the quest to bring non-state, economic actors within the international law fold has been hindered by the resistance put up not only, predictably, by the non-state actors themselves, but also, and more importantly, by the states, many of whom benefit directly from the economic activities of the non-state actors and are loath to adopt anything that might stem the flow.

The tussle over the human rights responsibilities of economic non-state actors marks out one of the most important and dynamic frontiers in international human rights law today, and it is one that is repeatedly addressed throughout this book. For the relationship is not just a matter of concern to the human rights lobby, but is also an issue that has shadowed the modern era of globalisation from the outset, and is today emerging into the full light of day as a key challenge for all actors in the global economy.

31 Andrew Clapham, *Human Rights Obligations of Non-State Actors* (New York and Oxford: Oxford University Press, 2006), p. 6.

Modern development of the global economy

As with my focus on the modern development of human rights, so my focus on the global economy is in its modern format, for that is where its impact has been most widespread and dramatic. To be sure, economic globalisation has ancient and pre-modern antecedents – 'rapid integration of the world economy occurred in the late nineteenth and early twentieth centuries'[32] – but it is the sheer scale, scope and speed of growth of the global economy today that marks it out as a subject of such interest, to economists and non-economists alike. It has been since the early 1990s that economic globalisation has really taken hold by way of the same force that W. H. Auden once remarked was the hope of all poets – that is, 'to be, like some valley cheese, local, but prized elsewhere'.[33]

How the global economy has grown during this time. In 1995, world output was $42.3 trillion. By 2005, world output amounted to $61.3 trillion (measured in purchasing power parity), representing a stunning 45 per cent increase over ten years.[34] The flow of cross-border investment – a quintessential barometer of globalisation – has had an extraordinary roller-coaster ride in this period. From the early 1990s when the global total of Foreign Direct Investment (FDI) hovered around $200 billion, it rocketed to a peak of $1,411 billion in 2000, collapsed to less that $600 billion in 2003, following the globally contagious Asian financial crisis, and has since recovered to $1,306 billion in 2006[35] (though the figures for 2008–9 are registering another significant contraction).[36] Historically, the developed economies have accounted for much of this growth and investment, but recently the most significant gains in percentage terms and in terms of material impact have been registered in developing countries. For example, according to the World Bank, year-on-year GDP growth in developing countries now far outstrips that in the developed countries, and the trend is set to continue, notwithstanding the projected global downturn, as Figure 1 illustrates. Significantly, this is not just the consequence of the celebrated growth of the Chinese and Indian economies, for if their figures are removed

32 Jagdish Bhagwati, *In Defense of Globalization* (New York: Oxford University Press, 2004), p. 10.
33 W. H. Auden, 'Shorts II', in *Collected Poems*, ed. Edward Mendelson (London: Faber and Faber, 1976), p. 639.
34 World Bank, *World Development Indicators 2007* (Washington, DC: World Bank, 2007), p. 185.
35 UNCTAD, *World Investment Report 2007* (New York and Geneva: United Nations, 2007), p. 3.
36 Institute of International Finance, 'Capital Flows to Emerging Market Economies', Report (27 January 2009) at www.iif.com.

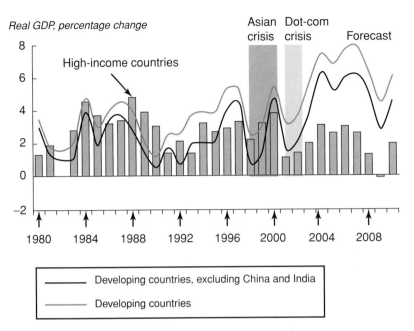

Fig. 1 GDP growth. *Source:* World Bank, *Global Economic Prospects 2009*, p. 18.

from the totals for all developing countries in 2006 and 2007 (7.5 and
7.4 per cent respectively), growth in the remaining developing economies
remains high at 5.9 per cent for 2006 and 5.7 per cent for 2007.[37]

More dramatically still, the same World Bank report calculates that
the number of those living in absolute poverty, classified as less than one
dollar per day, has been dropping steadily from 1.2 billion in 1990, and
will, it estimates, be half that figure (i.e. 624 million) by 2015, thereby
meeting one of the Millennium Development Goals.[38] The figure dipped
beneath 1 billion to 970 million in 2004.[39]

As a concept, globalisation, like the idea of God, is known to us all,
even if we do not all believe in or understand it. Unsurprisingly, there is
no uniformly accepted definition of the term. However, there is common

---

37 Source of figures: World Bank, *Global Economic Prospects 2008: Technology Diffusion in
the Developing World* (Washington, DC: World Bank, 2008), p. 21.
38 See MDG website at www.un.org/millenniumgoals/.
39 World Bank, *Global Economic Prospects 2008*, p. 17; the report adds the caveat that 'such
aggregate outcomes are not guaranteed, however, and performance across individual
countries is likely to be diverse'. It should be noted that following recent changes in the
way in which some economists classify the poor, these figures have been revised upwards;
see 'The Bottom 1.4 Billion', *The Economist*, 30 August 2008, p. 62.

agreement over certain basic characteristics, these being that globalisation represents the congruence of political philosophy, policy implementation and technological innovation. While stressing the importance of the consequences of their intersection, let me briefly deal with each of these in turn.

Ideologically, globalisation has been facilitated and accentuated by the prevalence of the political philosophy of liberalism and its hand-maidens, the promotion of individual freedoms, democratic governance, and (relatively) non-interventionist government. Capitalism, as the economic manifestation of these political characteristics, has indeed triumphed over the planned economy of post-war communism, and since 1990 has locked in its advantage globally, with even the hold-out communist states of China, and latterly Vietnam, aggressively embracing the market economy, through deregulation, divestment of state owned enterprises, and the cautious institution of private property rights. The triumph has not had the hyperbolic consequences asserted and prophesied by Francis Fukuyama in his 1992 opus *The End of History and the Last Man*, for, even accepting some degree of stylistic licence, his crude bipolarity of democratic liberalism versus communism ignored too much the burgeoning middle-ground phenomena of social welfarism, the promotion of *good* governance (which can be much more varied than the Anglo-American perceptions of democracy), and the idea of human rights conditionality that both informs and inhibits a state's political economy. While, as one reviewer put it, 'almost nobody bought' Fukuyama's thesis of liberalism's ultimate doctrinal victory, 'everyone agreed he had put his finger on something'.[40]

That 'something' has been avidly pursued in national and international policy initiatives since the mid 1990s – globalisation's second pillar. The corporatisation and privatisation of public utilities, the deregulation of financial markets and the promotion of competition through anti-trust laws and watchdog bodies have become hallmarks of developed economies that are now being effectively exported to emerging economies. The international yang to this domestic yin has been the successful revitalisation and extension of the liberalisation of international trade, and the establishment of the WTO in 1994 to oversee its implementation. The 153 countries, out of a total of some 193, that are now members of the WTO represent more than 90 per cent of global trade in goods.[41] No matter

---

40 Edmund Fawcett, 'Drop the Pilot', *Guardian*, 17 July 2004, p. 10.
41 Uri Dadush and Julia Nielson, 'Governing Global Trade' (2007) 44(4) *Finance & Development* 22.

the asymmetries in the application of the free trade policies and in the distribution of the benefits they yield, they are, nonetheless, the key conduits through which the theory of globalisation has been translated into practice.

The third pillar of globalisation is the extraordinary accommodation that technology has provided it. The notion of connectivity is central to the development of globalisation – just as the 'stringer' is to the shaping of a surfboard – and it has been hugely facilitated by the technological advances in recent years in transport, telecommunications, e-commerce, manufacturing, construction, power generation, and much else. For Thomas Friedman, technology has been *the* defining catalyst that shook the world out of its Cold War torpor into the new age of globalisation:

> In the Cold War the most frequently asked question was: 'Whose side are you on?' In globalization, the most frequently asked question is 'To what extent are you connected to everyone?' In the Cold War, the second most frequently asked question was: 'How big is your missile?' In globalization, the second most frequently asked question is 'How fast is your modem?' The defining document of the Cold War system was 'The Treaty'. The defining document for globalization is 'The Deal'.[42]

A key economic consequence of such technological advancements has been the dramatic lowering of the costs of connection and trade. Martin Wolf, for example, though wary of overstating the impact of technology, is nonetheless convinced that it is the intoxication of such cost savings that has ensured globalisation's success and made it 'more difficult to prevent'.[43] Indeed, by way of this observation, one completes the circle in terms of describing the pillars that support globalisation, for curbing its advancement requires determined and concerted state action (governmental policy born, at least in part, of political conviction), just as much as state action is required to facilitate its progress. For whatever else has been claimed of globalisation in its modern format, it is manifestly not the case that it requires the retraction of government intervention. State action is, according to Jagdish Bhagwati, one of the two coloured inks in which the story of globalisation today must be written (the other is coloured by technological change). The modern history of economic

---

42 Thomas Friedman, *The Lexus and the Olive Tree* (London: HarperCollins, rev. edn 2000), p. 10.
43 Martin Wolf, *Why Globalization Works* (New Haven, CT: Yale University Press, 2004), p. 17.

globalisation has been marked by its reliance on the deep connivance of states, in much the same way as modern conceptions of human rights make heavy demands on states in order to secure their protection and promotion.

Competing state responsibilities and interests

On the face of it, therefore, this circumstance effects a competition for the ear of the state, as well as for its resources, between capitalists and trade liberalists on one side, and human rights advocates and social welfarists on the other. Certainly, if one looks at the manner in which the two groups often portray each other today, their interests in what the state could and should provide appear to be mutually exclusive. But such a conclusion is superficial and wrong-headed. In fact the challenge for the state, and for all of us, is not to decide between two antagonists, but rather how to reconcile the different perspectives of two protagonists. That does not make the challenge any less daunting, of course, but it frames it in a way that might yield more tangible results. After all, there is scope for the state to mediate. On the one hand, as Christie Weeramantry argues, there is an economic substratum to all human rights, without which 'right[s] cannot possibly exist in practical terms, whatever the theory behind [them]'.[44] On the other hand, free marketeers and the captains of industry cannot, and generally do not, ply their trade free of any ethical concerns and social obligations.

A government's record of economic management, whether in a developed or a developing state, is today a chief gauge of how well it is performing. Such scrutiny of governments comes from the inside, mainly through the domestic political processes, and the outside, through the attentions of international institutions such as the World Bank and the IMF, the Organisation for Economic Co-operation and Development (OECD), and the EU. To some extent, legal regimes at both levels regulate their economic conduct – domestic taxation and public spending laws and policies, as well as constitutional and administrative laws, and international trade, banking and finance laws. Similarly, a government's record on human rights is subject to domestic and international avenues of scrutiny, albeit often more emotively and through different international bodies, e.g. the UN, the International Labour Organisation (ILO) and human rights Non-governmental Organisations (NGOs),

---

44   Christopher Weeramantry, 'Human Rights and the Global Marketplace' (1999) 25 *Brooklyn Journal of International Law* 27.

such as Amnesty International and Human Rights Watch. Domestic laws (covering constitutional, criminal, anti-discrimination, labour and social welfare issues) and international regimes (for example, the treaty regimes of the UN, the ILO, the Council of Europe, the Organisation of American States and the African Union) have also been established. But there is one factor that separates the two concerns and which has a direct and significant impact on the nature and extent of the respective responsibilities that they place on the shoulders of states. This is the viewpoint that it is the market that exerts the greatest pressure on governments.[45] A government's tax receipts, credit worthiness and borrowing capacity, monetary controls, balance of trade figures, inflation and employment levels, and prospects for economic growth are all subject to market fluctuations, however instigated, whether by the circumstances of the state in question or by those of other states. There is no equivalent in the human rights arena; no marketplace of norms.

Paradoxically, this makes it, at the same time, easier and more difficult for human rights to be adequately protected by states. Easier, because, unlike the unruly and, by definition, largely unregulated market standards, human rights standards are, comparatively speaking, more easily identified, as they are stipulated in treaties and statutes. The task is made more difficult, because in most cases the same impetus (national and/or international) to secure the best possible outcome is not there for states in respect of protecting human rights as it is for preserving healthy market conditions. Put simply, for states in which systematic and egregious human rights abuses are absent (which is the case for most), governments are far more committed to achieving their economic goals than their human rights goals, whatever their rhetorical proclamations. Government officials in China, as much as the United States, may protest that this does not mean that human rights do not form part of the equation; they do, but it is as derivative beneficiaries of the primary object of economic success. As I have made clear already, I have some sympathy for such a claim. Where my difficulty lies is in the fact that the human rights responsibilities of states are not brought forward in the equation, to the point where their compliance is an objective premise, rather than merely an optional derivation.

---

45 'Perhaps most important of all is the pressure on all governments to avoid burdening economic activity in such a way that competitive pressures reduce market opportunities and performance', as Richard Falk puts it in *Predatory Globalization: A Critique* (Cambridge: Polity Press, 1999), p. 101.

States are often at the very centre of both economic and human rights abuses. Thus, in economic terms, states may preside over the injustices that are caused by endemic, nepotistic corruption (as in Indonesia under former President Suharto, or in Russia today), unsustainable exploitation and asset stripping of natural resources (as in Brazil, China, Nigeria or Venezuela since the mid 1990s), or breathtaking mismanagement (as has brought the economies of Myanmar and Zimbabwe to their knees). In human rights terms, the abuses may comprise state-sanctioned ethnic cleansing (as in Rwanda, the former Yugoslavia or Sudan), systematic discrimination against women and homosexuals inspired by religious fundamentalism (as in Iran, Saudi Arabia and many Pacific Islands), or the blatant denial of civil rights (as with free speech in China, Vietnam and Singapore) or of economic and social rights (where politics gets in the way, as in the case of adequate health care for AIDS victims in South Africa, the poor in many states in the US, and aboriginal communities in Australia).

The consequences of all these state actions are grave. The invisible and largely uncontrollable hand of the market certainly impacts on the actions of states, but it does so with far more effect in the economic arena. In so far as it affects state actions regarding human rights, it does so indirectly, *through* the economy. States, therefore, can and should be taking their legally sanctioned human rights responsibilities more seriously, rather than relegating them beneath the economic imperatives by way of obfuscating variations of what Rhoda Howard critically refers to as the 'full belly' thesis.[46] That is, where it is argued that only when economic prosperity has been secured (the 'full belly') will the state be willing and able to set about protecting (other) human rights.

A state's human rights duties are equally unyielding to arguments about the so-called 'shrinking state', as public functions are increasingly divested into private hands. Certainly, governments cannot shift responsibilities along with their functions. For a start, as already made clear, human rights typically are attached to the state's duty to comply with its *legal* jurisdiction, not its *functional* jurisdiction. For the UN Human Rights Committee, which oversees the implementation of the International Covenant on Civil and Political Rights (ICCPR), this means that 'the positive obligations on States Parties to ensure Covenant rights will

---

46 Rhoda Howard, 'The Full-Belly Thesis: Should Economic Rights Take Priority over Civil and Political Rights? Evidence from Sub-Saharan Africa' (1983) 5(4) *Human Rights Quarterly* 467.

only be fully discharged if individuals are protected by the State, not just against violations of Covenant rights by its agents, *but also against acts committed by private persons or entities that would impair the enjoyment of Covenant rights*.[47] States are required to regulate both horizontal relations between individuals and vertical relations between individuals and themselves, in so far as they impact on people's human rights guarantees. As *The Economist* puts it more prosaically: 'it is the job of governments to govern; don't let them wriggle out of it'.[48]

In any case, the consequences of the outsourcing of public functions are in fact more to do with the manner and form of public power, rather than with the diminution of its quantum. Where once it was only the state that provided water, power and telecommunications services, and the state that ran hospitals, prisons, roads and railways, now these and other services are commonly partially or wholly provided by private corporations. However, in these circumstances, the state's supervisory and regulatory responsibilities are greatly enlarged to the point where they replace the direct provision of services as the paramount role of the state. It is difficult to overestimate how important this change in role has and will become. For as John Ralston Saul argues, '[t]he irony of deregulation is that the more freedom business is given, the more dependent it becomes upon government as the saviour of last resort'.[49] Words, incidentally, that are especially prophetic in light of the gargantuan rescue packages put together by the US Federal Reserve Bank in late 2008, in an attempt to save the financial services sector from complete collapse under the weight of the toxicity of so many bad assets held by so many key financial institutions.[50]

In their excellent study of the privatisation phenomenon, Feigenbaum, Henig and Hamnett argue that 'in shifting responsibilities from government to market, privatisation alters the institutional framework through

---

47 Human Rights Committee, *General Comment 31: Nature of the General Legal Obligation Imposed on States Parties to the Covenant*, UN Doc. CCPR/C/21/Rev.1/Add.13 (26 May 2004), para. 8, at www.unhchr.ch/tbs/doc.nsf/(Symbol)/CCPR.C.21.Rev.1.Add. 13.En?Opendocument; emphasis added.
48 'How Good Should Your Business Be?' *The Economist*, 19 January 2008, p. 13.
49 John Ralston Saul, *Voltaire's Bastards: The Dictatorship of Reason in the West* (Penguin, 1993), p. 418.
50 Including the US Federal Reserve Bank's bail-outs of investment bank Bear Stearns, mortgage underwriters Freddie Mac and Fannie Mae, and insurer AIG; as well as the umbrella $700 billion scheme established by the Bush Administration that was intended to underwrite the toxic assets held by many other banks, the extent of whose liabilities was yet to become apparent.

which citizens, companies and organisations articulate, mediate and promote their individual and shared interests'.[51] The result is, then, a reconfiguration rather than a repudiation of the state. As the level to which the
organs of the state impact directly on an individual's daily life is reduced,
so there is less scope for either direct infringement or fulfilment of human
rights by the state. But equally, as the regulatory role of the state expands,
so the state's proper concern for human rights protection *overall* is at least
maintained, if not increased.[52]

The significance, therefore, of the role of governments in the global
economy is not just to facilitate the conditions for productive, prosperous
and prudent commercial enterprise, but also to ensure that, in the process,
they do not renege on their social responsibilities to promote freedom,
equality, order and welfare as represented, in part, by their international
human rights law obligations. The real crux of the problem here is how to
ensure that the social 'ought' gains purchase in the context of the economic
'is', where the free market tenet of globalisation militates against the
regulatory inclinations of a typical mixed economy. Dani Rodrik argues
that the market, in this sense,

> undercuts the ability of nation-states to erect regulatory and redistributive
> institutions, and does so at the same time that it increases the premium
> on solid national institutions. Social safety nets become more difficult to
> finance just as the need for social insurance becomes greater; financial
> intermediaries increase their ability to evade national regulation just as
> prudential supervision becomes more important; macroeconomic man-
> agement becomes trickier just as costs of policy mistakes are amplified.
> Once again, the stakes are greater for developing countries, since they have
> weak institutions to begin with.[53]

The instruments and institutions of human rights can be used to miti-
gate these deleterious impacts in the areas of trade, aid and commerce, so
long as governments are willing and capable, individually and collectively.
Governments ought not to dominate or thwart the market, but equally
they must not be 'servant[s]' to the market, as Martin Wolf starkly advocates, albeit 'humble and honest' ones, as he adds.[54] This imperative that

---

51 Harvey Feigenbaum, Jeffrey Henig and Chris Hamnett, *Shrinking the State: The Political
Underpinnings of Privatisation,* (Cambridge: Cambridge University Press, 1999), p. 36.
52 These are the words I used in an unpublished 2001 conference paper entitled 'Human
Rights and the Shrinking State: The New Footprint of State Responsibility', at www.law.
monash.edu.au/castancentre/conference2001/papers/ kinley.html.
53 Dani Rodrik, *One Economics, Many Recipes: Globalization, Institutions, and Economic
Growth* (Princeton: Princeton University Press, 2007), pp. 195–6.
54 Wolf, *Why Globalization Works,* p. 76.

governments must not be beholden to the market is crucially important if only to guard against what John Maynard Keynes called the 'astounding belief' of capitalism – namely, 'that the most wickedest of men will do the most wickedest of things for the greatest good of everyone'.[55]

Current conflicts and complementarities

Behind the 'role of the state' debate, there lies a broader conceptual question about how the globalising economy and universalising human rights relate to each other today, whether in support, in opposition or indifference to one another. The boundaries of this relationship are aptly represented by Aesop's fable about the goose that laid golden eggs. Greed and avarice, so the tale goes, cause the owner to kill the goose (seeking to obtain all the eggs immediately and in one go), and in consequence he loses all future wealth. Adding an ironic twist to this tale, many globalisation protagonists argue that over-burdening the 'free market goose' with demands to recognise and respect human rights will kill it and end its golden issue. A great deal of the often fraught relationship between the global economy and human rights can be explained within the parameters of this metaphor.

On the one hand, the golden eggs of economic prosperity are essential ingredients in any plans or policies that seek better to protect and promote human rights, so to kill their progenitor or even to hinder significantly her fecundity would indeed be a serious problem. Uncompromising demands that the goose be neutered – that is, that the profit motive ought to be dispensed with, or the whole idea of trade liberalisation be abandoned, or aid be entirely decoupled from liberalist economic conditionality – are simplistic, counter-productive and today, thankfully, infrequently voiced arguments for better human rights observance. The implementation of free trade policies, the enterprise of private corporations and the utility of economic aid have together vastly increased global aggregate wealth, whatever one might say about their manifest imperfections, inequities and injustices. So the goose is certainly producing the golden eggs needed if there is to be any hope of securing to the poor and disadvantaged (but especially the poor) their human rights.

On the other hand, the *production* of golden eggs is not the object of the whole venture. It is the ends to which we put the wealth they provide –

---

55 Quoted in Michael Albert, *Moving Forward: Program for a Participatory Economy* (San Francisco and Edinburgh: AK Press, 2000), p. 128.

personal and social goods – that are the ultimate goals. While necessary, the golden eggs are not themselves sufficient to secure human rights. The circumstances under which they are produced and the conditions of the utilitarian divestment of the wealth are also vital dimensions in the quest to put the golden eggs to their best use. The 'before' and 'after', in other words, are just as important as the instant of production. The teleological demands that are made of the processes of wealth creation, as imposed by national and, less so, international laws, policies and practices, are not just important but integral to the whole globalised, free market enterprise. The 'ancient question', as Robert Kuttner puts it, remains 'how market forces need to be tempered for the greater good of the economy and society'.[56]

Pro- and anti-globalisation

The debate over whether and how human rights and the global economy intersect lies at the centre of the much more diffuse debate between supporters of globalisation and its detractors, the anti-globalisationists. Inevitably, therefore, the narrower debate has to some extent suffered from the excesses and inconsistencies of the wider one. When protestors carry placards proclaiming that globalisation kills children, or civil society activists are belittled as simplistic hypocrites, there is a tendency for such excesses to be self-perpetuating, as each side's perceived blindness and intransigence of the other begets more of the same in both. Henry Veltmeyer, in his edited collection of essays on *Globalization and Anti-globalization*, sensibly counsels against lumping together globalisation institutions (such as the Bank, the Fund, the WTO and TNCs), as their strategic motivations and operational practices differ, and, equally, against doing the same with the anti-globalisation movement, which 'is also divided as to strategic direction, ultimate goal and the appropriate forms of struggle'.[57]

All that said, especially zealous defenders of globalisation have at times been too ready to extol its virtues without any reference to, let alone addressing of, its problems. In part this has been due to philosophical convictions; for example, the fervent belief in the vitality of laissez-faire

---

56 Robert Kuttner, 'The Role of Governments in the Global Economy', in Will Hutton and Anthony Giddens (eds.), *On the Edge: Living with Global Capitalism* (London: Vintage, 2001), p. 163.
57 Henry Veltmeyer, 'Introduction', in Veltmeyer (ed.), *Globalization and Anti-globalization* (Aldershot: Ashgate, 2004), p. 8.

economics that characterised the Structural Adjustment Programs of the IMF and the World Bank in the 1980s despite their detrimental impact on the social welfare policies of recipient countries.[58] In part, it has been through blinkered vision, such as Mike Moore's bombastic account of his time as Director-General of the WTO, *A World without Walls*, in which he presumes rather than proves globalisation has spread democracy, alleviated poverty and secured freedom. Or the assertions of David Henderson, formerly a chief economist in the OECD, that 'corporate social responsibility' is not just misguided, but counter-productive, because it is wholly incompatible with the precepts of a globalised market economy (that is, despite manifest evidence to the contrary coming from the business community itself).[59]

The anti-globalisation movement that originated in the 1990s as a visceral reaction to the march of free market liberalism has been, if anything, even more strident. In its early stages the movement was entirely negatively defined – that is, as the antonym of its perceived adversary – and characteristically advanced the sort of uncompromising demands mentioned above, as well as more rabid rhetoric such as the Humane Society of the United States' depiction of the WTO as 'the single most destructive international organisation ever formed'.[60] Though spectacular in terms of the attention that the movement attracted through mass protests at the annual meetings of the World Economic Forum (WEF) in Davos and of the World Bank Group and the IMF in Washington DC, as well as the various G8 summits and the ministerial meetings of WTO trade rounds, the purely 'anti-' part of anti-globalisation had a limited shelf-life. Trenchant questions as to what precisely it is that globalisation does wrong, and why and how to repair or replace it, quite properly challenged the movement to redefine itself. The very fact that it was rather globalist in format and aspirations – the promotion of a unifying, global message, by building

---

58 See *The Realization of Economic, Social and Cultural Rights*, second progress report prepared by Mr Danilo Türk, Special Rapporteur for the UN Commission on Human Rights, UN Doc. E/CN.4/Sub.2/1991/17 (18 July 1991), at www.unhchr.ch/Huridocda/ Huridoca.nsf/(Symbol)/E.CN.4.Sub.2. 1991.17.En?Opendocument, especially paras. 49–206. The issue is endemic and long-standing. Türk quotes an earlier study of loan conditions by Susan George in her book *A Fate Worse than Debt* (London: Penguin, 1988) that 'counted 196 objectives of Fund programmes between 1964 and 1979, among which the aim to "protect the poor against possible adverse effects of programmes" occurs exactly once' (at para. 74).

59 *Misguided Virtue: False Notions of Corporate Social Responsibility* (London: Institute of Economic Affairs, 2001), Parts 3–6.

60 As quoted by Michael Weinstein and Steve Charnovitz, 'The Greening of the WTO' (2001) 80(6) *Foreign Affairs* 147, at 150.

global networks and communicating through global telecommunications media[61] – also added greatly to the need to rethink its rhetoric and outlook. In more recent times, therefore, the notions of '*alter*-globalisation', campaigning for 'global social justice' and the institution of a World Social Forum (WSF), as an annual alternative to the WEF, have appeared, all of which acknowledge and accept the benefits of globalisation, while striving to limit or eliminate its worst excesses and injustices. The WSF, for example, aims to do so by prescribing 'alternative' policies (political, social, legal and economic), that:

> are designed to ensure that globalization in solidarity will prevail as a new stage in world history. This will respect universal human rights, and those of all citizens – men and women – of all nations and the environment and will rest on democratic international systems and institutions at the service of social justice, equality and the sovereignty of peoples.[62]

Conditional dependency

We have reached a position today in which the interrelationship between human rights and the global economy can be characterised as one of conditional dependency. The key questions are now centred on what is the nature and extent of the conditionality. Thomas Pogge delineates a high-water mark from the perspective of moral philosophy. In the remarkable opening pages of his *World Poverty and Human Rights*, Pogge challenges the 'fortunates' and beneficiaries of the global economy (including, by definition, all reading his and these words) to justify the social consequences of the prevailing economic order. The human rights of many millions are routinely and egregiously denied, which situation is avoidable should the rich so choose. For Pogge, this can be done, not merely by helping the poor *within* the capacity of prevailing global economic circumstances, but by radically overhauling a 'coercive global order that perpetuates severe poverty for many who cannot resist'.[63] Even staying within the boundaries of the current economic order, noted economists

---

61 See Walter Truett Anderson, 'The Anti-Globalisation Movement Changes its Tune', 15 February 2002, at www.alternet.org/globalization/12423/.
62 As stated in the WSF's *Charter of Principles* (Principle 4), at http://wsf2008.net/eng/about.
63 Thomas Pogge, *World Poverty and Human Rights* (Cambridge: Polity Press, 2002), p. 23. The difference is critical for Pogge, who sees 'the distinction between causing poverty and merely failing to reduce it as morally significant', such that those engaged in the former are violating human rights precepts; *ibid.* p. 13.

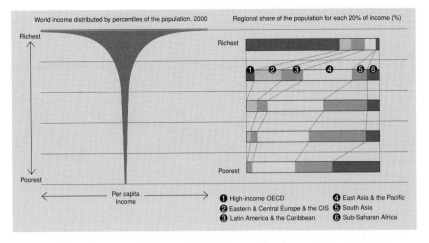

Fig. 2   Where the money is. *Source:* UNDP, *Human Development Report* 2005, at p. 37, fig. 1.16.

Jeffrey Sachs, in *The End of Poverty*, and Paul Collier, in *The Bottom Billion*, make the point that it is not beyond the wit of us and our governments collectively to devise and implement economic policies that would exploit the more than ample wealth (extant and potential) created by the global economy for the greater benefit of the most abjectly disadvantaged and dispossessed in our world today.

Poverty does not cause human rights abuse; the actions or inactions of governments and other institutions and organisations, as well as other individuals, *cause* human rights abuse, and they often do so by way of the impoverishment of those denied their rights.[64] However, the incidence of poverty is a reliable sign of attendant human rights problems. The asymmetry in the distribution of wealth between rich and poor countries, and between the rich and poor within countries, is indicative (though not completely so, as even the rich can be denied rights, but just less prevalently than the poor) of the relative enjoyment of human rights. The aptly named 'champagne glass' figurative depiction of global wealth distribution (see Figure 2) highlights the relative inequity – the lower 80 per cent of the world's population constituting the long, thin, gently widening stem of the glass (totalling 25 per cent of world income),

---

64 Philip Alston makes clear this distinction in 'Ships Passing in the Night: The Current State of the Human Rights and Development Debate Seen through the Lens of the Millennium Development Goals' (2005) 27(3) *Human Rights Quarterly* 755 , at 785–8.

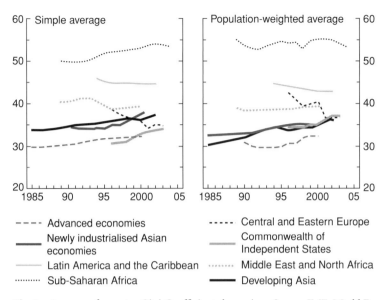

Fig. 3 Average of country Gini Coefficients by region. *Source:* IMF, *World Economic Outlook,* October 2007, p. 140, fig. 4.3.

and the top quintile representing the wide, flat glass head (totalling 75 per cent of world income).[65]

Digging beneath the surface of these statistics, the more sophisticated 'Gini Coefficient' exposes the extent of the distribution of income/wealth (or equality of income/wealth) within countries and how this compares on a state-to-state and region-to-region basis. Thus, for example, as Figure 3 shows, the IMF has calculated that inequality has increased (the Gini Coefficient has risen) since the late 1980s in all regions of the world, except the Commonwealth of Independent States, where it has fallen markedly, and Sub-Saharan Africa. It has risen most steeply in the poorest developing economies of Asia and Central and Eastern Europe, and in the advanced economies. The regions with the greatest inequality are, by far, Latin America and the Caribbean.

This is significant because it tells us how deep 'radical poverty' goes, and it highlights the economic incapacity, not only of those in extreme poverty, but also of those who are relatively poor, to realise their human rights needs, as compared with the capacity of the relatively rich. A key challenge arising out of the intersection between the global economy and human rights is, therefore, to devise a conceptual framework within

---

65 UNDP, *Human Development Report 2005* (New York: UNDP, 2005), p. 36.

which practical approaches can be developed to address the fundamental question of capacity.

To this end, the principal international organisations that focus more on social issues, such as labour, development and human rights, variously seek to impose conditions on states to regulate the global economy in such a way that, at the very least, the grossest inequities and injustices might be eradicated. The UN's Millennium Development Goals stress the need to 'develop further an open trading and financial system that is rule-based, predictable and non-discriminatory, [and] includes a commitment to good governance, development and poverty reduction – nationally and internationally', and to do so not only through the states themselves, but 'in cooperation with the private sector'.[66] The World Social Commission, established by the ILO to investigate the social dimensions of globalisation, issued a lengthy report in 2004, entitled *A Fair Globalization*, which carried a message of qualified support for globalisation based on the need to change its current path. The report argues that there are 'deep-seated and persistent imbalances in the current workings of the global economy',[67] that must be addressed by way of grand changes to structures of national and international governance (more democracy); more robust engagement with both civil society and the private sector in the formulation of development policies; more effective social justice oriented regulation of transnational trade and commerce; and more assiduous compliance by governments and international bodies with human rights laws and standards.[68] In respect of global trade, the UNDP 2003 Report on *Making Global Trade Work for People* concluded that 'trade liberalization has had mixed results for gender outcomes, especially in developing countries'.[69] Thus, for example, where more open trade appears to have led to increased female employment in many developing countries, very often 'there has *not* been a corresponding decrease in their household and care responsibilities', especially in countries where spending on social services has been cut due partly to lower revenue from erstwhile trade tariffs. 'Such cuts', the Report states, 'hurt women disproportionately because they must make

---

66 Millennium Development Goal 8; see www.un.org/millenniumgoals/.
67 ILO World Commission on the Social Dimension of Globalization, *A Fair Globalization: Creating Opportunities For All* (Geneva: ILO, 2004), at para. 12, www.ilo.org/public/english/wcsdg/docs/report.pdf.
68 *Ibid.*
69 See UNDP and Kamal Malhotra, *Making Global Trade Work for People* (London and Sterling, VA: Earthscan Publications, 2003) at www.networkideas.org/doc/mar2003/UNDP_Trade.pdf, p. 32.

up for the reduction in health care, safe water and the like by increasing their (unpaid) household work and care.'[70]

Pronouncements have been made by human rights specific, multilateral organisations that are similarly conditional. For example, the UN Office of the High Commissioner for Human Rights (OHCHR) has published separate Issues Papers on how business, trade and development interrelate with human rights.[71] The Human Rights Council passed a resolution in 2007 on *Globalization and its Impact on the Full Enjoyment of Human Rights*, in which it stated:

> globalization should be guided by the fundamental principles that under-pin the corpus of human rights, such as equality, participation, account-ability, non-discrimination, at both the international and national levels, respect for diversity and international cooperation and solidarity [for] while globalization offers great opportunities, at present its benefits are very unevenly shared and costs are unevenly distributed and . . . developing countries face special difficulties in meeting this challenge.[72]

All of these statements and stances represent the particular context in which the body of international human rights laws (IHRL), including labour rights such as those covered in ILO Conventions, operate. Clearly, they have a particular view of the role and use of the global economy. Essentially, it is a view that places the dignity and well-being of the individual at the centre of things. Frank Garcia characterises the normative underpinning of IHRL as being 'rooted in the liberal commitment to the equal worth of each individual regardless of their utility, and human rights themselves embody the minimum standards of treatment necessary in view of this equal moral worth'.[73] This he contrasts with how international economic law (IEL) accommodates the individual, whereby, for example, '[t]he *Homo Economicus* Model of human beings presupposed in trade law places little emphasis on the precise end of human

---

70 *Ibid.* pp. 32–3.
71 See www.ohchr.org/EN/PublicationsResources/Pages/SpecialIssues.aspx. Each of these papers is discussed in the related contexts of the following three chapters in this book.
72 Human Rights Council Resolution 4/5, 'Globalization and its Impact on the Full Enjoyment of All Human Rights', UN Doc. A/HRC/RES/4/5 (30 March 2007), at http://ap.ohchr.org/documents/E/HRC/resolutions/A-HRC-RES-4–5.doc. These were the almost identical words used by the Commission on Human Rights (which was replaced by the Human Rights Council in 2006), in its Resolution of the same title, in 2003, at http://ap.ohchr.org/documents/E/CHR/resolutions/E-CN_4-RES-2003–23.doc.
73 Frank Garcia, 'The Global Market and Human Rights: Trading Away the Human Rights Principle' (1999) 25(1) *Brooklyn Journal of International Law* 51, at 70.

activity, assuming it to be individual well-being through the satisfaction of individually determined preferences'.[74]

In fact, it can be seen that both perspectives are concerned with individual welfare. The critical difference between them lies in how such welfare is to be secured, with IHRL insisting on it as a presupposition to all else, whereas IEL *assumes* it will be the product of a properly functioning market. The first brokers no conditionality or qualification to the fulfilment of individual rights; the latter not only necessarily admits that market failure can distort the intended outcome, but also presumes that eventually the market will always deliver.

In practice, each of these purest standpoints is attenuated by virtue of being 'magnificently unprepared for the long littleness of life', as Frances Cornford delightfully puts it (albeit in an entirely different context).[75] Many prominent international human rights and social welfare organisations do indeed acknowledge the importance of the role played by the economy in achieving their goals. Concessions from the purest stance are also evident in prominent international economic bodies, in respect of both their goals and their modus operandi. Social welfare concerns are apparently central to the goals of the WTO, as the 1994 treaty establishing the organisation[76] requires the state parties to recognise

> that their relations in the field of trade and economic endeavour should be conducted with a view to raising standards of living, ensuring full employment and a large and steadily growing volume of real income and effective demand, and expanding the production of and trade in goods and services, while allowing for the optimal use of the world's resources in accordance with the objective of sustainable development, seeking both to protect and preserve the environment and to enhance the means for doing so in a manner consistent with their respective needs and concerns at different levels of economic development.

This is the first paragraph of the treaty's Preamble. The second stresses the particular need to ensure that developing countries 'secure a share in the growth in international trade commensurate with the needs of their economic development'. It is only in the third paragraph that the free market strictures of removing tariffs and trade barriers are stipulated and even then as a means to achieve the objects in the first two paragraphs.

---

74 *Ibid.* p. 71.
75 That is, in a poem written about Rupert Brooke: Frances Cornford, 'Youth', in *Collected Poems* (London: Cresset Press, 1954), p. 19.
76 The Marrakesh Agreement Establishing the World Trade Organization opened for signature 15 April 1994, 1867 UNTS 3 (entered into force 1 January 2005).

NEW YORK INSTITUTE
OF TECHNOLOGY

The stated purposes of the foremost organ in the World Bank Group – the International Bank for Reconstruction and Development – also talk of the need to raise standards of living and conditions of labour by boosting productivity not only by direct Bank assistance, but also by facilitating private foreign investment and promoting the development of local private sectors.[77]

Companies, too, have begun to incorporate social responsibilities into the language of their corporate agendas. The compendious 'Business and Human Rights' website[78] logs the number of major corporations that possess human rights policy statements (240, at the time of writing). The business case for incorporating human rights concerns was the basis upon which the path-breaking group of fourteen leading companies that constituted the Business Leaders Initiative on Human Rights (BLIHR) developed a framework for such integration that it hoped would help make human rights 'part of mainstream business consciousness and a natural component of business practice'.[79]

Language and leverage

Evidently language matters in this area. The correct mixture of economic enunciations and rights rhetoric, as the previous section makes clear, can build bridges, just as its absence can entrench opposition. But determining what is the proper balance and, further, what degree of sincerity lies behind the language used are vital questions for gauging the success of the crossovers and complementarities.

Given the wide range of disciplines that traverse human rights and the global economy, it is perhaps unsurprising to find – for instance – economists and lawyers disagreeing over the intent and interpretation of the same set of words. A striking example of this is provided by Jagdish Bhagwati's laissez-faire attitude towards the very words of the Preamble to the Marrakesh Agreement establishing the WTO quoted above. In declaring himself troubled by the WTO Appellate Body's use of the Preamble (specifically the notion of 'sustainable development') in assisting it to reach certain conclusions regarding the precise interpretation of

---

77 Articles of Agreement of the International Bank for Reconstruction and Development, Article 1.
78 www.business-humanrights.org.
79 Report 3: *Towards a 'Common Framework' on Business and Human Rights: Identifying Components* (2006), p. 21, at www.blihr.org/Reports/BLIHR3Report.pdf. At the time of writing, the Initiative was due to be wound up in March 2009.

substantive articles of the Agreement, he declares that '[m]any of us non-legal intellectuals and experts think that the preamble is like the overture at the opera: the audience is free to rustle through the libretto and even to whisper to friends until the real opera begins!'[80] One might like to ask Professor Bhagwati what he thinks therefore is the purpose of the Preamble, and, assuming as we must that he believes it serves some purpose, what its effect ought to be. (It cannot be, as with Alice in Wonderland, whatever any particular reader wants it to mean.)[81] More importantly, his remarks highlight the elasticity of the particular term he was concerned about. 'Sustainable development' is clearly a term capable of accommodating substantial economic as well as social and environmental features. In the context of trade, as well as aid, and to some degree commerce, such a contested notion certainly opens up opportunities for dialogue and agreement, but it can also result in monologues, as well as outright disagreement. There are many other terms that also straddle the two spheres: mixed economy, corporate social responsibility, ethical trade, socially responsible (or ethical) investment, human rights approaches to development, good governance, aid and trade conditionality, etc. All of these accommodating ideas, which are discussed throughout the following chapters, occupy both legal and policy arenas, albeit to different extents and with different outcomes.

There are, however, limits to the elasticity of such notions, in terms of concept and practice. Thus, for example, the subject matter of certain human rights claims has been extended in ways that relate directly to intersection between the global economy and human rights as a whole. So-called 'third generation rights' (or group or global rights),[82] such as the rights to a healthy environment and to development, are indistinctly legally founded (in the case of the right to a healthy environment), or are fundamentally contested (as in the case of the right to development). The many and various international environmental treaties are focused

---

80 'Afterword: The Question of Linkage' (2002) 96 *American Journal of International Law* 126, at 133; he was referring to the Appellate Body's decision in the so-called *Shrimp/Turtle* case (1998) which departed (in part) from the reasoning in the earlier *Tuna/Dolphin* case (1993). These and other relevant cases are discussed further in chapter 2 below.

81 In fact, the Vienna Convention on the Law of Treaties 1969 states specifically that in the interpretation of the purpose of a treaty, its Preamble is to be accorded a status no different from the text of the treaty (Art. 31(2)).

82 The term flows from the contentious claim that civil and political rights are first-generation and economic, social and cultural rights are second-generation rights. The 'group' or 'global' tags refers to the supposed application of the rights not to individuals *qua* individuals, but to groupings of individuals or to all humankind as a whole.

on mapping out the obligations, and more often aspirations, of the states parties, rather than bestowing rights on individuals or groups to seek their compliance.[83] And in so far as international human rights treaties embrace environmental protection, they do so in inexplicit and indirect terms. The UN's International Covenant on Economic, Social and Cultural Rights (ICESCR) and the EU's Charter of Fundamental Rights talk generally of the need to improve environmental standards;[84] the African Charter on Human and Peoples' Rights refers to a 'general satisfactory environment';[85] and environmental concerns have been taken into consideration when interpreting the right 'to the use and enjoyment of property' under the American Convention on Human Rights.[86]

The right to development has also been articulated in an international instrument, albeit in a non-binding form. The Declaration on the Right to Development was adopted in 1986 but, despite its strong rhetorical contribution to development debates, the initiative is hampered by a fundamental ambiguity over the purported rights-holder (whether individuals or states, or both) and, flowing directly therefrom, uncertainty as to who or what are the duty-bearers (states or the international community at large, or both). Indeed, this lack of consensus has contributed directly to the failure to transform the Declaration into a binding covenant.[87]

At the outer reaches of the expansion of the human rights empire there exist debates as to whether individuals might have a right to trade, what that means in practice and how it might complement or clash with other rights, or indeed with the whole ethos of human rights. Philip Alston, in one of his contributions to his notorious public debate with Ernst-Ulrich Petersmann over the issue, lambasted the latter's promotion of the idea of a right to trade as threatening to detach human rights from their foundations in human dignity by demoting them to 'instrumental means for the achievement of economic policy objectives'.[88] Outdoing even the notion of a right to trade, a new human right to globalisation has been

83 See Alexandre Kiss, 'Concept and Possible Implications of the Right to Environment', in Kathleen Mahoney and Paul Mahoney (eds.), *Human Rights in the Twenty-First Century: A Global Challenge* (Dordrecht: Martinus Nijhoff, 1993), p. 551.
84 Article 12 (right to health) and Article 37 (environmental protection), respectively.
85 Article 24.
86 See judgment of the Inter-American Court of Human Rights in *The Mayagna Awas Tingni Community v. Nicaragua* (2001), paras. 140–55.
87 See Stephen Marks, 'The Human Right to Development: Between Rhetoric and Reality' (2004) 17 *Harvard Human Rights Journal* 137. I discuss further the plight of the right to development in chapter 3 below, pp. 106–7.
88 Philip Alston, 'Resisting the Merger and Acquisition of Human Rights by Trade Law: A Reply to Petersmann' (2002) 13(4) *European Journal of International Law* 815, at 843. Petersmann's direct contributions to the debate are: Ernst-Ulrich Petersmann, 'Time

mooted by Michael Pendleton.[89] I mention it here, not because the idea has any merit (Pendleton's conceptual incoherence is truly breathtaking), but because it illustrates the extent to which some are keen to stretch the boundaries between human rights and the global economy in a way which, though welcome in so far as it encourages debate and engagement, also courts over-simplification and fantasy. Christiana Ochoa strikes just the right note of caution, in my view, in her assessment of the 'mingled dialect' (using Samuel Johnson's words), or 'alter-language' (using her own), that now marks much of the language shared by human rights advocates and international economic actors when they interact today.[90]

It is with the middle ground occupied by this shared language that this book is concerned. There is disagreement and talking at cross-purposes. In *The Soulful Science*, Diane Coyle's thoughtful exposé of what economists do and why it matters, she states that

> among people of more moderate opinions there is still a division of per-ception between those who believe global capitalism has been essentially beneficial but needs its problems ironing out, and those who believe it has brought some selective benefits but has essentially operated against the interest of the very poorest countries.[91]

But, in respect of the particular concern of human rights, rights advo-cates and globalisation protagonists are increasingly traversing the divide between these two camps. And therein, whatever the caveats, lies the attraction. The leverage that the translocation of some level of human rights language can obtain within economic discourse, and the potential benefits for human rights that might flow therefrom, is just too inviting a prospect to be passed over. The countermanding facts that, among the various institutions of the global economy, some resist the appropriation

for a United Nations "Global Compact" for Integrating Human Rights into the Law of Worldwide Organizations: Lessons from European Integration' (2002) 13(3) *European Journal of International Law* 621, and Ernst-Ulrich Petersmann, 'Taking Human Dignity, Poverty and Empowerment of Individuals More Seriously: Rejoinder to Alston' (2002) 13(4) *European Journal of International Law* 845.

89 Michael Pendleton, 'A New Human Right – The Right to Globalization' (1998–9) 22 *Fordham International Law Journal* 2,053. Professor Pendleton's body of academic work is, as far as I can tell, wholly focused on intellectual property law, save this amazing foray into human rights law, globalisation theory, religion and much else.

90 Christiana Ochoa, 'Advancing the Language of Human Rights in a Global Economic Order: An Analysis of Discourse' (2003) 23 *Boston College Third World Law Journal* 57: the phrase of Samuel Johnson's she draws from his reflections on commerce's corruption of language and depravation of manners.

91 Diane Coyle, *The Soulful Science: What Economists Really Do and Why It Matters* (Princeton: Princeton University Press, 2007), p. 65.

of human rights language and the potential obligations it brings (e.g. the WTO, certain corporations and corporate representative bodies) and others experiment with it (the World Bank), or even embrace it (some corporations and bilateral aid agencies), should ultimately be seen as opportunities, even if challenging, to harness essential means to achieve human rights ends. That harnessing is effected through the conditions of accountability that the language of human rights, and human rights law in particular, imposes not only on states, but also on these other global economic actors, both public and private. Whether and how this is to be done – to what extent and in respect of which human rights, at what pace, by what means (legal and otherwise), and by whom (nation states, international bodies, corporations or other private institutions) – are ultimately matters of political contestation.

It is an exploration of the problems and possibilities of this bringing together of human rights and the global economy that constitutes the overriding purpose of the book. The chapters that follow address these questions in the contiguous spheres of trade, aid and commerce (chapters 2, 3 and 4 respectively), and chapter 5 concludes with the prescription of who has responsibility for what, and an analysis of what we stand to gain, as well as what we stand to lose, if those responsibilities are not met.

2

Trade and human rights

Introduction

In the late nineteenth century, when faced with difficulties in establishing trading relations with the tiny island states of the South Pacific that were effectively self-sufficient, early German trading magnates had a neat solution. They simply created demand. They set up so-called 'smoking schools' to teach the locals how to smoke tobacco and thereby to inculcate in them the habit.[1] The company dispensed free pipes and tobacco and manufactured an aura that cigarette smoking was not only pleasurable, but sophisticated and a symbol of status.[2] The ploy worked and trade began to flourish as the islanders imported tobacco products paid for by exports of such natural resources as copra, exotic fruits, timber, herbs and spices, and phosphate.

This discomforting tale casts light on two fundamental features of international trade and its relationship with human rights. First it shows that it is corporations and not states that do the trading,[3] even if it is states that must establish the rules of international trade and police their observance. This adjectival role of states – individually and by way of their multilateral creations (for example, the WTO, the EU, the North American Free

---

1 See Stewart Firth, 'German Firms in the Western Pacific Islands, 1857–1914' (1973) 8 *Journal of Pacific History* 11, at 13. I am indebted to Christie Weeramantry for alerting me to this saga, which he unearthed during his time as Chairman of the Nauru Commission of Inquiry in 1987–8, before he was appointed to the International Court of Justice in 1991. See C. G. Weeramantry, 'Human Rights and the Global Marketplace' (1999) 25 *Brooklyn Journal of International Law* 28, at 42–4.
2 Tobacco companies today are accused of much the same sort of advertising, particularly in developing countries whose regulation of such corporate behaviour is often absent or ineffective and whose populations may be considered especially vulnerable; see the World Bank, *Curbing the Epidemic: Governments and the Economics of Tobacco Control* (Washington, DC: World Bank, 1999).
3 Of course states can trade through so-called 'State Owned Enterprises' (which even in communist states are being rapidly dismantled), but these are nevertheless corporations, not the state *qua* the state.

Trade Agreement (NAFTA) and the Asia-Pacific Economic Cooperation (APEC)) – is key to understanding how international trade laws work and what legitimate expectations might be required of such trading bodies as listed above in support of human rights. This is a theme traced through this chapter. It is also an illustration of the interrelationship and inter-dependency of corporations and trade, despite my separate treatment of them in this book.

The second illuminated feature is that the wave of economic globalisa-tion which swept the globe in the late 1800s and early 1900s, just as with the current wave, was powered by exponential advances in the technologies of production, communication, travel and trade. In both waves, mega-corporations deepened and widened their commercial empires along – and often ahead of – the lines drawn by the great economic powers of their time. New trading routes have been opened and old ones revitalised, as the ripple of global trade leaves few countries and communities unaffected. Economies, social and religious mores, political philosophies and envi-ronmental circumstances have all been affected to some degree or other. Human rights are evidently no exception. Thus, while at the time these smoking schools were being set up in the Pacific few people would have couched the episode in human rights terms, and certainly there existed no relevant international human rights treaties then, it is clear nonethe-less that there were human rights concerns. As we know of human rights now, these concerns would be in respect of the rights to life and to health care, freedom of information (being that part of the right to free speech that embraces the receipt as well as the dissemination of information – in this case the known addictive attributes of smoking tobacco, if not yet their carcinogenic properties), and even the right to privacy (not to be subjected to environmental pollution).[4]

Trade goes round the world and makes the world go round. It exerts an almost hypnotic effect on nations; balance of trade figures are part of the economic stories that make or break governments; the clamour to join the WTO – the membership of which, as noted in chapter 1, comprises nearly all countries (and all those, save Russia, of any economic significance) – has been achieved in less than a decade and a half, and is now paralleled, if not outstripped, by the enormous growth in bilateral trade treaties; and it is seen by many developing nations as the path to their potential economic salvation and a better life for their citizens.

---

4 It was upon such health and human rights concerns that the World Health Organisa-tion established the *Framework Convention for Tobacco Control* in 2003; see www.who. int/tobacco/framework/WHO_FCTC_english.pdf.

From the outset, the simple intention of trade has been to gain access to greater variety and quantities of commodities and services, and to make a profit from the selling of one's own wit and wares. *Free* trade was to trade without so-called protections, which, as Adam Smith counter-intuitively argued, do not protect at all. 'To the contrary, trade spurs the wealth of nations, increases the commonweal, regulates prices and wages, and harmonizes relations among nations.'[5] These remain the basic premises for trade and free trade today. But the modern, post-war, conceptions of international trade are overlain by another factor: one that is especially relevant to the concern of this book – namely, a utilitarian concern to ensure that trade benefits as wide a spectrum of humanity as possible, but above all the poorest and the least advantaged.

The overlay of international trade welfarism was an apparent concern of the delegates who gathered in Havana in 1947 to draw up a treaty for the establishment of the International Trade Organisation (ITO). As Clair Wilcox, the Vice-Chairman of the US delegation, put it in his reflections on the negotiations, '[t]he most violent controversies at the conference and the most protracted ones were those evoked by issues raised in the name of economic development'.[6] Though, inevitably, the product of these machinations bore the hallmarks of compromise, Article 1 of the resultant Havana Charter nevertheless stressed the need 'to foster and assist industrial and general economic development, particularly of those countries which are still in the early stages of industrial development' within its broad remit to 'increase production, consumption and the exchange of goods'. The Charter also expressly related the ITO's objects and *modus operandi* to the UN's general ambition 'to create conditions of stability and well-being which are necessary for peaceful and friendly relations among nations', and specifically to its concern to promote 'universal respect for, and observance of, human rights and fundamental freedoms', as stipulated in Article 55 of the UN Charter.

The Havana Charter never came into force. Its fate was sealed by the US Senate failing to consent to the Charter's ratification, largely because of other apparently more pressing international concerns facing Congress at the time, including the drawing up and implementation of the Marshall Plan and the conclusion of the North Atlantic Treaty.[7]

---

5 As Peter Dougherty puts it in his book *Who's Afraid of Adam Smith?* (New York: J. Wiley, 2002), p. 55.

6 *A Charter for World Trade* (New York: Macmillan, 1949), at p. 48.

7 'The Administration had its hands full getting other measures through Congress and could see no gain in loading one more controversial item onto a crowded schedule', is

Additionally, despite the US's initial role as principal advocate of the negotiation of the agreement, concerns were now being aired in Congress and in the Administration about the result.[8] So, the ITO never took its intended place alongside the World Bank and the IMF as the third pillar of the new superstructure of global economic institutions. That said, its development-oriented trade prescriptions (recognisably 'sustainable development' in today's terminology)[9] survived the intervening forty-seven years until the international community returned once again to the idea of creating a global trade body – this time successfully – when the delegates from 124 countries and the European Communities congregated in Marrakesh in 1994 and agreed to establish the World Trade Organisation (WTO). The key provisions that I quoted from the Preamble of the WTO Agreement in chapter 1[10] support this line of reasoning. Indeed, for Rob Howse and Makua Mutua it is clear that the Preamble 'does not make free trade an end in itself. Rather, it establishes the objectives of the [WTO] system as related to the fulfillment of basic human values, including the improvement of living standards for all people and sustainable development, [and] . . . these objectives cannot be reached without respect for human rights.'[11] John Jackson, a leading light within international economic and trade law circles today, also revealingly concludes in a paper discussing the relationship of trade and peace that the inclusion of such 'peace-related trade goals' as poverty reduction and

how William Diebold put it, in *The End of the ITO*, Essays in International Finance No. 16 (Princeton University, 1952), p. 6. By the time President Truman sent the ITO Charter to Congress for approval in April 1949, Congress was preoccupied with the formation of NATO and the descent into the Cold War, such that, as Simon Reisman notes, 'there was no time and no enthusiasm for what had become a rather stale and disappointing enterprise'; 'The Birth of a World Trading System: ITO and GATT', in Orin Kirshner (ed.), *The Bretton Woods–GATT System: Retrospect and Prospect after Fifty Years* (Armonk: M. E. Sharpe, 1996), p. 86.

8 The result of the Havana conference failed to appeal to the protectionists, the promoters of free trade or the pragmatists in the US trade debate, since it contained, respectively, either too many concessions, too many exceptions, or too little in terms of concrete and timely outcomes; see Reisman, 'Birth of a World Trading System', p. 85.

9 That is, reflecting the ethos behind the term as promoted by the Brundtland Commission's iconic report *Our Common Future* published in 1987 in which sustainable development was defined as 'development that meets the needs of the present without compromising the ability of future generations to meet their own needs'; see The World Commission on Environment and Development, *Our Common Future* (1987), Australian edition (Melbourne: Oxford University Press, 1990), p. 87.

10 Above, p. 31.

11 Robert Howse and Makau Mutua, 'Protecting Human Rights in a Global Economy: Challenges for the World Trade Organisation', p. 3; available at the Rights & Democracy website: www.ichrdd.ca/english/commdoc/publications/globalization/wtoRightsGlob.html.

sustainable environmental development in the list of the WTO's objectives has important deductive consequences. Namely, that 'while none of these goals expressly mention human rights or democracy, you can see various connections with those concepts in each of the goals and thus ultimately yet more connections tying the WTO via democracy and human rights to peace'.[12]

There is no shortage of commentators identifying the sorts of rights that are relevant to trade, as well as those rights that are especially affected by trade. These include the right to a fair trial, freedom of movement and association, participation in (or election of) government, personal safety, property protection, non-discrimination, education, health and labour rights.[13] The problem has always been, however, that the trade theory (or at least that represented by these broad legal prescriptions) is not always borne out in trade practice as prosecuted by economists, trade officials and commercial enterprises. In respect of the international regimes in general, and the WTO in particular, such stated objectives – even when enshrined in treaties that bind the states that sign them – are not always interpreted as such, and in fact (as illustrated by the Bhagwati opera metaphor noted at the end of the last chapter) are more likely to be overlooked or ignored by many. Even the most socially sympathetic trade lawyers like Andrew Lang warn us against the temptation to overestimate 'the extent to which the normative vision of the trade regime is deducible from the text of trade agreements'.[14]

Within the operational framework of the WTO, law is subsumed within the dominant concerns of economics; lawyers are viewed as procedural plumbers, rather than as policy-makers or strategists. Frieder Roessler, the former Director of the Legal Affairs Division of the General Agreement on Tariffs and Trade (GATT),[15] provides us with a personal reflection on the historical embeddedness of this attitude:

---

12 John Jackson, 'Reflections on the Trade and Peace Relationship', in Padideh Ala'i, Tomer Broude and Colin Picker (eds.), *Trade as Guarantor of Peace, Liberty and Security?* (Washington, DC: The American Society of International Law, 2006), p. 28.

13 See *ibid.*; and Caroline Dommen, 'Raising Human Rights Concerns in the World Trade Organization: Actors, Processes and Possible Strategies' (2002) 24 *Human Rights Quarterly* 1.

14 Andrew Lang, 'Reconstructing Embedded Liberalism: John Gerard Ruggie and Constructivist Approaches to the Study of the International Trade Regime' (2006) 9 *Journal of International Economic Law* 81, at 94.

15 The GATT came into force in 1947 and was, and today remains, the principal international trade treaty. Since 1994 it has constituted one of the sixty-odd agreements, annexes, decisions and understandings administered by the WTO.

> The small secretariat of the GATT did not have a legal service when I became a staff member in 1973. Eager to use my education in international law, I asked the Director-General of the GATT at a staff meeting whether he intended to create a legal service. To my surprise and embarrassment, my enquiry met with a chuckle from the assembly. After the meeting, an older colleague explained in a patient tone of voice that the GATT did not believe in law, but in pragmatism.[16]

Robert Hudec, the father of modern international trade law, labelled the sort of law that emerged from these straitened circumstances 'a diplomat's jurisprudence', which is a 'jurisprudence puzzling to lawyers, for it is primarily the work of diplomats . . . [who] have developed an approach toward law which attempts to reconcile, on their own terms, the regulatory objectives of a conventional legal system with the turbulent realities of international trade affairs'.[17]

Hudec was concerned especially with the particular mechanics of dispute settlement under the GATT, but his point about treaty provisions being implemented in the context of the realities of international trade applies as much, if not more so, to their broad social and economic goals. While a key economic reality of international trade is, of course, the prevailing ethos of trade liberalisation coupled with economic efficiency, so too are the social concerns of trade to improve the living standards, employment conditions and development prospects of the poor part of that reality. The two are clearly linked, in that – broadly speaking – economic success through trade *can* facilitate social improvements. Even orthodox free-traders – indeed, they more especially – will promote precisely this line. Clive Crook of *The Economist* argues against globalisation sceptics by maintaining that the market economy theory of international trade provides that the poor, as well as the rich, *should* gain.

> [G]ains-from-trade logic often arouses suspicion, because the benefits seem to come from nowhere. Surely one side or other must lose. Not so. The benefits that a rich country gets through trade do not come at the expense of its poor-country trading partners, or vice versa. Recall that according to theory, trade is a positive-sum game [in that] . . . in all these transactions, both sides – exporters and importers, borrowers and lenders, shareholders and workers – can gain.[18]

16 Frieder Roessler, 'Foreword' to Robert Hudec, *Essays on the Nature of International Trade Law* (London: Cameron May, 1999), p. 10.
17 Robert Hudec, 'The GATT Legal System: A Diplomat's Jurisprudence' (1970) 4 *Journal of World Trade Law* 615, at 615.
18 Clive Crook, 'Grinding the Poor', in Simon Cox (ed.), *Economics and Making Sense of the Modern Economy* (London: The Economist and Profile Books, 2nd edn 2006), p. 15.

However, what is missing in this analysis is any acknowledgement of the declared intention of international trade laws to try to *ensure* that international trade delivers on this potential. This is the central problem with trade's adoption of the notion of economic efficiency as its fundamental normative principle. Typically, it treats such issues as human rights as 'externalities'. As such, they are not, or cannot be, 'internalised' in the construction process of the model, and so they are discounted from any evaluation of the outcomes.[19] The simple reliance on human rights protection by way of the conditional incidence of the benefits of trade is not enough. Rather, the prosecution of international trade must be directed towards that outcome. Free trade, after all, is not a promise of trade without regulation, but rather trade regulated with the intention to make it flow freely so as to fulfil its aims of greater prosperity for all, including and especially the poor, and thereby to assist in the promotion of base social and human rights standards. How this 'trying to ensure' can be done, how it is being done, and how it should be done better, are questions that together constitute the framework for my analysis of trade and human rights in this chapter.

I turn now to look at the theory and practice of the impact of trade (and trade law) on human rights, followed by a specific analysis of what is the present and possible future role played by the WTO, and finally a review of specific international initiatives that 'link' access to trade opportunities to human rights performance.

'A rising tide lifts all boats'?

This idiom – mostly famously invoked by J. F. Kennedy to emphasise the breadth of the purported beneficial impacts of his economic policies – is often used in respect of trade, to emphasise the purported beneficial impact of its liberalisation on the balance of payments of states and the hip pockets of their citizens. The highlighting of the notion of equality – that is, the flat application of the benefits to all, regardless of their current position – is quite deliberate. All will benefit, it asserts. However, implicit in the phrase is, of course, an acknowledgement that existing disparities between boats will remain: dinghies will be floating higher than before, but so will the cruisers and the liners. As a matter of principle, the maintenance

---

19 See Lorand Bartels, 'Trade and Human Rights', in Daniel Bethlehem *et al.* (eds.), *The Oxford Handbook of International Trade Law* (Oxford: Oxford University Press, forthcoming 2009), p. 576.

of inequality in relative terms may be more acceptable than its maintenance in absolute terms, but it still raises difficult problems of justice. The fact that in reality, far from showing that the relative differentials between countries are being maintained, data are pointing to their growth (in some cases exponentially so)[20] adds to the moral unease. Ha-Joon Chang, in his acclaimed book *Kicking away the Ladder*, attributes this circumstance in large measure to the fact that the economic advantages of protectionism, captured markets, and selective liberalisation exploited by the developed countries of today when they were climbing the development ladder, are being systematically denied to presently developing countries, ironically – some say hypocritically – in the name of equality and fairness.[21]

Historical analysis of theory and practice

Belief in the personal, social and political as well as economic benefits of free (or freer) trade has a long history. John Stuart Mill, a doyen of the liberalist philosophy, is well known for his articulation of the conceptual and practical arguments for the promotion of individual liberty within the political and social spheres, stating that 'the only part of the conduct of any one, for which he is amenable to society, is that which concerns others. In the part which merely concerns himself, his independence is, of right, absolute. Over himself, over his own body and mind, the individual is sovereign.'[22] But Mill also insisted on the importance of the intersection of individual liberty with the 'social act' of free trade to the wide fulfilment of international peace, order and security, saying that trade is 'the principal guarantee of the peace of the world, is the great permanent security for the uninterrupted progress of the ideas, the institutions, and the character of the human race'.[23]

The liberalisation of trading relations between states is considered to yield broad benefits which are only imperfectly identified when described

20 The UNDP noted that in 2003 '18 countries with a combined population of 460 million people, registered lower scores on the human development index (HDI) than in 1990 – an unprecedented reversal', and 'in human development terms the space between countries is marked by deep and, in some cases, widening inequalities in income and life chances'. UNDP, *Human Development Report 2005: International Cooperation at a Crossroads: Aid, Trade and Security in an Unequal World* (New York: UNDP, 2005), p. 3.

21 Ha-Joon Chang, *Kicking Away the Ladder: Development Strategy in Historical Perspective* (London: Anthem Press, 2002), especially chapter 2.

22 John Stuart Mill, 'On Liberty' (1859) in *On Liberty and Other Essays*, ed. John Gray (Oxford and New York: Oxford University Press, 1998), p. 14.

23 John Stuart Mill, *Principles of Political Economy* (1848), introduced by Sir John Lubbock (London: George Routledge and Sons, 1891), p. 395.

in economic or commercial terms. Trade, it is believed, increases competition, innovation and productivity growth. But it is the fact that these factors in turn generate greater prosperity and produce better living standards that provides trade with its ultimate worth and indeed its *raison d'être*. The process of trade is important, but by insisting on a focus on the consequential outcomes, the process is put in perspective. In this regard, there is no doubting the brilliance of David Ricardo's construction of the notion of 'comparative advantage' as an explanation and description of how and why trade between states is sought out and sustainably pursued. For many economists the beauty of the concept is in its classical identification of the factors of the efficient allocation of scarce resources. Cross-border trade necessarily agitates for the exploitation of comparative advantage by 'mov[ing] output in the direction of activities that offer domestic factors of production the highest returns', as Martin Wolf describes it.[24] This is why today the West engages in comparatively little manufacturing, and provides the bulk of the world's services industries, whereas in China it is the other way around. And yet, for Ricardo himself, the wider social, political and economic consequences of understanding trade in this way were just as (if not more) important.

> This pursuit of individual advantage is admirably connected with the universal good of the whole. By stimulating industry, by rewarding ingenuity, and by using most efficaciously the peculiar powers bestowed by nature, it distributes labour most effectively and most economically; while, by increasing the general mass of productions, it diffuses general benefit, and binds together, by one common tie of interest and intercourse, the universal society of nations throughout the civilised world.[25]

Nonetheless, it was not until the concerted efforts to reform the apparatus of the international economy at the end of the Second World War that these broader social and political dimensions were institutionalised; that is – to adopt John Ruggie's term – when liberalism was 'embedded' within broader social concerns, such as achieving full employment and improving living standards, that were shared across the industrialised world at the time. This embedded liberalism marked a shift from the 'unembedded' or orthodox laissez-faire liberalism that held sway in the international trading order during the latter part of the nineteenth century and the first

24 Martin Wolf, *Why Globalization Works* (New Haven and London: Yale University Press, 2004), p. 81.
25 David Ricardo, *On the Principles of Political Economy and Taxation* (1817), Great Minds Series (Amherst, MA: Prometheus Books, 1996), p. 93.

part of the twentieth century, and to some extent represented the international community's desire expressly to recognise the integration of the social, political and economic concerns of states on the international plane.

> The task of postwar institutional reconstruction...[was] to devise a framework which would safeguard and even aid the quest for domestic stability without, at the same time, triggering the mutually destructive external consequences that had plagued the interwar period. This was the essence of the embedded liberalism compromise: unlike the economic nationalism of the thirties, it would be multilateral in character; unlike the liberalism of the gold standard and free trade [that prevailed from the late 1800s until the early 1930s], its multilateralism would be predicated upon domestic interventionism.[26]

In respect of international trade, the enunciated aspirations of the GATT, and the ITO before it, discussed earlier, reflected this embedded liberalism. In practice, however, it may be said that the early post-war years proved to be something of a high point for the idea, for as global trade gathered pace during the 1960s and 1970s, the compromise between domestic stability and international economic liberalisation began to unravel. So much so that, despite the fact that the words 'free trade' appear nowhere in the text of the GATT, and the drafters of the GATT 'were far from doctrinaire advocates of unfettered markets',[27] the language and practice of free trade orthodoxy came to dominate international trading relations. A dramatically increasing global economy driven by waves of international trade and investment, and tigerish international financial markets characterised by highly mobile (or 'footloose') capital, has led to nations increasingly qualifying the scope and depth of domestic welfare programmes,[28] and consequentially diminishing the economic and social rights that such programmes (where they exist at all) are designed to protect. Indeed, a controversial report by the UN Commission on Trade and Development (UNCTAD) in 2004 maintained that trade liberalisation had, on the whole, not aided those least developed countries (LDCs) that had adopted such policies, especially in terms of efforts to combat poverty. The report argued:

---

26 John Ruggie, 'International Regimes, Transactions, and Change: Embedded Liberalism and the Postwar Economic Order' (1982) 36(2) *International Organization* 379, at 393.
27 Jeffrey Dunoff, 'Globalization and Human Rights' (1999) 25(1) *Brooklyn Journal of International Law* 125, at 130.
28 *Ibid.* at 136.

that the potential positive role of trade in poverty reduction is not being translated into reality in a large number of LDCs. The major policy challenge in linking international trade to poverty reduction in the LDCs is to bridge the gap between the positive role of trade . . . and the often neutral, and even negative, trade–poverty relationship which . . . currently exists in too many LDCs.[29]

It must be said that the 'immiserising trade effect' that the authors of the report claimed their research demonstrated was forthrightly rejected by, among others, *The Economist*. While acknowledging the report's value in identifying worrying trends of some of the poorest and weakest states doing badly when they formally opened their markets to international trade (average income rising only marginally and the incidence of extreme poverty remaining static), the journal was scathing about the report's assumptions and methodology failing to take into account factors other than trade that might have negatively impacted on these states, and the fact that so much of the economic enterprise in the poorest countries is beyond measurement, being informal and subsistence rather than part of the formal market and therefore recordable.[30] In fact, neither the report nor its criticism is conclusive. More important than the disagreements is the acceptance by both camps of the continuing, severe economic and social problems experienced by many of the poorest states in the world. How to ensure that trade, under whatever conditions, plays a positive part in their revival on all fronts, including human rights, is the key concern.

Linking human rights and trade

Given this historical progression, it is unsurprising therefore that among commentators on international relations generally, and on international trade in particular, there has been a burgeoning interest in reasserting the original post-war sentiments of balancing the benefits of robust global trade with the needs of domestic social order and welfare.[31] Equally predictably, this movement has itself been rebutted by the defenders of the present format of globalisation. The canvas upon which this debate has been painted has been, of course, the emergence of the WTO with its own particular representation of wide social and economic aspirations to be achieved through the mediated expansion of multilateral trade relations.

---

29 UNCTAD, *The Least Developed Countries Report 2004: Linking International Trade with Poverty Reduction* (New York and Geneva: United Nations, 2004), at p. 123.
30 'Nothing to Sell', *The Economist*, 29 May 2004, pp. 73–4.
31 As chartered by Lang, 'Reconstructing Embedded Liberalism'.

Wolfgang Benedek, for example, argues that the international economic system as a whole, and that of the WTO in particular, ought to take greater heed of the exhortation in Article 55 of the UN Charter (to which, of course, all members of the WTO are parties), better to reconcile its economic, social *and* human rights objectives.[32] Dani Rodrik demands a more radical approach, when he insists on a rehabilitation of the lost soul of trade by re-educating those who dictate its current form and direction. Within the world trading regime there needs to be, he maintains, a 'shift from a "market access" mind-set to a "development" mind-set'.[33] Thereby, the currently debilitating preoccupation with maximising trade flow (seen too often as an end in itself) would be replaced by one that focuses on how to maximise the possibilities for the socio-economic development of states individually and as a whole (which would require using trade flows as a means to an end).[34]

Adopting *and* implementing a development-oriented approach to trade would necessitate critical assessment not only of circumstances in which developing countries suffer from too much free trade, but also when there is too little. That is, when the West (in particular) does not open all of its markets evenly and substantially to developing states (especially, for example, in the agricultural sector), while at the same time insisting on wholesale dismantling of trade barriers of those same developing countries. Either way, these conditions are established in negotiations between states in which, as Thomas Pogge puts it, 'our [developed country] governments enjoy a crushing advantage in bargaining power and expertise'.[35]

Joseph Stiglitz also bemoans international trade's lack of earnest and effective focus on the economic development of the poorer states and sees the solution lying in its better management and regulation rather than philosophical orientation. He too suggests such better management would require a mixture of both more trade liberalisation (the West opening up *all* of its markets unconditionally to trade from the developing world), and more protectionism (in the sense of extending the preferential treatment given to trade from developing countries).[36]

---

32 Wolfgang Benedek, 'The World Trade Organisation and Human Rights', in Benedek *et al.* (eds.), *Economic Globalisation and Human Rights* (Cambridge: Cambridge University Press, 2007), p. 165.
33 Dani Rodrik, *One Economics, Many Recipes: Globalization, Institutions, and Economic Growth* (Princeton: Princeton University Press, 2007), p. 234.
34 *Ibid.*
35 Thomas Pogge, *World Poverty and Human Rights* (Cambridge: Polity Press, 2002), p. 21.
36 Joseph Stiglitz, *Making Globalisation Work* (New York: W. W. Norton, 2006), pp. 82–7.

Such critiques, however, have attracted robust defences of trade liberal-isation in its current guise. Jagdish Bhagwati is optimistic about what the empirical evidence of trade shows for the plight of the world's poor and the states in which they live and work. Trade generally rewards 'outward-oriented economies' (as he labels them), whether poor or rich, for they are best able to exploit export opportunities overseas and thereby finance and expand their own import markets.[37] Martin Wolf devotes a complete chapter in his book on *Why Globalization Works* to countering critics whom he sees are unnecessarily, and at times illogically, 'traumatized by trade'.[38] Kent Jones goes further and argues that, at least among his own tribe of 'economists and trade professionals', most 'regard the WTO as the catalyst for economic growth and emergence from poverty' through the democratic and social reforms, and the increased regard for human rights and the environment, that tend to flow from increased trade.[39]

In fact, the gap between the critics and the defenders is far less than at first it seems. When one reads these accounts closely, it is clear that most of what they rail against are caricatures. The plainly ill-conceived or unsupported criticisms of free trade, and equally of free trade critics, ought to be dismissed as untenable by all observers who have invested the time and effort to inform themselves of both sides of the debate. Examples of the outlandish have been rightly condemned by commentators such as Kent Jones, in his targeting of what he calls 'WTO bashers' (as opposed to 'WTO skeptics') who 'see irreconcilable conflicts between human rights, social justice, and the global environment on the one hand, and a market driven trading system on the other',[40] and Martin Wolf, who gives short shrift to claims that any employment of children occasioned by new trading opportunities is *necessarily* bad for the children and an infringement of their rights to education, health and not being exploited.[41] In fact, regarding the latter, the 1989 UN Convention on the Rights of the Child (which, incidentally, is by far the most heavily ratified of all human rights treaties) specifically acknowledges that children can and do undertake employment; it is the type and intensity of such work that Article 32 of the Convention seeks to limit. Similarly, the ILO Convention No. 182 is

---

37 Jagdish Bhagwati, *In Defense of Globalization* (New York: Oxford University Press, 2004), pp. 60–4.
38 Wolf, *Why Globalization Works*, chapter 10.
39 Kent Jones, *Who's Afraid of the WTO?* (Oxford and New York: Oxford University Press, 2004), p. 147.
40 *Ibid.* p. 5.   41 Wolf, *Why Globalization Works*, pp. 187–8.

concerned with prohibiting the worst forms of child labour, rather than child labour per se.

We might fairly conclude, therefore, that today the trade and social justice lobbies appear to share some important common goals. The majority of economists, claims Jagdish Bhagwati, *do* see trade as a 'powerful weapon in the arsenal of policies that we can deploy to fight poverty'.[42] However, the devil is in the detail of how that weapon is deployed, what conditions (if any) are imposed upon it, and what expectations are made of its impact, immediate and long-term, that constitute grounds of difference and dispute between free trade protagonists and development, social justice and human rights advocates. In specific relation to human rights, what this boils down to is the question of 'linkage': whether and how trade and human rights are linked to one another. In answering this question, not only must we draw from the relative legal bases of both fields, but we must also place them within the relevant political context of their interaction.

The political context of law-based linkage

The interactions between trade and human rights laws – both extant and projected – are not conducted in a vacuum, but rather are dominated by the demands of international relations, domestic politics, and perceptions of economic advantage or necessity.[43] In terms of its facilitation by international trade law, the most that can be said with certainty of the relationship between trade rules and human rights is that it is diffuse. 'The theoretical, empirical and policy issues raised by this discussion are complex and much remains unclear. In this regard, the normative aspects of the debate in terms of "*what should be*", have dominated.' This is how Hoe Lim insightfully described it in 2001.[44] Lim lamented the lack of in-depth analysis of *what is*, and set about starting to correct this in his article. In the years since, a large body of work has been devoted to both the present and future tenses of the relationship within the particular context of WTO law and policy.

---

42 Bhagwati, *In Defense of Globalization*, p. 82.
43 As Philip Alston noted more than twenty-five years ago: 'trade policy is foreign policy', and 'the promotion of respect for human rights is an important goal of foreign policy'. Having said that, Alston also conceded that such statements do not lead inexorably to any sort of certainty over the nature of the link between trade and human rights; 'International Trade as an Instrument of Positive Human Rights Policy' (1982) 4 *Human Rights Quarterly* 155, at 156–7.
44 Hoe Lim, 'Trade and Human Rights: What's at Issue?' (2001) 35(2) *Journal of World Trade* 275.

When trade increases then adverse pressure can, especially in developing countries, be placed on labour rights (including in respect of occupational health and safety), the rights of women and children, ethnic minority rights, and rights to food, health, education, housing and a clean environment. Positive pressure on such rights can also occur; sometimes, paradoxically, alongside the negative impacts. Thus, for example, while there have been valid causes for concern over the conditions of employment of women in garment manufacturing in Bangladesh, which has grown massively since the early 1990s in line with the country's export drive in clothing and footwear, the very fact that the women are now employed has been seen as a tremendous step forward in empowering them and permitting them greater access to exercising not only their economic and social rights, but also their civil and political rights. The confidence of women workers, born of rising trade union solidarity and the steady rise in the number of female leaders in the trade union movement, has led to significant advances in the political voice of women. 'Ten years ago you didn't see women on the streets of Bangladesh, and the garment industry has meant a massive change in the profile of women as paid workers', as Naila Kabeer argues.[45]

It was precisely this sort of mix of good, bad and unknown implications that my colleague Hai Nguyen (from the Ho Chi Minh National Political Academy, Institute for Human Rights) and I found in our study of the human rights impact of Vietnam's accession to the WTO in 2007. So, for example, while there have been undoubted social advantages borne on the back of Vietnam's booming economy over the years since it opened its doors to international trade in the late 1990s, there will be, inevitably, severe dislocations in certain areas of the economy such as agriculture, which is already raising serious human rights concerns.

> There is a coalition of economic, social and human rights reasons that warrant singling out the agriculture sector as a special case. Agriculture employs 60 per cent of Viet Nam's labour force, and 45 per cent of the rural population live below the poverty line. Indeed, it is in rural areas that 'more than 90 per cent of the country's poor people live and work'. The opening up of the sector to the forces of international trade will, at least in the short term, very likely compound this problem given the size and antiquated practices that predominate in the sector: farms are typically low yield, subsistence based and small – the average farm size being 0.7 hectare per household. The World Bank predicts that, as land transactions

45 Quoted by Annie Kelly, 'Battle Is Joined in the Fight for Equality', *Guardian Weekly*, 22 February 2008, p. 7.

become easier, the less productive (presumably poorer) households could be forced to sell some of their land to the more productive households, as market forces favour efficiency over egalitarianism. It is envisaged that the size of rural sector employment will drop dramatically over the next five to ten years as people are 'pushed' out of the sector by competition, and 'pulled' out by the draw of alternative employment in the industrial and manufacturing sectors. The human rights implications of these swift and significant shifts in circumstances of rural communities, and especially of the poor, will, at least in the short term, be profound.[46]

Given these circumstances, we might ask what should be expected of the rules and operations of the WTO to advance the beneficial aspects of trade for human rights protection and to minimise the adverse consequences? Are the rules 'rigged' against the interests of the poor and their attendant human rights concerns and in favour of the rich states and their human rights concerns, as Oxfam asserts in its influential 2004 Report,[47] or rather is it just that as a matter of practice trade deems human rights to be irrelevant and simply ignores them?[48] Paradoxically, it is a bit of both. Within the strict confines of the WTO, there is precious little room for human rights to be considered. That is despite the fact that the WTO's legal regime is to some extent subject to the constitutional goals and objectives of the UN. Articles 55 and 56 of the UN Charter mandate the UN (including all its organs and associated agencies),[49] and all member states of the UN,[50] respectively, to promote and strive to achieve the purposes of the UN which include 'universal respect for, and observance of, human rights and fundamental freedoms for all without distinction as to race, sex, language, or religion' (Article 55). Article XXI of the GATT

46 David Kinley and Hai Nguyen, *Viet Nam, Human Rights and Trade: Implications of Viet Nam's Accession to the WTO*, Dialogue on Globalization, Occasional Paper No. 29 (Geneva: Friedrich-Ebert-Stiftung, 2008), p. 25 (footnotes omitted).

47 Oxfam, *Rigged Rules and Double Standards: Trade, Globalisation and the Fight against Poverty* (Oxford: Oxfam, 2002).

48 'Economists and government representatives in the WTO dictate the content of its policies without assessing their impact on human rights', as Floris van Hees puts it: 'Protection v. Protectionism: The Use of Human Rights Arguments in the Debate for and against the Liberalisation of Trade' (2004), p. 13, available at http://web.abo.fi/instut/imr/norfa/floris.pdf.

49 Though the WTO has no formalised association with the UN, its founding charter, the Marrakesh Agreement, provides (under Article V(1)) that the WTO's General Council 'shall make appropriate arrangements for effective cooperation with other intergovernmental organizations that have responsibilities related to those of the WTO'.

50 Which, of course, include all the current 153 members of the WTO (though not, as Lorand Bartels has pointed out to me, the customs territories of the EU, Taiwan, Hong Kong and Macau).

expressly gives primacy to UN Charter obligations of states regarding international peace and security over any GATT rules, which obligations are increasingly based on the grounds of gross violations of human rights. Furthermore, Article 31(3)(c) of the Vienna Convention on the Law of Treaties (1969) – in an (unsuccessful) effort to prevent the fragmentation of international law into all its different subject areas – provides that in the interpretation of treaties 'any relevant rules of international law applicable in the relations between the parties' shall be taken into account. On the face of it, this stipulation requires the WTO dispute settlement bodies to consider shared international human rights obligations in their deliberations. Somewhat controversially, this is not quite how the WTO has since interpreted the provision.[51]

What is more, certain international human rights treaties impose obligations on states in respect of their intercourse with each other, including in trade. The UN Committee on Economic, Social and Cultural Rights has repeatedly stated that, under the terms of Article 2 of the ICESCR, signatory states[52] are obliged both to refrain from any actions that might result in human rights breaches in other countries (negative obligations), and to act in ways that aid and facilitate the efforts of other countries to protect human rights within their jurisdictions (positive obligations).[53] An inherent difficulty with such extended obligations is how they are applied in practice. So much depends on there being a sufficient degree of causal nexus between the legal measure and the effect, which, given the complex nature of both trade and human rights, is extremely difficult to ascertain with any degree of precision.

Certainly, there are surrogate or companion notions more openly acknowledged (such as strengthening the rule of law in member states by way of the lengthy and detailed legal processes of their accession and subsequent compliance measures),[54] and recognition of the importance of antecedent or parallel concerns (such as labour conditions and standards of living, as discussed earlier), but the addressing of human rights issues

---

51 In the *EC–Biotech* case (2007), briefly discussed below, a WTO dispute settlement panel ruled that this provision would only apply in WTO cases where *all* WTO members were signatory to the particular treaty at issue.

52 As at July 2008, there are 159 parties to the ICESCR.

53 For a compilation of such statements, see Bartels, 'Trade and Human Rights', p. 577, at footnote 27.

54 And without at least the rudiments of the rule of law, a state will simply be by-passed by global trade, resulting in 'black holes in the world economy... from which little but desperate people and capital flight emerge', as Wolf puts it: *Why Globalization Works*, p. 79.

expressly is limited to a few highly disputed cases before the WTO's dispute settlement panels (discussed below). Even Director-General Lamy's welcome and much vaunted declaration on the need to 'humanize globalization' by launching a more welfare-oriented 'Geneva Consensus' to counter-balance the perceived neo-liberalism of the 'Washington Consensus' in international trade relations does not once refer directly to human rights.[55]

In international trade law and relations outside the WTO, there is greater evidence of, and opportunity for, incorporating human rights matters. This is perhaps most strikingly apparent in respect of certain bilateral trade agreements (especially those concluded with the EU) which have standard human rights clauses. Indeed, generally, the incidence of developing countries linking access to trade benefits for developing states with their meeting certain human rights conditions is evidently growing. At the same time, the crude use of trade sanctions, which 'the WTO dispute settlement system is simply neither mandated nor competent to handle',[56] for reasons that might include human rights abuses, appears to be on the decline. I further discuss 'conditionality' in all of these senses in the final part of this chapter.

The trade and human rights debate has been gathering pace since the years immediately before and after the birth of the WTO in 1994. There have been a number of ambient political factors that have pushed it along, including the extension of free trade into Eastern Europe, Asia and, to some extent, South America in the 1990s, as well as the greater consciousness of the relevance of human rights issues in international relations generally, and specifically in respect of capitalism and private enterprise. There was also, of course, the fanfare establishment of the WTO, itself. Above all, however, there have been three developments that have stood out as being of especial importance to the development of the trade and human rights relationship.

The first of these was the awareness-raising impact of China's long road to accession to the WTO, which began in 1987 and concluded in December 2001. The process coincided with the early indications of how quickly China's economy was opening up and expanding, while its apparatus of state remained authoritarian and its social order controlled – a circumstance that some have labelled ' "market Leninism" in which centralised political control co-exists with (and indeed may depend upon)

---

55 Pascal Lamy, 'Humanising Globalisation', speech, 30 January 2006; available at www.wto.
    org/english/news_e/sppl_e/sppl16_e.htm.
56 Lim, 'Trade and Human Rights', at 286.

opening to global markets'.[57] The juxtaposition of China's striving for greater trade opportunities and its abject record of human rights violations was quickly latched onto as a high-profile subject of debate and a basis for demands. For some (mostly human rights activists), the situation provided an opportunity to leverage the prospect of entry into the WTO to try to extract concessions from China regarding its hard-line attitude towards human rights. For others (mostly trade specialists), such a course of action was not only unwise but counter-productive, and they argued that the best hope for better protecting human rights in China through instituting the rule of law, promoting greater transparency and representation in government, and the construction of a viable and vibrant civil society, lay with liberalising its economy and the opening up of its borders to global trade.[58] As for China itself, it has routinely argued in its periodic 'White Papers' on human rights that 'the human rights of its 1.3 billion people are being met by its economic development, which has seen standards of living rise tremendously'.[59] In any event, the resultant debate certainly projected the linkage of trade and human rights into public domains, in the West in particular, as a matter of interest and concern.

The second development was an initiative instigated in 1995 by the OECD further to liberalise global capital through its Multilateral Agreement on Investment (MAI).[60] The MAI – which was drafted in private (or in a 'black hole', as Noam Chomsky put it)[61] – was met by unprecedented and widespread condemnation and it was abandoned in 1998 when France, the host nation, withdrew its support. It comprised a suite of measures that would oblige states to dismantle their individual domestic financial regulations, as well as the myriad bilateral schemes created

---

57 Alison Brysk (ed.), *Globalization and Human Rights* (Berkeley: University of California Press, 2002), p. 12.
58 See for example, John Dorn, a China specialist with the CATO Institute in the US, 'Advancing Human Rights in China' (1999) at www.freetrade.org/node/181.
59 Paul Reynolds, 'Whisper if You Mention Human Rights in China', *BBC News* (18 January 2008), at http://news.bbc.co.uk/1/hi/uk_politics/7196086.stm. For China's latest 'White Paper' on human rights, entitled 'China's Progress in Human Rights in 2004' (Beijing: Information Office of the State Council of the People's Republic of China, 2005), see http://english.gov.cn/official/2005-07/28/content_18115.htm.
60 The Multilateral Agreement on Investment – Draft Consolidated Text (22 April 2008) OECD document DAFFE/MAI(98)7/REV1, available at www1.oecd.org/daf/mai/pdf/ng/ng987r1e.pdf.
61 'A black hole reserved for topics rated unfit for public consumption'; Noam Chomsky, 'Domestic Constituencies', *Z Magazine* (May 1998) at www.chomsky.info/articles/199805–.htm.

by Bilateral Investment Treaties (BITs), and instead abide by a new, uniform international regime which included provisions for corporations to sue states that had not sufficiently complied with the Agreement's deregulatory demands. The opposition to the Agreement was remarkable on account of the prominence accorded to the perceived adverse human rights consequences (alongside environmental and labour standards concerns) of the MAI, especially in developing countries, where it was believed that it would seriously compromise countries' sovereign budgetary controls by giving the providers of foreign direct investment immoderate financial leverage over governments and leaving states at the mercy of the savage short-termism of the financial markets.[62] The anti-MAI movement fed into the growing anti-globalisation movement at that time which was so visibly expressed in the public protests that dogged G8 summits, WTO ministerial meetings, and the annual meetings of the World Economic Forum and of the World Bank and the IMF, from Seattle and Washington DC, to Genoa and Melbourne.

The whole MAI episode proved to be something of a watershed event on account of both the Agreement's uncompromised abandonment and its coinciding with the Asian financial crisis (1997–8), which was precipitated (or at least exacerbated) by the extreme fluidity of finance and instances of swift and massive capital flight. If it was not already a 'dead man walking', the Asian financial crisis effectively sealed the fate of the MAI, and indeed also convinced many – including many economists and trade liberalists – of the economic *and* social dangers posed by opening up capital markets even further to the hyperbolic nature of capital, its flights of fancy and swamping invasions.[63] Amidst the damage done to a number of exposed South American economies in the years following the turmoil in Asia, Brazil's experience provided further evidence of the manifold dangers of such financial crises, even for apparently robust emerging economies, as well as grounds for pointing fingers at who or what was to blame. Political analyst Gary Younge tells the compelling story of how Luiz Inácio Lula da Silva, the then newly elected Brazilian President in 2002, was 'cruelly mugged' by the mounting crisis:

---

62 One of the most comprehensive analyses of these (and other) implications of the MAI was conducted by the Joint Standing Committee on Treaties of the Australian Parliament; see its *Multilateral Agreement on Investment: Interim Report* (May 1998), at www.aph.gov.au/house/committee/jsct/reports/report14/report14.pdf.

63 See Robert Kuttner, 'The Role of Governments in the Global Economy', in Will Hutton and Anthony Giddens (eds.), *On the Edge: Living with Global Capitalism* (London: Vintage, 2001), p. 147, at pp. 161–3.

In the three months between his winning the vote and being sworn in, the nation's currency plummeted by 30%, $6 billion in hot money had left the country, and some [global credit] agencies had given Brazil the highest debt-risk ratings in the world.

'We are in Government but not in power', said Lula's close aide, Dominican friar Frei Betto. 'Power today is global power, the power of the big companies, the power of financial capital.'[64]

There are today greater efforts being made to understand and coordinate the interface between trade and finance – in terms of both their respective goals and their *modus operandi*.[65] The US sub-prime lending contagion that sparked the most recent global financial crisis has even prompted no less a devoted free-trade organ than *The Economist* to declare that, after thirty years of dominance over public policy, belief in the power of the market might be waning and that the 'growing calls from all sides for bold re-regulation' might have to be heeded.[66] Clearly, even advanced economies have a hard time reining in the excesses of free range, capital markets, so the prospects for developing economies doing so, when they have neither the administrative capacities nor the human capital, as Dani Rodrik and Arvind Subramanian point out, are even less promising. Embracing 'financial globalization', as they label such free market capital, is not a policy priority for such states when they have so many other, more basic and pressing, economic challenges to overcome.[67]

The third factor that played an instrumental role in promoting the idea of linking trade and human rights was the much heralded establishment of the Doha Round of trade talks in 2001 (which President Bush once embarrassingly referred to as the 'Darfur Round', albeit it with some unintended appropriateness).[68] The aim of the Round was to focus on development and thereby, derivatively, provide for better levels of human rights protection. The trade ministers who put their names to the Declaration that launched the round pledged to 'continue to make positive

---

64 Gary Younge, 'Obama Faces the Pressure of High Hopes', *Guardian Weekly*, 13 June 2008, p. 18.
65 Thus, for example, in her review of existing cooperation between the IMF and the WTO, Christine Kaufmann identifies 'trade as a new factor in preventing balance of payments crises': 'Aid for Trade and the Call for Global Governance', paper delivered at the International Monetary Fund and Financial Crises Conference, University of Cambridge, April 2008, draft, p. 3.
66 'Fixing Finance', *The Economist*, 5–11 April 2008, p. 15.
67 Dani Rodrik and Arvind Subramanian, 'Why Did Financial Globalization Disappoint?' (24 March 2008), p. 10, at http://ksghome.harvard.edu/~drodrik/Why_Did_FG_Disappoint_March_24_2008.pdf.
68 'Just Do It', *The Economist*, 13 January 2007, p. 64.

efforts designed to ensure that developing countries, and especially the least-developed among them, secure a share in the growth of world trade commensurate with the needs of their economic development'.[69] It was the ninth negotiating round since 1947, and the first under the auspices of the WTO (the other eight having been within the GATT system). It was intended to be something of a redress for developing countries of the developed-country emphasis in all the prior rounds on the dismantling of tariff and non-tariff barriers and, latterly, the expansion of liberalisation into the fields of intellectual property, services and textiles and (to a more limited extent) agriculture. In fact, as Joseph Stiglitz and Andrew Charlton note, the 'unfinished business' of the previous round (the Uruguay Round), especially in respect of services and agriculture,[70] has dominated the Doha Round and has been an important cause of its current sclerotic state, which has been lingering since the first efforts to bring the negotiations to a close began in early 2006.

With one striking exception, the human rights dimension of Doha has been implicit rather than explicit. The exception concerns the formulation of the Doha Declaration on the TRIPS Agreement and Public Health (2001)[71] which reiterated the TRIPS provision[72] allowing developing states to negotiate (or exceptionally, compulsorily to acquire) the rights to manufacture so-called generic drugs (i.e. very cheap copies) on the grounds of the needs of public health, despite any existing patent restrictions.[73] The conclusion of the Declaration was assisted by the extraordinary case in 1998 of the forty-two transnational pharmaceutical companies that sued the South African government in the local courts on the grounds that the latter's actions in permitting the local manufacture of generic anti-retroviral AIDS drugs breached both its obligations under TRIPS and the protection of intellectual property rights under the South African Constitution (Article 25). No matter what the legal merits

---

69 *Ministerial Declaration*, adopted 14 November 2001, WTO Doc. WT/MIN(01)/DEC/1, para. 2.
70 Joseph Stiglitz and Andrew Charlton, *Fair Trade for All: How Trade Can Promote Development* (New York: Oxford University Press, 2005), pp. 52–3.
71 *Declaration on the TRIPS Agreement and Public Health*, adopted 14 November 2001, WTO Doc. WT/MIN(01)/DEC/2.
72 That is, Trade-Related Aspects of Intellectual Property Rights (TRIPS) Articles 27 and 31.
73 For examples of such agreements between the Brazilian Government and a group of US pharmaceutical companies, see Davina Ovett, 'Making Trade Policies More Accountable and Human Rights-Consistent: An NGO Perspective of Using Human Rights Instruments in the Case of Access to Medicine', in Wolfgang Benedek, Koen de Feyter and Fabrizio Marrella (eds.), *Economic Globalisation and Human Rights* (Cambridge: Cambridge University Press, 2007), p. 17.

of the case were (and there are grounds to believe that they were weak and the main aim of the litigation was simply aggressively to assert commercial interests), the political overtones of the case were incendiary.[74] The global public outcry over what was widely perceived to be the avaricious, amoral and politically inept stance of the corporations was as predictable as it was damning, and the case was settled out of court.[75] For the South African Government there was clearly an important economic imperative to take the course of action it did; however, it was also based on sound human rights grounds. The obligation to promote and protect the right of access to adequate health care is enshrined in Article 12 of the ICESCR, to which South Africa is a party, and which is incorporated in its national constitution (Article 27). Faced with an HIV/AIDS crisis of epidemic proportions, the Government thought that it had sufficient grounds to trigger the public health exception to the patent protections recognised in TRIPS, and so had passed legislation accordingly. The pharmaceutical companies thought otherwise, believing that the Government had neither acted constitutionally, nor sought with sufficient intent to engage with them in discussions over alternative ways to address the problem.[76]

The Doha Round, its development aspirations and its impact on human rights protections remain uncertain. But at least the profile of their intersections has been raised even in (indeed, especially in) the minds and words of such arch-conservatives as Paul Wolfowitz, who in 2005 (when he was still President of the World Bank) pronounced that:

> The Doha development round of trade talks will be judged by one simple test: does it enable people in poor countries to sell more of their goods overseas, creating more jobs and lifting their incomes? If the answer is yes, the round will succeed in enabling tens of millions of people to lift

74 See Margo Bagley, 'Legal Movements in Intellectual Property: TRIPS, Unilateral Action, Bilateral Agreements and HIV/AIDS' (2003) 17 *Emory International Law Review* 781, at 785.

75 *Ibid.* It beggars belief that someone – whether lawyer or not – within the corporations' team contemplating this action could so catastrophically fail to foresee how badly the case would be received publicly, and not have sought some other, less patently aggressive, course of action.

76 A subsequent decision of the General Council of the WTO in August 2003 (later formalised in December 2005) provided certain concessions to states seeking to issue compulsory licences in respect of medicines used to combat epidemics provided they complied with a newly established notification process – see *Implementation of para. 6 of the Doha Declaration on the TRIPS Agreement and Public Health*, Decision of the General Council, 20 August 2003, WTO Doc WT/L/540. Though the scheme was initially not used by any states (see discussion below), it was invoked in 2007 by both Canada and Rwanda in respect of the manufacture of anti-retroviral HIV/AIDS drugs.

themselves out of abject poverty over the next decade and give them and
their children a chance to lead a better life – in some cases, it will be
the difference between a healthy life or an early death from a preventable
disease.[77]

Overlapping jurisdictions?

Still, despite this promising political context in which some important socio-political connections have been established between the two
domains, these are the exceptions more than the rule. In legal and institutional terms, human rights and trade remain largely separate. It is on this
basis that a report from the relatively newly established 'trade and human
rights' programme of the OHCHR calls for the 'increasing dialogue on
human rights and trade' across a wide spectrum of institutions and actors
at both international and domestic levels, including trade, finance, environmental and human rights practitioners, ministries and relevant agencies and other public bodies, civil society groups, academic commentators
and of course international organisations representing trade and human
rights interests.[78] Building on certain parallel instances of such dialogue,
this comprehensive exchange is being pursued through the Enhanced
Integrated Framework which comprises two UN agencies (UNCTAD and
the UN Development Program (UNDP)), the World Bank, the IMF, the
International Trade Commission and the WTO itself, as well as through
the so-called cooperation (that is, consultative) agreements that the WTO
has signed with both Bretton Woods institutions.[79]

Shared jurisdictional grounds do appear to be there. It is easy to agree
with Amartya Sen's proclamation, for example, that there exists:

> a remarkable empirical connection that links freedoms of different kinds
> with one another. Political freedoms (in the form of free speech and
> elections) help to promote economic security. Social opportunities (in the
> form of educational and health facilities) facilitate economic participation.
> Economic facilities (in the form of opportunities to participate in trade
> and production) can help to generate personal abundance as well as public
> resources for social facilities. Freedoms of different kinds can strengthen
> one another.[80]

77 Paul Wolfowitz, 'Everyone Must Do More for Doha To Succeed', FT. com., 23 October
2005, p. 1.
78 Report of the UN High Commissioner for Human Rights, 'Human Rights, Trade and
Investment', UN Doc. E/CN.4/Sub.2/2003/9 (2 July 2003), para. 62.
79 *Agreements between the WTO and the IMF and the World Bank*, General Council Decision,
WT/L/194 (18 November 1996).
80 Amartya Sen, *Development as Freedom* (Oxford: Oxford University Press, 1999), p. 11.

Yet, this is only part of the story. Questions remain as to how this does, or could, reflect what human rights international law provides for, and how the relevant international institutions actually operate in practice. For a long time the linkage between the fields of international trade law and international human rights law was best described as no more than coexistence: 'interactions have existed since their inception, but remained marginal or largely ineffective', according to Cottier, Pauwelyn and Bürgi.[81] Since the mid 1990s, however, there have been pushes from within both fields to reinterpret and promote their relationship as being one of interdependence. To some degree this constitutes a part of a wider movement to link trade with any number of non-trade issues, such as peace and security, the environment, labour and culture,[82] but it is also a reflection of a number of essentially legal concerns. These are, first, the fear among human rights lawyers that the WTO's reinforcement of the dispute settlement mechanisms within trade law would effectively give primacy to trade rules over less well enforced international laws such as human rights standards; second, in direct response to the first, a movement to seek out ways in which human rights might be located within trade law and thereby harness the perceived enforcement power of the trade regime in ways that might advance human rights ends; and third, the analogue drawn by some commentators between the intermeshing of economic and trade polices and human rights protections within state constitutional arrangements, and that which might be aspired to at the level of international law. In this latter respect, Ernst-Ulrich Petersmann leads the charge, fuelled by what he sees as the instructive example of international constitutionalism of the EU.[83]

81 Thomas Cottier, Joost Pauwelyn and Elizabeth Bürgi, 'Introduction', in Cottier *et al.* (eds.), *Human Rights and International Trade* (Oxford: Oxford University Press, 2005), p. 2.

82 On the last mentioned, see Hélène Ruiz Fabri's analysis of the tense relationship that exists between trade enhancement and the preservation of cultural diversity, for both developed and developing states: 'Games within Fragmentation: The Convention on the Protection and Promotion of the Diversity of Cultural Expressions', in Sarah Joseph, David Kinley and Jeffrey Waincymer (eds.), *The World Trade Organization and Human Rights: Interdisciplinary Approaches* (London: Edward Elgar, forthcoming 2009).

83 Ernst-Ulrich Petersmann, 'Human Rights and International Trade Law: Defining and Connecting the Two Fields', in Cottier *et al.* (eds.), *Human Rights and International Trade*, p. 37. It is perhaps worth noting here that this aspirational stance of Petersmann's contrasts starkly with Philip Alston's focus on what is possible under *current* circumstances. As such, the vividly combative dispute between the two referred to in chapter 1 has been interpreted by some observers as a classic case of a *dialogue des sourdes*: Thomas Cottier, Joost Pauwelyn and Elisabeth Bürgi, 'Linking Trade Regulation and Human Rights in International Law: An Overview', in *ibid.* p. 7.

The taxonomy of linkage is, as David Leebron charts it, broad and complex. This is so not just in terms of the areas in which linkage is sought as noted above,[84] but also in terms of the various reasons for, and forms of, linkage. Leebron identifies linkages that are substantive in nature (where trade and other norms overlap in object or relative impact on each other), others that are strategic (where there is no connection between the two sets of norms themselves but they share approaches and processes), and some that are both.[85] He also lists a host of different means by which linkages are pursued, ranging from simple inter-regime negotiations to intricate legal arguments as to jurisdictional boundaries.[86]

Fundamentally, the linkages between trade law and human rights law are of two sorts: either they concern the status of human rights standards within the rules and adjudicatory procedures of trade regulation, or they concern the status of trade rules within human rights laws and adjudicatory formats.[87] Ancillary to these base models there are institutional interactions which, at the international level, are still in their nascent stages (i.e. such as the joining of the WTO and the UN's OHCHR in informal, information-gathering or scoping exercises),[88] and interactions born of efforts to construct the conceptual frameworks that explain or justify the degree of instantiation of each regime within the other. The law, evidently, is an important format within which intersections between trade and human rights occur, even if motivations and outcomes are much more widely framed. As such, it is to the details of the nature and form of the inter-linkages between international trade law and human rights law, presently and possibly, that I now turn: first to consider the specific circumstances of the WTO and human rights protection, and then, in the final part of this chapter, to address the questions of human rights concessions and conditionality within trade, and the use of trade sanctions for human rights ends.

---

84 And see further José Alvarez, 'Symposium: The Boundaries of the WTO: Foreword' (2002) 96 *American Journal of International Law* 1, at 2.
85 David Leebron, 'Linkages' (2002) 96 *American Journal of International Law* 5, at 11–15.
86 *Ibid.* 15–24.   87 See Cottier *et al.* (eds.), *Human Rights and International Trade*, p. 3.
88 Including four separate reports by the OHCHR on the impact on human rights of, respectively: TRIPS (2001), the Agreement on Agriculture (2002), the General Agreement on Trade in Services (GATS) (2002) and investment (2003). For an excellent discussion of their methodology, analysis and conclusions, see James Harrison, *The Human Rights Impact of the World Trade Organisation* (Portland, OR: Hart, 2007), pp. 127–40.

The limits and possibilities of the WTO protecting human rights

The term 'human rights' does not appear anywhere in the Agreement establishing the WTO, nor in any of the sixty or so agreements and decisions over which it presides. Yet, there appears to be ample room for the relevance of human rights to be established. The WTO's constitutive instruments range widely across specific industry sectors – such as agriculture, textiles and clothing, maritime transport, sanitary and phytosanitary standards, financial services and intellectual property protections, through to technical issues – such as the process of dismantling tariff and non-tariff trade barriers, conditions of government procurement, dispute settlement procedures, negotiating protocols, environmental protection and accession arrangements.[89] This does not mean to say that the door is closed to human rights in WTO law, just that in so far as it finds its way in, it does so by ways other than through the front door. This, historically, has been the case with trade law, where other terms have been used to permit a human rights angle to be run. Stephen Powell notes that 'dozens of the trade agreements predating the GATT routinely linked "moral" with "humanitarian" goals through an exception for "moral and humanitarian reasons"'.[90]

Today, in the GATT itself and in the multitude of trade instruments that have followed it, the opportunities for inserting human rights demands still arise in ulterior forms – that is, as possible exceptions or legitimate excuses, not to be bound by the otherwise mandatory rules to dispense with tariffs and subsidies, to treat all trading partners equally, and to make no distinctions between domestic and foreign produced or sourced goods and services. Typically, these 'exceptions clauses' are based on such notions as the protection of public health, of morals and of the environment (or at least animal and plant life), as well as the prohibition of prison labour and where the interests of national security require. I will look at the jurisprudence associated with the interpretation, application and enforcement of these exceptions in a moment. First, however, I want to stress the importance of certain structural dictates of international trade

89 See the WTO's online data base on 'Legal Texts', at www.wto.org/english/docs_e/legal_e/legal_e.htm.
90 Stephen Powell, 'The Place of Human Rights Law in World Trade Organisation Rules' (2004) 16 *Florida Journal of International Law* 219, at 223 n18. See also Nicolas Diebold, 'The Morals and Order Exceptions in WTO Law: Balancing the Toothless Tiger and the Undermining Mole' (2008) 11 *Journal of International Economic Law* 43, who charts the lineage of such interpretations of key phrases in the GATT and GATS.

law generally, and the institution of the WTO in particular, within which the intersection with human rights occurs.

Structural dictates

There are some basic features of the international trade regime that remain constant and which to some significant extent dictate whether and to what extent human rights can civilise trade. The first of these is the fact that the WTO is an inter-governmental organisation: a creature of states, effectively directed by them, as administered by a secretariat charged with little or no significant capacity (not jurisdictionally, nor politically, nor in terms of manpower, and certainly not financially)[91] to operate outside the remit given to it by the member states. Unlike other international organisations such as the UN, the World Bank or the IMF, the mandates of which provided various levels of institutional autonomy, the WTO is held under the sway of being a 'member driven organisation', with the Director-General and secretariat having no independent, organic mandate to develop policy or issue binding determinations or interpretations. It is a legal regime, therefore, that is more open than others to being governed by the demands of domestic politics rather than international comity, and this includes attitudes towards human rights and the extent to which they should be accommodated within the WTO framework.

That said, while in the WTO regime there is abundant evidence of states pursuing self-interest and of their coercion, it is not, as Jack Goldsmith and Eric Posner argue in their über-realist treatise, that these are the *only* factors at play; there being no room for the normative influence of international comity and laws (beyond their mere coincidence with self-interest), that is the target of the authors' polemic.[92] Surely manifest statal desires to promote international comity and laws are themselves key parts of self-interest, or form parts of the reason for coercion, whether coincidental or not.[93] The evidence I refer to is the fact that the most politically and economically powerful states have been able to

---

91 The organisation employs a total of 625 people and has an annual budget of only $183 million (in 2007 figures), which is allocated almost entirely to salaries and running costs.

92 Jack Goldsmith and Eric Posner, *The Limits of International Law* (Oxford and New York: Oxford University Press, 2005), especially chapter 5 on international trade.

93 Neils Petersen suggests that the pursuit of such ends is better explained by way of a 'deliberative approach' than by adopting the blinkered instrumental approach of rational choice; see 'Rational Choice or Deliberation? Customary International Law between Coordination and Constitutionalization' (1 July 2008). Max Planck Institute, Collective Goods Preprint, No. 2008/28; available at http://ssrn.com/abstract=1161123.

exert their influence over the operations of the WTO, and thereby to promote their interests – across the board – ahead of those of other states. This is despite the fact that, formally, the voting authority of all member states is the same (which, incidentally, is also in stark contrast to the complicated weighted voting structures of both the IMF and the World Bank).

The WTO's 'one member, one vote' format was intended to dilute the bargaining power of the powerful, at least in formal terms, even if in practice a host of exogenous factors (such as differences in expertise, and the striking of back-room deals – 'Green Room'[94] negotiations, as they are colloquially known) has meant that this has not been borne out in practice. The GATT was in fact designed to do something similar. It was a 'disarmament treaty', to use Martin Wolf's imaginative phrase, in that it intentionally sought to restrict the nature and scope of the erstwhile untrammelled freedom with which trade negotiations were conducted between states, and between states and merchants.[95] But for nearly the whole life of GATT and the first five or so years of the WTO, the rich nations had been able to guide the multilateral trade ship across the sea of liberalisation more or less unchecked, save in the important respect of disagreements between themselves. This led to a situation in the late 1990s where there was a mounting demand from developing countries for a collectively greater voice in the WTO. For while decisions are indeed taken by consensus, 'developing countries complain about not being able to defend their interests, as an important part of the decision-making is done between a selected group of (developed) countries outside the formal meetings in the hallways and "green rooms" of the WTO'.[96]

Signs that developing countries might be gaining entry into the ship's wheelhouse became apparent in the late 1990s with moves that led to the launch of the Doha Development Round in 2001 (as discussed above), and when coalitions of developing countries and mixtures of developing and

---

94 A metaphorical allusion, for, as noted on the WTO website, 'the term "Green Room" has its origins in British theatre and refers to the room where performers would wait when they were not needed on stage'. It adds that 'Green Room meetings serve a useful purpose in that their informal nature allows negotiators to explore new approaches to settling difficult issues'; at www.wto.org/english/tratop_e/dda_e/meet08_org_e.htm#green_room. Green Room discussions are conducted under the stewardship of the Director-General.

95 Wolf, *Why Globalization Works*, p. 91. Which circumstances led to the ironic situation today where to agree to liberalise is now seen as a concession rather than a gain (the presumption being that protectionism is natural or best); *ibid.*

96 Van Hees, 'Protection v. Protectionism', p. 13.

developed countries began to emerge or were revitalised with the express object of pooling political, legal and economic resources against US and EU domination. Examples of coalitions include the Cairns Group of agricultural exporting countries,[97] the African, Caribbean, Pacific group of states,[98] and more recently the International Sugar Trade Coalition of sugar exporting countries that trade with the US.[99] The Ministerial Meetings in Cancún in 2003 and Hong Kong in 2005 proved to be something of watershed events in the power struggles within the WTO, with a large and diverse group of developing nations (the G90) staging a walk-out and effectively scuppering the negotiations in Cancún. In Hong Kong, decisions were made to refocus on core trade issues (agriculture, services and industrial goods) and ditch the attempts to pursue discussion on governance matters (the so-called 'Singapore Issues'),[100] which were strongly disliked by developing states, and to launch the 'aid for trade' initiative,[101] all in an effort to prevent a repeat performance of mass disaffection. These efforts were not enough, however, to prevent the debilitating failure to bring the Doha Round to a close in July 2008 when developed and developing states could simply not 'bridge their differences'[102] over levels of agricultural subsidies and special provisions enabling developing countries to protect their farmers from import surges and sudden price falls in staple crops. It remains to be seen whether and how, once again, the Round will rise, Phoenix-like, from these ashes.

At one level, the empowering of the developing states within the WTO framework can readily be seen as potentially very good for their economies, social orders and human rights protections – that is, to the extent that the relevant governments direct the resultant increases in economic prosperity towards the upkeep of the other two. At another level, however, it can also be considered to be a setback for social welfare and human rights, if the developing states are only, or primarily, interested in the economy, and view any pressure to deliver on these other outcomes

---

97 See www.cairnsgroup.org.   98 See www.acpsec.org.

99 Established in 2006; see www.sugarcoalition.org.

100 Primarily, greater transparency in government procurement; enhanced 'trade facilitation', investment and more effective competition policies. Incidentally, this realignment was built on agreement brokered in the previous year by Pascal Lamy, the EU Trade Commissioner, and Robert Zoellick, the US Trade Representative, now the Director-General of the WTO and the President of the World Bank, respectively.

101 Discussed further below.

102 As Pascal Lamy reported to an informal meeting of the Trade Negotiations Committee: 'Chairman's Opening Remarks', 29 July 2008, at www.wto.org/english/news_e/news08_e/meet08_chair_29july08_e.htm.

as sovereignty-invading conditionality. This is an important point, but one that is characterised by great complexity and sensitivity, as such conditionality is open to misuse and misunderstanding. The situation is, in fact, an inevitable consequence of the WTO's legal structure, as well as the interpretation and implementation of the various exceptions clauses.

While some limited level of human rights conditionality is available through exceptions in many treaties within the WTO regime (and much more outside the WTO), it cannot be utilised as a disguise for protectionism or other trade restrictive practices,[103] which is what many developing states believe to be the real reasons behind developed states' use of exceptions. Thus, for example, the concerted effort of the EU and the US to force the issue of labour standards onto the agenda of the 1999 Seattle Ministerial was greeted with near-universal suspicion and condemnation among developing states. 'They saw it', to repeat Nigel Grimwade's words, 'as having one purpose only – to provide developed countries with *carte blanche* to introduce trade restrictions on their products under the guise of protecting human rights.'[104] In particular, developing countries see international pressure to have them raise their domestic labour standards (despite the 1996 Singapore Ministerial Declaration's apparent stipulation to the contrary)[105] as challenging the single most important comparative advantage many of them have – namely, cheap labour. Certainly, there is something of a conflict of interest when trade unionists in the North push for higher labour standards in the South, if not blatant cynicism. One high-ranking American trade union leader, for example, was reported as saying in a private conversation with a senior aide to the WTO: 'We don't give a damn about workers in the Third World. We just want to protect our members' interests.'[106] The tension and mutual suspicion extends beyond developing countries' relationship with Northern trade unions, to cover nearly the whole community of Northern NGOs working on trade issues, despite, that is, their shared goals of a 'democratic and accountable WTO

---

103 See GATT, Article XX (chapeau), as outlined below.
104 Nigel Grimwade, 'The GATT, the Doha Round and Developing Countries', in Homi Katrak and Roger Strange (eds.), *The WTO and Developing Countries* (Houndmills and New York: Palgrave Macmillan, 2004), p. 25.
105 Paragraph 4 of the Declaration expressly states that the comparative labour advantage of developing countries should not be limited, though it then adds that labour standards cannot be used for protectionist purposes; *Singapore Ministerial Declaration*, 13 December 1996, available at www.wto.org/english/theWTO_e/minist_e/min96_e/wtodec_e.htm.
106 Philippe Legrain, *Open World: The Truth about Globalisation* (London: Abacus, 2002), p. 64.

that is more concerned with the problems of poverty and development and . . . a more just and equitable trading system'.[107]

Of course, Machiavellian manoeuvring is not the preserve of the rich states alone. The governments of developing states can be gallingly insincere when they throw up accusations of such protectionism as a smokescreen to cover their inability or unwillingness to meet their human rights responsibilities. There can be little doubt that oft-repeated pleas not to interfere with a country's poor labour conditions and wage levels, in order to preserve its attractiveness to foreign investment and the cheapness of its exports, can lead quickly into blatant worker exploitation as developing countries compete with each other for global trade and business opportunities in 'a race to the bottom'.

In 1999, President Clinton captured the thrust of the issue when he addressed the ILO on the occasion of the US signing of the ILO Convention No. 182, on the Elimination of the Worst Forms of Child Labour:

> The step we take today affirms fundamental human rights. Ultimately, that's what core labor standards are all about, not an instrument of protectionism or a vehicle to impose one nation's values on another but about our shared values, about the dignity of work, the decency of life, the fragility and importance of childhood.[108]

This is a statement of principle, and one with which I agree. It is not, however, a representation of *Realpolitik*; nor does it purport to be so. The actions taken within the institutional confines of the WTO that bear on the relations between trade and human rights are, as James Harrison has trenchantly argued, much more equivocal and often contradictory.[109] We are, as yet, far from the comfort of being able to declare with the certainty of Christine Breining-Kaufmann and Michelle Foster that the debate has 'moved beyond the stage of questioning whether the link is appropriate and legitimate'.[110]

All that said, the WTO's 'Dispute Settlement Mechanism' (DSM) has been the focus a great deal of attention and expectation as a possible vehicle

---

107 Daniel Bradlow, ' "The Times Are A'Changin": Some Preliminary Thoughts on Developing Countries, NGOs and Reform of the WTO' (2001) 33 *George Washington International Law Review* 503.

108 President Clinton, 'Remarks by the President at Signing of ILO Convention #182', Seattle, Washington, 2 December 1999; see http://clinton6.nara.gov/1999/12/1999-12-02-remarks-by-the-president-at-signing-of-ilo-convention.html.

109 Harrison, *The Human Rights Impact of the World Trade Organisation*, pp. 76–81.

110 Christine Breining-Kaufmann and Michelle Foster, 'Introduction', in Frederick Abbott *et al.* (eds.), *International Trade and Human Rights: Foundations and Conceptual Issues* (Ann Arbor: University of Michigan Press, 2006), p. 4.

to carry human rights issues further into the heartland of international trade.

Human rights in the WTO's Dispute Settlement Mechanism?

Alongside the new trade policy apparatus that the WTO established, its other significant innovation was the creation of a legal regime for the enforcement of trade rules and the settlement of disputes between member states to replace that which existed under the GATT. There is, as indicated earlier, very little scope for considering human rights within the DSM. As such accommodation was not in the minds of the drafters, this is perhaps not that surprising. The argument, therefore, to raise the profile of human rights within the deliberations of the dispute panels and the appellate body that constitute the DSM is an uphill struggle. And yet great struggle there has been. In part, faith in the quest has been drawn from the belief in the power of rule enforcement and formalised adjudication, especially as the WTO's DSM is perceived to have real teeth, unlike international human rights tribunals (all of which, except, notably, the European and American Courts of Human Rights, are advisory only). The fact, then, that the DSM definitively determines winners, and losers, and metes out punishments to the latter, has been a great attraction – a sort of 'penance envy', to use Joel Trachtman's delightfully mischievous phrase.[111]

There are, however, a number of aspects of the DSM as it presently operates that together caution against too much investment in its capacity to deliver on human rights goals. First, there are some commentators who challenge the notion that the DSM is indeed at all, or even primarily, about rigidly enforcing rules. Steve Charnovitz perceptively notes 'the WTO may have the best dispute settlement system of any international organization, but it does not have the best compliance system'.[112] In a similar vein, Andrew Lang (approvingly) reports the following argument made by Jeffrey Dunoff at a conference in London in 2005:

> Compliance, he suggests, has never been the sole nor even the highest value of the dispute settlement processes in the WTO. Instead, he suggests, we should see such processes as a compromise between the need to ensure compliance and the need to provide a degree of flexibility – a complex and

---

111 As quoted by Alvarez, 'Symposium: The Boundaries of the WTO: Foreword', at 2.
112 Steve Charnovitz, 'Rethinking WTO Trade Sanctions' (2001) 95 *American Journal of International Law* 792, at 832.

evolving compromise between legalism and pragmatism, between rule-
and power-based approaches to dispute settlement.[113]

This compromised approach might of course open up greater room for
human rights concerns to be heard, but that is only possible within the
boundaries of relevant legal provisions that may tolerate some flexibility. In any case, flexibility does not get over the fact that the scope for
the accommodation of human rights concerns in the WTO's constitutive treaties is limited. Article XX of the GATT is the most important of
the exceptions clauses and typifies those found in other WTO treaties. It
permits states to employ potential, or actual, restrictive measures when
trying to protect public morals, and human (or plant or animal) life;
when blocking products of prison labour, or conserving exhaustible natural resources, or when trying to secure the essential acquisition or distribution of products in short supply, *provided* that such measures are
necessary, non-arbitrary and, above all, not mere disguises for protectionist policies. Article XXI of the GATT also permits the imposition of
restrictive measures where they are deemed necessary to protect national
security. Articles XVIII and XIX of the GATT also allow poorer states,
exceptionally and for limited periods, to protect fragile markets through
export subsidies and/or import restrictions. Human rights may be read
into each of these exceptions to different degrees. But most are relatively
little used and, with the exception of the protection of human and animal
health, very little litigated (and not at all in the case of the prison labour
exception).

   As with all rule systems, the very fact that they seek to define what is
and is not permissible invites dispute, avoidance and evasion. Take, for
example, the reprehensible, but legal, scam cooked up by EU and US
biofuel manufacturers and merchants to ship huge quantities of biodiesel
from Europe to the US 'where a small quantity of fuel is added, allowing traders to claim 11 pence [US 21 cents] a litre of US subsidy for the
entire cargo,'[114] before it is shipped straight back to Europe. The subsidy was intended, of course, for genuine, significant 'blending' of bio
and fossil fuels, but has inadvertently allowed this violation of *l'esprit de
la loi*, if not its letter. Neither the above environmental nor the health
exceptions would seem to permit the arrest of this 'splash and dash'
practice.

---

113 Lang, 'Reconstructing Embedded Liberalism', at 94.
114 Terry McAllister, 'US Biofuels Loophole Allows Trading Scam', *Guardian Weekly*, 4 April
     2008, p. 6.

The jurisprudence that is trotted out as evidence of some potential to argue human rights points in Article XX (and its siblings in other treaties) is, if the truth be told, tangential, eclectic and inconsistent. It is further, bizarrely, somewhat dependent on the fate of various attempts to protect fauna (especially aquatic), and their indirect relevance to protecting human beings and their rights. Thus, for example, in cases involving challenges to restrictions imposed for health reasons – the US complaining about the EC's import ban on American hormone-treated beef (1998), and Canada's challenge to Australia's ban on the former's uncooked salmon (1998)[115] (both cases argued under the Sanitary and Phytosanitary Agreement (SPS))[116] – separate dispute-settlement panels decided against the respondent states. The arguments of both Australia and the EC were dismissed on the grounds that their respective scientific analysis had been inadequate, based more on supposition than on proof. Explicitly, the panels rejected arguments suggesting that the precautionary principle (borrowed from international environmental law) should be applied and thereby allow the bans, until such time as scientific proof was established to settle the matter one way or the other.

These decisions – and especially the dismissal of the precautionary principle as irrelevant to trade law – were criticised in non-trade circles for being blinkered, unnecessarily pedantic and detrimental to people's rights to health and food safety. And indeed, shortly afterwards, in 2001, the use of the very same 'protection of health' exception (this time under the GATT) was upheld by a dispute settlement panel. In this case, France's ban on the importation of asbestos products from Canada on public health grounds was allowed to stand, despite the fact that there was no unanimity in expert scientific opinion regarding the precise risks posed by various uses of the products in question.[117] But this might best be viewed

---

115 Respectively: Panel Report, *European Communities – Measures Concerning Meat and Meat Products (Hormones) – Complaint by the United States*, WT/DS26/R/USA, adopted 13 February 1998, as modified by the Appellate Body Report, WT/DS26/AB/R, WT/DS48/AB/R; and Panel Report, *Australia – Measures Affecting Importation of Salmon*, WT/DS18/R and Corr. 1, adopted 6 November 1998, as modified by the Appellate Body Report, WT/DS18/AB/R.

116 In effect, the whole of the SPS agreement is an 'exception clause', in that its very purpose is to allow restrictions on the basis of the preservation and protection of animal or human life. Article 2.4 of the Agreement provides that any measure taken in conformity with the SPS agreement would be per se consistent with the GATT (in particular with Article XX(b)).

117 Panel Report, *European Communities – Measures Affecting Asbestos and Asbestos-Containing Products*, WT/DS135/R and Add. 1, adopted 5 April 2001, as modified by Appellate Body Report, WT/DS135/AB/R.

as something of an aberration, for as a rule the insistence on scientific backup, where it is required by the relevant treaty provisions, would otherwise appear to be unstintingly pursued. This is clearly illustrated by the so-called Genetically Modified Organisms (GMOs) case in which a number of countries challenged the EC's general moratorium on the approvals of biotech products (including GMOs), as well as certain health related safeguard policies that some EU member states had also mounted against biotech products, under the SPS Agreement. The challenge was successful, in part due to the fact that the Panel found that the EC had failed to undertake adequate scientific risk analyses and/or to demonstrate sufficiently clearly the presence of a risk to human health.[118]

There seems, perhaps, to be more room to pursue rights-type arguments in such 'non-scientific' areas as the protection of public morals and public order, as illustrated in the *US – Gambling Services* case. In this case, the WTO Appellate Body accepted that the US's banning of on-line gambling services emanating from some Caribbean states was justifiably necessary on public morals grounds, as provided by Article XIV of the GATS (albeit that, in the end, it found against the US on the legislation's infringement of another aspect of the Article).[119]

The picture is different again regarding trade restrictions based on reasons of environmental protection. At the heart of a clutch of cases concerning fishing practices and their effect on certain protected or endangered species was the question of whether the WTO rules could or should permit states to restrict goods that have been produced (or harvested, as in these cases) by allegedly environmentally harmful methods. Initially, in the two *Tuna/Dolphin* cases (*Tuna/Dolphin I* (1991) and *Tuna/Dolphin II* (1994)), decided under the old GATT dispute settlement system, the relevant panels clearly rejected any suggestion that process and production methods (PPMs) could be used as a basis for the US to ban tuna imports from Mexico (*Tuna/Dolphin I*) and the EC (*Tuna/Dolphin II*), on the grounds that the 'purse seine' methods employed by the fishing fleets from these states to catch tuna also, incidentally, killed significant

---

118 Panel Report, *European Communities – Measures Affecting the Approval and Marketing of Biotech Products*, WT/DS291/R, WT/DS292/R, WT/DS293/R and Corr. 1, adopted 21 November 2006.

119 Appellate Body Report, *United States – Measures Affecting the Cross-Border Supply of Gambling and Betting Services*, WT/DS285/AB/R, adopted 20 April 2005. The hurdle the ban failed to clear in the view of the Appellate Body was the requirement, under the chapeau of Article XIV, that any measures taken are not applied in a way that is unjustifiably or arbitrarily discriminatory.

numbers of dolphins.[120] At the time, these decisions were also heavily criticised on the grounds that, by simply focusing on trade equity concerns, they overlooked the wider and vitally important environmental implications. It was argued, further, that the Panel's reasoning would, by extension, result in cases where bans imposed on goods produced, for example, by child labour or by forced labour would be deemed impermissible. (As an aside, it should be noted that in part response to just this type of concern, the recent Economic Partnership Agreement between the European Community and the forum of Caribbean states (Cariforum) expressly states in its 'general exceptions clause' (which is modelled on the GATT original) that 'measures necessary to combat child labour shall be deemed to be included within the meaning of measures necessary to protect public morals or measures necessary for the protection of health'.)[121]

Shortly after the establishment of the WTO, the opportunity arose to review the principle established by the *Tuna/Dolphin* cases, this time in a case involving a US ban on the shrimp caught in nets that were not equipped with 'turtle excluder devices'.[122] In this case it was India, Malaysia, Pakistan and Thailand who complained that the ban constituted an unjustified restraint of trade. The US responded by claiming that the ban was allowable as it sought to conserve an 'exhaustible natural resource' (the sea turtles) as provided by Article XX(g) of the GATT. The WTO Appellate Body agreed that the ban was justifiable on this basis, but, ultimately, the US measure failed to satisfy the non-discriminatory demands of the chapeau to Article XX and the ruling went against the US.[123] Predictably, again, there was anger and even a little despair in environmentalist camps. As one activist group put it:

> The outlook for sea turtles is bleak. The WTO has always ruled against environmental measures when they conflict with commerce. This ruling has set the wheels in motion for the dismantling of the US law. The WTO

---

120 Panel Report, *United States – Restrictions on Imports of Tuna*, GATT DS21/R, 3 September 1991 ('Tuna/Dolphin I') and Panel Report, *United States – Restrictions on Imports of Tuna*, GATT DS29/R, 16 June 1994 ('Tuna/Dolphin II').

121 *Economic Partnership Agreement between Cariforum and the EC and its Member States*, Article 224 (footnote 30); see www.normangirvan.info/cariforum-ec-epa-annexes/. At the time of writing (mid 2008), the agreement had been initialled but not yet signed by the parties. I am indebted to Lorand Bartels for bringing this to my attention.

122 If netted, the turtles drowned, being unable to surface for air.

123 Appellate Body Report, *United States – Import Prohibition of Certain Shrimp and Shrimp Products*, WT/DS58/AB/R, adopted 6 November 1998.

is creating the path for the rapid destruction of our global resources and the plundering of local economies.[124]

The perceived intransigence of the WTO dispute resolution bodies, and the attendant trade myopia as represented by this latest decision in the shrimp/turtle case, certainly contributed to the growing anti-WTO and anti-globalisation movements in the late 1990s, which may or may not have had some effect on the outcome of the final case in this particular dispute. In 2001, Malaysia alone pursued the US over what it believed to be the latter's incomplete compliance with the initial decision. The Panel decided in this case that the US's continuing ban on shrimp not caught in nets with turtle excluder devices was indeed justifiable under GATT Article XX(g) – a decision that was subsequently confirmed on appeal.[125] And yet, despite the more subtle balancing of the interests of protecting (animal) health against the disguised or arbitrary protection-ism employed in this latter case,[126] the implications for the protection of human rights of the decision are tangential rather than substantial. Apart from the benefits we gain from protecting vibrant and diverse ecosystems, the only other relevant consequence is that this decision (together with the decision in the asbestos case) might precipitate more openness on the part of the dispute-settlement panels to entertain non-core trade issues in their deliberations, including, possibly, human rights concerns – an openness, what is more, that that should not be blocked by any misplaced arguments over limited jurisdiction and applicable laws. The Interna-tional Law Commission's landmark *Fragmentation Report* in 2006 made it plain that while acknowledging that the WTO's legal regime does indeed limit both its jurisdictional reach and its competence to entertain issues arising under human rights and environmental law treaties, nonetheless, 'when elucidating the content of the relevant rights and obligations, WTO bodies must situate those rights and obligations within the overall context

124 Sea Turtle Restoration Project, 'The Story of the WTO versus the Sea Turtles', at www.seaturtles.org/article.php?id=68.

125 Panel Report, *United States – Import Prohibition of Certain Shrimp and Shrimp Products – Recourse to Article 21.5 of the DSU by Malaysia*, WT/DS58/RW, adopted 21 November 2001, as upheld by Appellate Body Report, WT/DS58/AB/RW. See Press Release of the US Trade Representative, 22 October 2001, at www.ustr.gov/ Document_Library/Press_Releases/2001/October/US_Wins_WTO_Case_on_Sea_Turtle_ Conservation.html.

126 As followed through in the context of human health in the *Brazil – Retreaded Tyres* case: Panel Report, *Brazil – Measures Affecting Imports of Retreaded Tyres*, WT/DS332/R, adopted 17 December 2007, as modified by Appellate Body Report, WT/DS332/AB/R.

of general international law (including the relevant environmental and human rights treaties)'.[127]

In review, all this is a thin gruel for hopeful human rights advocates to feed on, and far from a wholesale, long-term solution. 'The WTO is not an appropriate forum for enforcing human rights law, and Article XX is not a legal backdoor', as Tatjana Eres starkly warns in the conclusion to her review of the jurisprudence.[128] Furthermore, there is something clearly problematic about the prospect of seeking to rely on specialists in the settlement of trade disputes, to interpret, apply and enforce human rights standards to any significant degree. Functionally, the panels and the Appellate Body as they stand today are ill suited for such a task. Procedurally as well, the DSM exhibits features that are not especially conducive to the addressing of human rights concerns, at least not in any systematic way. Gregory Shaffer's illuminating work in this area reveals not only how the nature of the disputes submitted to the DSM are becoming increasingly skewed towards private commercial interests (as opposed to public economic interests, let alone social issues), but also that the burdens on developing countries to hold anything like their own against the EU and the US, in terms of legal capacity and expertise to run these trade disputes, are especially onerous.

> The growing interaction between private enterprises, their lawyers, and US and European public officials in the bringing of most trade claims reflects a trend from predominantly intergovernmental decision-making toward multilevel private litigation strategies involving direct public–private exchange at the national and international levels.[129]

Shaffer unearths the extent to which corporations are the driving force behind so many disputes pursued by states and the degree to which they underwrite the resultant legal costs. There is nothing illegal about this, and on reflection it is unsurprising, given the often enormous commercial interests at stake. But it is unsettling, nonetheless.

Historically, developing countries have had great difficulties matching the developed states in terms of their capacity (legal, financial and

---

127 *Fragmentation of International Law: Difficulties Arising from the Diversification and Expansion of International Law*, Report of the Study Group of the International Law Commission, Finalized by Martti Koskenniemi, UN Doc. A/CN.4/L.682 (2006), para. 170 and see also para. 45.

128 Tatjana Eres, 'The Limits of GATT Article XX: A Back Door for Human Rights?' (2003–4) 35 *Georgetown Journal of International Law* 597, at 635.

129 Gregory Shaffer, *Defending Interests: Public–Private Partnerships in WTO Litigation* (Washington, DC: Brookings Institution Press, 2003), p. 4.

bureaucratic) to mount or defend challenges, and the privatisation of disputes noted by Shaffer is likely only to make the playing field even less level.[130] Sylvester Stallone once said polo was like playing golf in an earthquake;[131] it might be said that the same sense of bewilderment engulfed many developing, and (especially) least developing, countries when they tackled the machinations of the DSM. Despite all, however, Shaffer believes that the stronger developing nations at least are 'learning to use the dispute settlement system more effectively',[132] and they are finding some institutional support in the form of an Advisory Centre on WTO Law established in 2001, that provides subsidised legal services to developing countries engaged in WTO disputes.[133]

Fundamentally, in my view, within the current operational parameters of the WTO's DSM, there is only limited opportunity to develop means and methods of protecting human rights. Calls for greater accommodation by, and reforms of, the DSM continue to be made from within and without the WTO. John Jackson believes that the dispute-settlement system needs some 'fine-tuning' if it is to be more amenable to such non-core trade issues as human rights. He suggests that hearings ought to be conducted in public; that there should be greater room for NGO participation, and for Panels to accept and consider amicus briefs. To these suggestions, James Harrison, in his thoughtful and prodigiously researched book on human rights and the WTO, adds a number of proposals that he believes would broaden the scope for ensuring that the WTO not only refrains from negatively affecting human rights, but also positively promotes their advancement. These include: monitoring the effects of trade rules on human rights protections (by way of human rights impact assessments, for example); the promoting of understanding among trade specialists and members of the WTO's dispute-settlement bodies of the jurisprudence of international human rights laws; and the insertion of express human rights reference in certain key WTO treaties.[134]

Perhaps most significant, however, is Gabrielle Marceau's trenchant assessment of what changes need to be made to the dispute-settlement regime within the context of the current situation. Marceau, formally a Counsellor in the Legal Affairs Division of the WTO secretariat, and who

---

130 Gregory Shaffer, 'The Challenges of WTO Law: Strategies for Developing Country Adaptation' (2006) 5 *World Trade Review* 177.
131 Michael Booth, 'Argentina: Where the Polo Crowd Swing Swing', *Independent*, 4 February 2001, available at www.independent.co.uk.
132 Shaffer, 'The Challenges of WTO Law', at 197.   133 See www.acwl.ch.
134 Harrison, *The Human Rights Impact of the World Trade Organisation*, pp. 225–45.

now works in the Cabinet of the Director-General, is in no doubt that WTO law cannot be interpreted and applied in isolation. She stresses the importance of the fundamental principle of international law that states are presumed always to negotiate all their international treaty obligations in good faith.[135]

> Therefore [she argues], all WTO members must comply with their human rights obligations and with their WTO obligations at the same time without letting a conflict arise between the two sets of legislations. Hence, it is only reasonable to expect that the WTO adjudicating bodies would interpret WTO provisions taking into account all relevant obligations of WTO disputing states.[136]

What needs to be done to ensure that this 'reasonable expectation' is better fulfilled, Marceau suggests, is that human rights expertise and evidence should, where relevant, be accommodated by the panels and the Appellate Body, and that greater efforts should be invested in having inter-state conflicts between human rights and trade laws reach negotiated settlements rather than proceed to formal adjudication. She also, rightly, points out that if adjudication there must be on these trade and human rights issues, then it is a mistake to rely *solely* on WTO apparatus. The dispute-settlement mechanisms of human rights treaty regimes must also be engaged, which necessitates that they be strengthened to 'reduce the attractiveness of the WTO['s]'.[137]

Conditionality, concessions and sanctions

Trade sanctions

For many people, trade sanctions are perhaps the first thing that comes to mind when they consider how trade is linked to human rights. And indeed economic sanctions, almost invariably executed with some measure of military backing, have an ancient history as a means to punish, pressure and persuade – from Troy and Carthage, through Xiangyang and Derry, to Leningrad and Sarajevo.

135 That is, the principle of *pacta sunt servanda*, as stipulated in Article 26 of the Vienna Convention on the Law of Treaties 1969.
136 Gabrielle Marceau, 'The WTO Dispute Settlement and Human Rights', in Abbott *et al.* (eds.), *International Trade and Human Rights*, p. 234. Her last point is underlined by the Vienna Convention on the Law of Treaties 1969, Article 31(3)(c), which provides that in the interpretation of treaties 'any relevant rules of international law applicable in the relations between the parties' must be taken into account.
137 *Ibid.* p. 235.

International law's gradual relegation of the use of military force to a mechanism of last resort in dispute resolution between nations, culminating in the UN Charter of 1945,[138] has had the effect of elevating the importance of economic sanctions (*without* military backing) as an instrument of pressure in international conflicts. The UN Charter expressly authorises the Security Council to decide what measures are necessary to implement its decisions, including calling upon member states to institute measures that effect 'complete or partial interruption of economic relations' (Article 41), though this power is constrained by the loosely defined stipulations in Article 2(3) and (4) that such actions must not themselves endanger international peace and security, nor threaten the territorial integrity or political independence of any state.

Since 1945 there has been no shortage of examples of sanctions imposed for human rights reasons – against the Apartheid regime in South Africa; communist regimes in China, Cuba, the USSR and Vietnam; military regimes in Burma and Pakistan; dictatorships in Iraq, Indonesia, Libya, North Korea and Uganda; kleptocracies in Cambodia and Zimbabwe; and repressive theocracies in Afghanistan and Iran. Some of these have been backed by the UN, but many have been minimally multilateral, or even unilateral (such as the US embargo of Vietnam from 1975 until 1995).

Despite their number, variety and longevity (the West's sanctions against North Korea have lasted more than fifty years), sanctions are widely acknowledged as being crude exercises of political and economic power. They can be very effective in imposing economic and social hardships (and thereby themselves occasioning human rights violations), but are seldom effective in promoting political change. The poor, the sick, the marginalised and children all tend to be especially seriously affected, as sanctions almost invariably increase the costs of staple foods, essential medicines and power, and they starve welfare services, food security programmes, water and sanitation services, health care and schools of necessary public funding. Unsurprisingly, embargoed countries will turn elsewhere for economic as well as social and political support: for example, Cuba's reliance on USSR assistance (until 1990) and Burma's current reliance on trading relations with China and to a lesser extent India. Economic sanctions are also often honoured as much in their breach as in compliance, for example Barclays Bank's continuation,

---

138 Chapter VII, 'Action with Respect to Threats to the Peace, Breaches of the Peace and Acts of Aggression'.

albeit disguised, of investment in South Africa in the 1980s, and in the 2000s the Australian Wheat Board's subversion of the UN 'Oil for Food' programme (which programme was a specialised form of conditional sanction).

That said, one should never underestimate how sanctions can be symbolically important or psychologically significant, especially for those directly suffering from the government actions that have prompted the sanctions. Nelson Mandela has always been clear about how much store he set by the sanctions levied against South Africa's Apartheid governments, calling them a 'potent weapon'.[139] But, even with the benefit of hindsight, it has been extremely difficult to discern any clear causal relationship between the sanctions imposed, and the ending of Apartheid in 1994, the election of Mandela himself as President, and the subsequent enactment of a Constitution with extensive human rights provisions. As the economist Philip Levy concludes in his case-study of the sanctions and Apartheid: 'while foreign companies doing business in South Africa experienced pressure in their home countries to disinvest, it is difficult to distinguish the effects of this pressure from South Africa's diminishing appeal as a borrower'.[140] Political, economic and social changes, in the end, come from complex combinations of internal dissatisfaction and unrest, as well as exogenous factors such as border conflicts, or the death or displacement of a despot, in which sanctions may well play a part, but are never the sole or even the primary cause of change.

As a consequence of the obligation to treat equally all nations with which a member state trades (the principle of the universalising 'Most Favoured Nation' (MFN) status) imposed by the WTO Agreement and the GATT before it, the use of economic sanctions would appear to be barred on the basis that they are necessarily discriminatory. Member states have effectively 'contract[ed] away the right to impose unilateral, trade-restrictive measures to enforce human rights in another Member's territory'.[141] Such a conclusion is what some human rights advocates fear is an especially reprehensible outcome of the WTO, forbidding 'trade

---

139 Nelson Mandela, 'Closing Address to the 48th National Conference of the African National Congress' (1991), at www.anc.org.za/ancdocs/history/mandela/1991/sp910700-03.html.

140 Philip Levy, 'Sanctions on South Africa. What Did They Do?', Center Discussion Paper No. 796 (Economic Growth Center, Yale University, 1999), p. 5; at www.econ.yale.edu/growth_pdf/cdp796.pdf. Levy also notes that to the extent that sanctions did exert pressure on the former governments, it was that coming from the private sector, rather than from the states, that was most effective; *ibid.* p. 2.

141 Eres, 'The Limits of GATT Article XX', at 611–12.

sanctions even in response to violations of human rights or other norms of international law', as Carlos Manuel Vásquez puts it.[142] After all, the whole post-war trade law apparatus has been likened, as mentioned earlier, to a disarmament treaty; with multilateral initiatives expressly intended to regulate trade relations by, inter alia, providing a rule-based adjudicatory system for the settlement of disputes, to replace the use of the unregulated armament of trade sanctions.

The problem has always been when the causes of trade disputes are situated outside trade, as is the case of claims of human rights abuse. If, then, the international trade law regime is to deal with the problem, it must necessarily reach out beyond the boundaries of trade, or at least ensure that its legal borders are sufficiently porous to permit entry of non-trade issues. With some liberal interpretation, the public morals, human health and national security exceptions under the GATT (Article XX(a), (b) and Article XXI respectively) might be read so as to justify some measure of trade sanctions, though there has been little or no jurisprudence on these provisions.[143] Trade sanctions have, however, had some airing in the DSM. In 1997, the EU and Japan challenged the US over Massachusetts' *Act Regulating State Contracts with Companies Doing Business with or in Burma (Myanmar)* of 1996, which barred any companies (US *and* foreign) who had business dealings with Myanmar/Burma from bidding for state government contracts. The legislation was inspired by ongoing human rights abuses perpetrated on the people of Myanmar by the ruling military junta there. Dispute settlement proceedings were initiated, based mainly on complaints that the law breached the WTO Agreement on Government Procurement which prohibits such discriminatory practices and provides no exception that would justify the Massachusetts law.[144] However, the case lapsed in 2000, after domestic litigation mounted against the legislation led to a judgment from the US Supreme Court pronouncing the law to be unconstitutional.[145]

Related to these specific WTO concerns, there is also a wider debate within international law about the legality of trade sanctions. Sarah

---

142 Carlos Manuel Vásquez, 'Trade Sanctions and Human Rights – Past, Present and Future' (2003) 6(4) *Journal of International Economic Law* 797, at 801.

143 *Ibid.* 809–10.

144 See *United States – Measure Affecting Government Procurement – Request for Consultations by the European Communities*, WT/DS88/1, 26 June 1997; and *United States – Measure Affecting Government Procurement – Request for Consultations by Japan*, WT/DS95/1, 21 July 1997.

145 *Crosby v. National Foreign Trade Council*, 530 U.S. 363 (2000).

Cleveland has shown in her work[146] how the foundational legal bases for economic sanctions overlap with international human rights law, with somewhat unclear results. She notes the importance of *jus cogens* principles, which can be understood to bear directly on economic sanctions in two ways. First, they appear to permit states to take appropriate actions (including trade sanction actions) against human rights transgressors to stop violations. But secondly, at the same time, they constrain states from taking actions that would result in the infringement of such basic human rights as protection from slavery and torture, either directly by actions of the sanctioning state, or indirectly, by actions of the sanctioning state that prevent the target state itself from providing adequate protection.

The International Court of Justice (ICJ) has insisted upon the transnational interest that all states have in the preservation of certain fundamental rights and the prevention of their infringement by any nation in the seminal *Barcelona Traction* case (1970).[147] Further, the Court appeared partially to endorse the use of sanctions in *Nicaragua v. US* (1986), when it chose *not* to admonish the US for its termination of economic aid to Nicaragua (rather, its proscriptions were aimed at the active support the US was providing to the Contras both inside and outside Nicaragua).[148] The latter point is perhaps surprising, given the fact that Article 60 of the Vienna Convention on the Law of Treaties (1969) explicitly states that the normal rule that a material breach of a bilateral treaty by one party entitles the other party to terminate the treaty does *not* apply when the treaty is humanitarian in nature.[149]

To this inconclusive state of affairs, international human rights law, alas, brings no obvious resolution. Though some human rights treaties may be read to imply some level of endorsement (see, for example, the earlier discussion on the ICESCR), none provides any unambiguous authority

---

146 Sarah Cleveland, 'Human Rights Sanctions and the World Trade Organisation', in Francesco Francioni (ed.), *Environment, Human Rights and International Trade* (Oxford and Portland: Hart, 2001), p. 119, at pp. 208–13 *et seq.*

147 *Barcelona Traction, Light and Power Company, Limited (Belgium v. Spain)(Second Phase)* [1970] ICJ Reports 3, at 32 (paras. 33–4).

148 *Military and Paramilitary Activities in and against Nicaragua (Nicaragua v. USA) (Merits)* [1986] ICJ Reports 14.

149 As underscored by the International Court of Justice, which has noted a 'general principle of law that a right of termination on account of breach must be presumed to exist in respect of all treaties, except as regards provisions relating to the protection of the human person contained in treaties of a humanitarian character (as indicated in Art. 60, para. 5 of the Vienna Convention)'; in *Legal Consequences for States of the Continued Presence of South Africa in Namibia (South West Africa) notwithstanding Security Council Resolution 276 (1970)*, Advisory Opinion, [1971] ICJ Reports 16, at p. 47.

for the use of economic sanctions in order to safeguard human rights. This, Sarah Cleveland points out, is in contrast to international environmental agreements which commonly condone trade sanctions in express terms.[150]

So, there is 'no clear trump card'[151] provided either by *jus cogens* principles or by human rights treaties for the use of economic sanctions for human rights ends over the objections that such actions are illegal. And trade sanctions still occur. It can be concluded, therefore, that while international law does have an important normative influence on the conduct of international relations in this area (as in many others), evidently it is not determinative. Where other pressures demand (for example, non-trade relations with other countries, or domestic politics), then trade laws can and will be flouted, or their provisions interpreted imaginatively by states. An illustration of this is provided by the postscript to the demise of the above-mentioned Massachusetts statute targeting corporations doing business in Myanmar. Shortly after the Supreme Court decision, President Clinton issued an Executive Order prohibiting all federal executive agencies from purchasing goods produced 'wholly or in part by forced or indentured child labor'.[152]

Preferential treatment and conditionality

Special and differential treatment has always been a controversial aspect of trade liberalisation, precisely because it appears to counteract the main tenet of the liberalising agenda, namely that trading partners should all be treated equally as between each other, and also that there should be little or no distinction between a country's treatment of domestic and foreign corporate enterprises. Some of this disquiet is voiced by those outside a preferential trade deal – such as many critics of the Lomé Convention and the Cotonou Agreement which until very recently[153] gave the ACP

---

150 Cleveland has compiled a list of such treaties, which includes instruments covering transboundary movement of hazardous wastes, ozone depletion and the protection of endangered species; Cleveland, 'Human Rights Sanctions and the World Trade Organisation', at pp. 210–11.

151 *Ibid.* p. 213.

152 As noted by Raul Pangalangan, 'Sweatshops and International Labor Standards: Globalizing Markets, Localizing Norms', in Alison Brysk (ed.), *Globalization and Human Rights* (Berkeley: University of California Press, 2002), p. 104.

153 Now being replaced by 'European Partnership Agreements' (EPAs) which, in respect of the ACP, have been heavily criticised for their classical free trade demands that access and liberalisation be reciprocal. See Oxfam, *Partnership or Power Play? How Europe*

(African, Caribbean, Pacific) group of countries privileged access to the EU Market – and some by those within such a deal, over the nature and extent of the conditions imposed on them, including meeting certain human rights standards, in order to gain the preferences on offer.

Special and differential treatment is in fact endemic through trade agreements. It is recognised in various formats including in Accession Agreements; bilateral and regional trade agreements; certain sector-specific treaties (e.g. in the Agreement on Agriculture);[154] 'Generalised System of Preferences' arrangements (GSPs); and most recently the suite of initiatives launched under the banner of 'Aid for Trade' which 'aim to help developing countries, particularly LDCs, to build the supply-side capacity and trade-related infrastructure that they need to assist them to implement and benefit from WTO Agreements and more broadly to expand their trade'.[155] All of these attach conditions on target states usually based on some combination of economic goals (e.g. reciprocal tariff and subsidy reductions, or export targets), and what can be called social and political welfare issues (e.g. labour standards, good governance practices and human rights goals).

Despite its prevalence, there is a sizeable body of literature that sees such conditionality, taken as a whole, as counter-productive. Referring generally to the phenomenon of conditionality in relation to economic deals that developed countries strike with developing ones, Balakrishnan Rajagopal, for example, is very critical about the manner in which conditions are chosen and the form in which they are expressed.

> Selectivity is the idea that donors should be more discriminating about the governments they are willing to support. The criteria for such discrimination are by no means self-evident but are supposed to include a good policy environment and a clean government that has not engaged in massive repression, such as the Burmese Junta. These criteria are in the end

Should Bring Development into its Trade Deals with African, Caribbean and Pacific Countries, Oxfam Briefing Paper No. 110 (April 2008); www.oxfam.org/en/policy/ briefingpapers/bp110_EPAs_europe_trade_deals_with_acp_countries_0804.

154 Article 6 of the Agreement on Agriculture, which governs domestic support, and Article 9 of the same Agreement concerning export subsidies, both contain provisions which give special or differential treatment to developing country members, being Articles 6.2 (exempting investment subsidies for agricultural development from domestic support reduction commitments) and 6.4(b) (increasing the level of the *de minimis* exception for developing countries), and Articles 9.2(b) and 9.4 (providing less onerous export subsidy reduction commitments for developing countries during the first six years of the Agreement's implementation).

155 These are the words used in paragraph 57 of the *Hong Kong Ministerial Declaration* (adopted 18 December 2005), WT/MIN(05)/DEC, that mandated the initiative.

contradictory or self-defeating. It is the absence of good policy that leads to the financial crisis that calls for conditionality-based intervention in the first place; therefore, a good policy environment could not be a criterion for positive discrimination.[156]

In practice, this apparently circular problem is circumvented by, as Rajagopal notes, setting the threshold criterion very low, and by the liberal and pragmatic employment of attitudes of hope over expectation when engaging states in negotiations about such conditions. This broad contextual setting of conditionality bears directly on the specific instance of the impact of human rights conditionality in trade agreements with which I am concerned.

The principal trade-related vehicle through which express human rights conditionality is pursued is the GSP mechanism. GSPs are a specific kind of preferential trade arrangement. Their basic premise is broadly to provide calibrated exceptions to the universalised MFN principle for a wide range of developing countries, in order initially to encourage the maturation of their fragile or emerging economies by giving some targeted privileged access to the host state's markets, and, ultimately, to propel them towards the point where such preferential treatment is no longer required. Their legal legitimacy is obtained through the WTO's so-called 'Enabling Clause'[157] which in effect provides a permanent waiver to the MFN stipulation, by permitting 'differential and more favourable treatment to developing countries', provided it has the intention 'to facilitate and promote the trade of developing countries', and does not, in consequence, 'raise barriers to or create undue difficulties for the trade of any other contracting parties'.[158] The delicate task of facilitating trade for developing states while at the same time not impeding trade relations between other states is the fulcrum upon which the whole apparatus of GSPs balances.[159]

---

156 Balakrishnan Rajagopal, 'From Resistance to Renewal: The Third World, Social Movements and the Expansion of International Institutions' (2000) 41 *Harvard International Law Journal* 529, at 575.

157 Entitled: 'Decision on Differential and More Favourable Treatment, Reciprocity and Fuller Participation of Developing Countries', adopted by Member States under the GATT, 28 November 1979 (L/4903).

158 *Ibid.* para. 3(a).

159 As demonstrated in the reasoning of the Panel and Appellate Body reports in *European Communities – Tariff Preferences* (Panel Report, *European Communities – Conditions for the Granting of Tariff Preferences to Developing Countries*, WT/DS246/R, adopted 20 April 2004, as modified by Appellate Body Report, WT/DS246/AB/R) in which India challenged the specific conditions set down in the EU GSP regarding trading incentives for certain developing countries taking measures to counteract illegal drug trafficking.

Currently, there are thirteen GSPs,[160] covering every developing country, and although all of them are broadly concerned with the promotion of good political and economic management, there are only two that make specific reference to labour and human rights standards – namely those of the US and the EU.

The US GSP, which has been periodically renewed since 1974, has two categories of target states: (i) some 131 developing states eligible for duty free access to 3,400 lines of products imported into the US, and (ii) further preferences for 42 least developed states that have duty free access to an additional 1,400 product lines.[161] Eligibility for membership of the GSP depends on meeting certain criteria – that the state is non-communist,[162] is not engaged in acts supportive of terrorism, and does not otherwise act in ways contrary to US national interests; acts to protect intellectual property rights and (since 1984), respects core international labour rights (for example, trade union membership, rights to collective bargaining, prohibitions against child labour and forced labour).[163] Continuance of membership depends on avoiding transgressions of these same criteria. Though over the years there have been many hundreds of petitions filed claiming breaches (a great many of which were lodged by American trades union), suspension of a state's membership has occurred relatively rarely.[164]

More telling, I think, has been the maintenance of punitive 'Watch Lists' issued under section 301 of the US *Trade and Tariff Act* 1984,[165] which by virtue of their selective application (notably in respect of states suspected

160 See UNCTAD website on GSPs: www.unctad.org/Templates/Page.asp?intItemID=1418 &=1.

161 Office of the United States Trade Representative, *US Generalized System of Preferences Guidebook* (Washington, DC: USTR, March 2008), pp. 3, 6.

162 Though this appears to be relaxable where the state is a member of the WTO; thus it is understood that, at the time of writing, the US Trade Representative is considering granting GSP beneficiary status to Vietnam, which joined the WTO in 2007.

163 For the text of the relevant statute, see 19 USC § 2461 *et seq.*

164 There have been only nineteen suspensions since the programme's inception in the mid 1970s, according to data extracted from United States Government Accountability Office, *US Trade Preference Programs: An Overview of Use by Beneficiaries and US Administrative Reviews*, Report to the Chairman, Committee on Finance, US Senate, and Chairman, Committee Ways and Means, House of Representatives (27 September 2007), table 4: 'Changes in Countries' GSP Beneficiary Status since Program Implementation', pp. 68–71.

165 The statutory provision authorises the withdrawal of trade benefits and/or the imposition of duties on goods from countries deemed not to have provided protection for US intellectual property interests. A compilation by the *IP Justice* in the US indicates that Section 301 was utilised against fifty-nine countries (most repeatedly so) between

of flaunting intellectual property laws) have been described by Eric Smith, President of the International Intellectual Property Alliance, as having 'done more than any other provision of U.S. trade law to improve the level of worldwide protection of U.S. products embodying copyright',[166] rather than necessarily promoting the protection of human rights in the target countries.

In their detailed study of the implementation and enforcement of all aspects of the US GSP over twenty years, Lance Compa and Jeffrey Vogt reach the conclusion that 'geopolitics and foreign policy are the chief considerations for applying the GSP labour rights clause, not the merits of a country's compliance or non-compliance with the law'.[167]

In terms of its capacity to contribute to the protection of human rights, what is perhaps the most significant limitation of the US GSP is that its rights component is focused solely on labour rights – and even then on what Bob Hepple calls 'idiosyncratic interpretations' of labour rights. Hepple notes, for example, one bizarre instance in which 'the murder of a trade union leader has been classified as a violation of "human rights" not of a "worker right" and so excluded from the GSP program'.[168]

The EU has also had a continuing cycle of GSPs since 1971, with the latest version established in 2005 to run for three years having been extended for a further three years from 1 January 2009.[169] As with the US regime, the EU GSP provides potential concessions to all developing countries, and additional concessions to some fifty least developed countries.[170] These twin base-line GSP arrangements have been supplemented under the EU scheme by a third arm referred to as 'GSP Plus', which is designed as a sort of human rights compliance 'carrot'. It offers still greater reductions in access barriers to 'vulnerable countries' (picked on economic criteria), provided that the state complies with an expanded list of sixteen human

---

2001 and 2007; see compilation of *United States Trade Representative (USTR) Section 301 Annual Reports (2001–2007)*, http://ipjustice.org/wp/wp-content/uploads/2008-Section-301-Table-IPJustice.htm.

166 As quoted by Susan Sell, 'Industry Strategies for Intellectual Property and Trade: The Quest for TRIPS, and Post-TRIPS Strategies' (2002) 10 *Cardozo Journal of International and Comparative Law* 79, at 101.

167 Lance Compa and Jeffrey Vogt, 'Labour Rights in the Generalised System of Preferences: A 20 Year Review' (2001) 22 *Comparative Labor Law and Policy Journal* 199, at 236.

168 Bob Hepple, *Labour Laws and Global Trade* (Oxford and Portland, OR: Hart, 2005), p. 95.

169 Council Regulation No. 732/2008 of 22 July 2008 [2008] OJ L211/1.

170 The additional concessions for LDCs effectively widen duty free access to product lines that include 'everything but arms'.

rights and labour rights conventions, as well as a further eleven treaties covering environmental protection, narcotics and governance.[171]

Compared to the US enforcement against transgressions of eligibility, the EU has been more hesitant about invoking the ultimate sanction of withdrawing preferences, which was always intended to be an action of last resort.[172] Thus far, there have only been two clear sanctions (Burma, in respect of forced labour in 1997, and Belarus, regarding restrictions on trades union in 2006), and one inquiry into the use of child labour in Pakistan (in 1996). That said, it is fair to conclude that the EU's GSP scheme, with its much broader inclusion of human rights instruments, possesses the greater potential to impact positively on the target states' levels of human rights protection.

While it appears that there can be certain economic benefits of the scheme (see, for example, the gains noted by Ludo Cuyvers and Stijin Verherstraeten in respect of the Association of South-East Asian Nations (ASEAN) countries that are among the greatest potential beneficiaries of the EU GSP),[173] it is very difficult to gauge what impact it is having in human rights terms. This is as true for the US GSP as for that of the EU, despite the former's more aggressive record. Attempts that purport to measure the human rights impact of GSP regimes do not withstand scrutiny, tending too easily to 'mistake motion for action', as Ernest Hemingway warned us against doing in all aspects of life.[174] For example, Emilie Hafner-Burton's survey of the influence of preferential trade agreements 'on government repression' in 177 countries between 1972 and 2002[175] falls prey to the simplistic temptation of interpreting coincidence of compliance or non-compliance as evidence of direct causal relationship with the conditionality of the preferential trade agreements.[176] The complexity

---

171 Council Regulation No. 980/2005 of 27 June 2005 [2005] OJ L169/1. The relevant conventions are listed in Annex III to the Regulation.

172 As noted by Barbara Brandtner and Allan Rosas, 'Trade Preferences and Human Rights', in Philip Alston, Mara Bustelo and James Heenan (eds.), *The EU and Human Rights* (Oxford: Oxford University Press, 1999), p. 699, at p. 717.

173 Ludo Cuyvers and Stijin Verherstraeten, *The EU's Generalized System of Preferences and its ASEAN Beneficiaries: A Success Story?* CAS Discussion Paper 47 (December 2005), pp. 11–19.

174 As attributed.

175 Emilie Hafner-Burton, 'Trading Human Rights: How Preferential Trade Agreements Influence Government Repression' (2005) 59(3) *International Organization* 593.

176 Consider for example the enormous assumptions as to governmental motivations regarding trade and human rights (let alone regarding all the other manifest concerns that impact on day-to-day governmental decision-making) in the construction of her remarkable 'repression formula'; *ibid.* at 614–23.

of reasons why states do or do not adopt certain human rights protec-tions, together with the many gradations of their actual compliance, is so substantial that the only real value of efforts such as Hafner-Burton's is to demonstrate how lacking the human rights and trade communities are in respect of rigorous methodologies to address such important questions of cause and effect. An exposure, let me say, that is both long overdue and telling.

Alongside the GSP, the EU also has a long history of inclusion of human rights provisions in its many bilateral and multilateral trade treaties. Typ-ically, these comprise a standard ('essential elements') exhortation to abide by democratic principles and respect international human rights standards generally, the inclusion (where necessary) of specific human rights concerns peculiar to the parties, and sanctions provisions regard-ing non-compliance.[177] But these too, despite their promise, have yielded little by way of clear human rights benefits. In his review of their appli-cation and enforcement, Lorand Bartels concludes that, 'compared to the range of *possible* scenarios in which human rights clauses might be applied, their actual impact on the EU's external human rights policies has been relatively modest... [with] limited use of human rights clauses to suspend benefits provided under agreements'.[178] Amnesty International has even called the 'essential elements' clause a 'dead letter';[179] which damned status is most graphically confirmed by the absence of human rights clauses from so-called sectoral agreements, and some bilateral agreements with certain states – for example, in respect of China (the biggest single benefactor of the EU's preferential trade agreements), and much of South East Asia.[180]

The general tenor of the whole of the EU's apparatus of human rights conditionality in trade relations is one of potential power, but timidity in practice – like 'a shiver waiting for a spine to climb up', as former Australian Prime Minister Paul Keating once put it in a very different context.[181] Some commentators believe that the spine is now there to be climbed – the new EU GSP model being viewed as 'a step forward' in that

---

177 As discussed in Commission Communication (COM 216/1995) of 23 May 1995 on the Inclusion of Respect for Democratic Principles and Human Rights in Agree-ments between the Community and Third Countries, available at http://ec.europa.eu/external_relations/human_rights/doc/com95_216_en.pdf.
178 Lorand Bartels, *Human Rights Conditionality in the EU's International Agreements* (Oxford: Oxford University Press, 2005), pp. 37–8.
179 As quoted in *ibid.* p. 38.   180 *Ibid.* pp. 34–5.
181 Unsurprisingly, perhaps, in light of Keating's acerbic reputation, this was his *ad hominem* assessment of the then leader of the Opposition (and the next Australian Prime

direction[182] – while others continue to call for greater efforts to be made to strengthen the backbone of human rights conditionality within trade relations, by, for instance, focusing much more on the most economically vulnerable countries (e.g. small island states and land-locked states) where leverage is greater and substantial assistance potentially more effective.[183]

Whatever the precise format of human rights conditionality in the EU or US schemes, their application in practice has to be focused on assisting (and cajoling) 'governments to deliver the human rights entitlements of their people in the course of their financial [and trade] programs, not on making demands as conditions for assistance'.[184] The impact is more likely to be more effective and actively embraced by the target states where the approach is facilitative rather than when it is intended and viewed as being admonitory and coercive.

Conclusion

In the late 1990s the UN Sub-Commission on Human Rights boldly declared that 'human rights are the primary objective of trade, investment and financial policy'.[185] In the intervening years, while much has been said and written about the relationship between trade and human rights, there have been few steps taken within trade circles towards demonstrating agreement with such a statement, let alone clear, positive steps taken towards its fulfilment.

To be sure, there has been the establishment of grounds for a better understanding of what the economic benefits of trade can and have done for economic development, social welfare and political stability, and thereby for better standards of human rights observance. But in terms of trade practice, we are still some way from ' "delinking" international trade strategy from the theory of neo-liberalism and setting a high priority

Minister), John Howard; as reported by David Fickling, 'Strewth! Australian Prime Minister Tells Larrikins to Mind Their Tongues', *Guardian*, 10 July 2004, p. 3.

182 Harrison, *The Human Rights Impact of the World Trade Organisation*, pp. 120–1.

183 See Bartels, *Human Rights Conditionality in the EU's International Agreements*, pp. 42–4, and also Lorand Bartels, 'The WTO Legality of the EU's GSP+ Arrangement' (2007) 10(4) *Journal of International Economic Law* 869, at 883–4. In the latter Bartels admits, of course, that such a truncated but more intrusive scheme would be politically difficult to sell within (and outside) the EU.

184 Adam McBeth, 'Global Rules for Global Players: International Economic Actors and Human Rights', PhD thesis 2007, on file with author, p. 210. McBeth was here drawing on the arguments of Jorge Daniel Taillant, *Human Rights and the IFIs*, paper for Sustainable Justice Conference, Montreal (June 2002), part 1.

185 Sub-Commission on Human Rights Resolution 1998/12 (20 August 1998).

on compliance with human rights norms', which, Gig Moon argues, remains a key and, as yet, unfulfilled objective of global trade relations.[186]

The development orientation of the WTO, as the unchallenged lodestone of multilateral trade policy development, rule creation and dispute resolution, holds the promise to do more in these respects. There are both legal and political (or rhetorical) avenues within the WTO down which human rights concerns have travelled. The legal avenues are restricted, however, in jurisdictional, capacity and cultural terms, as the above discussions on the limited accommodation for human rights arguments in the 'exceptions clauses', and the ad hoc and piecemeal formats of the US and EU GSP schemes illustrate. There are indications of change, such as with the advances in the access to certain essential medicines in the developing world through the amendments to the TRIPS compulsory licensing scheme,[187] which prove 'that change is indeed possible . . . however slow and cumbersome' it may be, as Adam McBeth puts it.[188]

Nonetheless, the legal route is not – at least not alone – the basket into which to put all one's trade and human rights eggs. The philosophical, political and diplomatic arenas are predominantly important at this stage; it is, fundamentally, a case of winning over 'hearts and minds', more than winning legal cases. Marking the tenth anniversary of the WTO, the lacklustre Sutherland Report in 2005 did little to inspire this cause. Joost Pauwelyn describes it as 'a missed opportunity'. 'The overall message of the report', he laments, 'is an unabated defense of the WTO largely unchanged [save the (unoriginal) calls for greater transparency] and, for the most part, to be kept safely secluded from other international efforts to correct market failures and accompany free trade with social and other non-economic safety nets.'[189] Reflecting, in part, these sorts of criticisms, Pascal Lamy, who was appointed as the new Director-General of the WTO shortly after the publication of the Sutherland Report, has

---

186 Gillian Moon, 'The WTO-Minus Strategy: Development and Human Rights under WTO Law' (2008) 2 *Human Rights & International Legal Discourse* 37, at 78.

187 Initially, developing countries have preferred to strike deals with large pharmaceutical companies to obtain access to heavily subsidised drugs, rather than invoking the compulsory licensing option, though certainly the threat of the latter has proven to be a powerful bargaining chip; see Adam McBeth, 'When Nobody Comes to the Party: Why Have No States Used the WTO Scheme for Compulsory Licensing of Essential Medicines?' (2006) 3 *New Zealand Yearbook of International Law* 69, at 97–8.

188 *Ibid.* 99.

189 Joost Pauwelyn, 'The Sutherland Report: A Missed Opportunity for Genuine Debate on Trade, Globalization and Reforming the WTO' (2005) 8(2) *Journal of International Economic Law* 329, at 329–30.

pursued (as earlier discussed) a 'humanising globalisation' agenda, which has included the WTO-led 'Aid for Trade' initiative.[190] Such enterprise, even if beholden to the desires and determinations of the member states of the WTO, nevertheless represents the sort of broad spaces in which discussions of trade and human rights might be fruitfully pursued. That is, if and when the member states extricate themselves from the politically charged textual intricacies of closing the current Doha Round.

Speaking personally, I have lost count of the number of trade specialists (lawyers, economists, national and international bureaucrats, and academics) who roll their eyes whenever mention is made of human rights and trade, followed immediately by pained pronouncements that of course there is a great deal of misunderstanding over what that can and does mean in terms of how trade operates and how it is regulated. It is likely that they have heard many unfounded criticisms and bad arguments. But there are a number of valid, well-reasoned arguments why trade and human rights are and can be linked – many of which are represented in this chapter. There is a very great difference between those who use their experiences of bad arguments to justify both their supercilious response that their area of expertise is much misunderstood and their subsequent disingenuous dismissal of *all* talk of a trade and human rights linkage, and those whose awareness of the awfulness of some human rights and trade arguments is matched by their preparedness to accommodate the better ones.

Such open-mindedness together with the adoption in certain quarters of broader perspectives on trade and human rights linkages is certain to become even more significant as bilateralism increasingly becomes the vehicle of choice for new trade and investment negotiations.[191] Alongside much else, this movement towards bilateralism has important implications for human rights. The manifest 'inequality of arms' experienced by many developing nations (and all of the least developed states) in bilateral trade negotiations with rich states presents not only opportunities for their economic exploitation by the latter, but also opportunities to advance human rights compliance agendas with those same countries,

---

190 For an overview of which see the joint OECD/WTO, *Aid for Trade at a Glance 2007: First Global Review* (Paris: OECD; Geneva: WTO, 2007).

191 In respect specifically of the now more than 2,500 Bilateral Investment Treaties (BITs) there are particular human rights implications relating to the treaty provisions that limit host states' ability to meet their international human rights obligations, in favour of the interests of the home state investor. I discuss this issue in further detail in chapter 4.

whether earnestly intended as such, or as disguised protectionist measures (or a little of both). For trade-related human rights programmes to
have lasting impacts in developing states they must reach beyond merely
the export sector, otherwise 'there is a danger that [they] will fail to make
a difference to working conditions in the usually much larger informal
and non-export sectors'.[192]

No matter the re-emergence of robust trade bilateralism, the WTO
will still, of course, figure largely in the picture (as will other multilateral
organisations more concerned with human rights, such as the UN). But
the important human rights impacts of trade, both positive and negative,
will also occur in forums that operate alongside or outside the WTO, even
if they too hinge upon the demands and dispositions of states parties,
their representative politicians and their bureaucrats.

192 Harrison, *The Human Rights Impact of the World Trade Organisation*, p. 114.

3

Aid and human rights

Introduction

The relationship between human rights and economic aid is fundamentally different from that which human rights have with trade and with commerce, even if the problems of conceptual tension and institutional practice and culture turn out to be somewhat similar. Aid's *raison d'être* to alleviate poverty by promoting economic and social development is more *directly* focused on achieving human rights goals. With the trade or commerce components of the global economy, human rights are seen as possible *derivative* beneficiaries of the principal concerns of trade liberalisation and commercial enterprise.

Development thinking has, at least in certain quarters, always seen the relevance and importance of human rights. When the UN Economic and Social Council was established under the UN Charter it had functions and powers that related equally to 'international economic, social, cultural, educational, [and] health matters', and to 'promoting respect for, and observance of, human rights and fundamental freedoms for all' (Article 62). The very essence of what development means to the individual was initially captured in Article 25 of the UDHR 1948, which states that:

> Everyone has the right to a standard of living adequate for the health and well-being of himself and of his family, including food, clothing, housing and medical care and necessary social services, and the right to security in the event of unemployment, sickness, disability, widowhood, old age or other lack of livelihood in circumstances beyond his control.

This expression of development goals in human rights terms was repeated in various subsequent UN human rights treaties, in particular the International Covenant on Economic, Social and Cultural Rights 1966, the Convention on the Elimination of All Forms of Discrimination against Women 1981 and the Convention on the Rights of the Child 1990, and variously reiterated in numerous statements of each of their overseeing committees. There is even a body of opinion that asserts a right to development and a UN Declaration in 1986 that proclaims such right, though this is not without contestation as I further discuss later in this chapter. The interdependency of the two notions has also been expressly recognised and relied upon. Thus, the final communiqué of the first World Conference on Human Rights held in Teheran in 1968 pronounced that 'the achievement of lasting progress in the implementation of human rights is dependent upon sound and effective national and international policies of economic and social development';[1] and Kofi Annan, in his *In Larger Freedom* report in 2005 which heralded a reconfiguration of parts of the UN's human rights and humanitarian apparatus, identified development as inextricably linked to both the enjoyment of human rights and security.[2]

However, despite the effort invested in asserting their interrelationship in formal, declaratory terms, in practice the outcomes fall well short of the ideal. As Philip Alston and Mary Robinson note in the introduction to their jointly edited collection of essays on *Human Rights and Development*,

> debates in the United Nations and in other international fora do not necessarily translate into change on the ground, let alone within the different disciplines which need to adjust their working assumptions and methods in order to embrace, or at least accommodate, change. While the human rights community had recognized the need to engage with their [*sic*] development counterparts, they were not necessarily prepared to change their modus operandi. And, perhaps unsurprisingly, the latter group proved generally reluctant to engage in debates about international legal obligations and how to reflect the relevant norms in policies at the domestic and international levels.[3]

Responding to poverty

To understand why there is this dislocation and what its implications are, it is necessary to place the debate within the context of the wider development movement. The South-driven 'New International Economic Order' movement in the 1970s initially captured the imagination of the UN and, it seemed, many rich states in the North, with its strident call

1 Proclamation of Teheran, Final Act of the International Conference on Human Rights, Teheran, 22 April to 13 May 1968, UN Doc. A/CONF. 32/41 at 3 (1968), para. 13.
2 *In Larger Freedom: Towards Security, Development and Human Rights for All* (2005), www.un.org/largerfreedom, para. 17.
3 'The Challenges of Ensuring the Mutuality of Human Rights and Development Endeavours', in Philip Alston and Mary Robinson (eds.), *Human Rights and Development: Towards Mutual Reinforcement* (Oxford and New York: Oxford University Press, 2005), pp. 1–2.

for a radical rebalancing of global wealth, even if it was eventually to falter in the face of dissipating commitment among developed states and disagreement among the developing states.[4] It was only during the 1980s, driven by visions of what Bob Geldof called the 'pornography of poverty that is on our news screens' relating to the successive famines in the Horn of Africa countries, and popular movements such as the high-profile campaigns of Oxfam, War on Want, Save the Children, and the Geldof-orchestrated fund-raising Live Aid concerts (and the Band Aid and Comic Relief that followed them), that the alleviation of abject poverty became politicised for many people and governments in the West.

The particular association between human rights and development aid is also relatively young, even if accepting that it has amorphous roots dating back at least to the mid 1960s. As Katarina Tomasevski reports, it was in 1966 that the UN stated that: 'It may be said that, in a broad sense, everything that is being done by the United Nations family of organiza-tions . . . to promote economic and social development contributes to the implementation of human rights.'[5] That said, Tomasevski places the real genesis of the movement in the clearer linkages between development and human rights that emerged in the 1970s in the thinking of Western governments as well as international organisations such as the UN, the World Bank and the EEC (as it then was) as they wrestled with how to deal with blatant human rights abusing states such as Chile, Ethiopia, Kampuchea (now Cambodia), Sri Lanka and Haiti.[6] In the case of these countries, many donors chose to use the withdrawal of aid as a means to punish the human rights abusing governments. And while such action was controversial at the time – being considered by some to be counter-productive to human rights ends – it certainly highlighted to many the linkages between human rights and development aid.

At about the same time as all these deliberations were taking place, a junior economics professor at Chittagong University in Bangladesh was formulating a radical, home grown, aid programme in poor villages that surrounded the university campus that was to prove to be something of a harbinger for wholesale changes in the ways that the rich Western government aid agencies were to frame and administer there own aid programmes. Shocked by the appalling scenes of the consequences of

---

4 See Craig Murphy, *Emergence of the NIEO Ideology* (Boulder, CO: Westview Press, 1984).
5 UN, *Human Rights and the United Nations Family* (1966), para. 309, as quoted by Kata-rina Tomasevski, *Development and Human Rights* (London: Pinter Publishers, 1989), p. 21.
6 *Ibid.* chapter 5.

the famine that gripped Bangladesh in 1974, Muhammad Yunus was profoundly moved to act both personally and, crucially, professionally.

> I used to get excited teaching my students how economics theories provided answers to economic problems of all types. I got carried away by the beauty and elegance of these theories. Now all of a sudden I started having an empty feeling. What good were all these elegant theories when people died of starvation on the pavements and on door steps.
>
> My classroom now seemed to me like a cinema where you could relax because you knew that the good guy in the film would ultimately win. In the classroom I knew, right from the beginning, that each economic problem would have an elegant ending. But when I came out of the classroom I was faced with the real world. Here, good guys were mercilessly beaten and trampled. I saw daily life getting worse, and the poor getting poorer. For them death through starvation looked like their only destiny.
>
> Where was the economic theory that reflected their real life?[7]

The Grameen Bank, a micro-credit banking system that Yunus established in an effort to address abject poverty from the ground up rather than from the classroom down, developed into an enormous success and proved 'that the poor are bankable'.[8] It was, and still is, essentially a self-help scheme through which the bank lent very small amounts (often less than the equivalent of $10), at very low interest, to be paid back in tiny, but regular, instalments over a relatively short period. Crucially, it lent only to women, precisely because 'they constitute the majority of the poor, the under-employed and the economically and socially disadvantaged'.[9] Not only did this revolutionary tack empower women personally and socially, that investment of confidence and respect was literally repaid by remarkably high rates of compliance with the repayment schedules.[10] The loans enabled women and their families to break free from the vicious cycles of hand-to-mouth, subsistence living financed (or rather extorted) by old-fashioned usuries. They could invest even these tiny amounts of

---

7 *Banker to the Poor: The Story of the Grameen Bank* (London: Aurum Press, 1999), p. 4.
8 *Ibid.* p. 24. In terms purely of turnover, it grew astonishingly 'from $27 lent to forty-two people in 1976 to $2.3 billion lent to 2.3 million families by 1998'; p. 13. And, as I write, the *Washington Post* reports on the recently opened offices of the Grameen Bank in New York (the first in a developed country), and records the fact that loan disbursements in Bangladesh to date now total some $6 billion, spread across 7.4 million borrowers; Robin Shulman, 'Small Loans, Significant Impact', *Washington Post*, 10 March 2008, p. A03. Muhammad Yunus was awarded the Nobel Peace Prize in 2006.
9 *Ibid.* p. 89.
10 The repayment rate ranges between 92 and 98 per cent. P. K. Rao, *Development Finance* (Berlin and New York: Springer, 2003), p. 66.

capital into raw materials to be used to make tradable goods and so build up a micro-business: the first step on the ladder to financial independence.

The aid package that the Grameen Bank represents is certainly not typical. It is private sector based, commercial (though on a break-even rather than a profit maximisation basis), targeted at, and directly delivered to, the poorest of the poor, strategically long-term in its objectives, remarkably free of corruption or wastage. It delivers, what is more, palpably concrete results with businesses established, lands cultivated and houses built. Yunus pithily sums up his philosophy as follows: 'Poverty is a chronic disease. It cannot be cured with *ad hoc* measures. There may be short-term measures, but one must have a long-term strategy in mind when taking a quick tactical step.'[11]

During the late 1980s and the 1990s the same concerns with systemic, long-term approaches to poverty alleviation increasingly became the focus of national and multilateral aid agencies worldwide. The 1980s experiment with 'structural adjustment' planning – whereby severe and instant austerity measures in respect of public spending, monetary supply and fiscal accountability were imposed upon states as conditions of any assistance rendered either by the World Bank or the IMF – is now widely regarded as a failure. Danilo Türk's biting 1991 critique of the wider development and human rights implications of the structural adjustment programmes concluded that:

> [t]he 1980s . . . will go down in history as the 'lost decade' for development. In spite of remarkable progress (due in part to the availability of external financing) during the 1960s and 1970s for virtually all social and economic indicators, those covering the 1980s show largely either negligible improvement or in many cases dramatic decline. To cite but one example, over two thirds of the world's developing countries registered negative or negligible economic growth during this decade.[12]

The economic interventionist focus of structural adjustment gradually gave way to increased attention on the facilitation of institutional reforms in governments and also, latterly, greater engagement with the private sector in integrated efforts to bolster economic development and to install self-sustaining market economies in target states. Indeed these developments represented two strands to what amounts to a revolution in aid, the

---

11 *Ibid.* p. 103.
12 *The Realisation of Economic, Social and Cultural Rights*, Second Progress Report prepared by Mr Danilo Türk, Special Rapporteur, UN Doc. E/CN.4/Sub.2/1991/17, 18 July 1991, para. 55.

implications of which are still apparent today and which have direct bearing on the relationship between aid and the protection and promotion of human rights.

The first strand manifested itself in a shift away from the more traditional objects of aid and modes of delivery, namely the provision of a mixture of untied grants and loans and the underwriting of major infrastructure projects such as building bridges, dams, pipelines and power stations, roads, schools and hospitals. There has been a move towards substantial investment in governmental and institutional capacity-building through technical assistance, training and education, underpinned by a belief in the principles of good governance, transparency, combating corruption, strengthening civil society, the rule of law and respect for human rights. Indeed, defining governance broadly to include all of these principles and activities, it is estimated that about one quarter of the total of the World Bank's annual allocated budget is now directed towards governance-related projects. Somewhere between 10 and 25 per cent of each of the budgets of key bilateral aid agencies – including, for example, Australia, Canada, Denmark, the Netherlands, Sweden, the UK and the US – is also dedicated to improvements in governance.[13] Paul Collier's illuminating research considers 'the trap of bad governance' to be one of the most important points of leverage for aid today. In his book *The Bottom Billion* he describes three ways in which aid can be used to help turnarounds in the governance of poor states: (i) as an incentive to improve (or continue improving); (ii) as the provision of skills (directly, or indirectly by way of education and training); and (iii) as a reinforcement of sudden or tipping-point, positive changes in a country's political circumstances.[14] In Collier's view the three ways have various degrees of success, but, that aside, what his analysis demonstrates is that seeking ways to improve governance in poor countries has become big business within aid agencies. What makes the governance movement significant for my purposes is that it also encompassed particular human rights oriented initiatives. The joint UNDP–OHCHR programme for Human Rights Institutional Strengthening (HURIST), for example, though relatively

---

13 It is very difficult to be any more accurate because each agency breaks down its aid 'sectors' differently. However, according to OECD Development Assistance Committee (DAC) statistics for 2006, the total of all DAC donor countries allocations to the 'Government and Civil Society' sector was $14.4 billion, which represented nearly 15 per cent of all DAC official development assistance (ODA) for that year. See OECD-DAC Statistics Online, *Dataset 3: ODA by Sector*, at http://stats.oecd.org/wbos/Index.aspx?DatasetCode=ODA_SECTOR.

14 Paul Collier, *The Bottom Billion: Why the Poorest Countries Are Failing and What Can Be Done about It* (New York: Oxford University Press, 2007), pp. 108–17.

short-lived, managed to encourage the growth of national human rights commissions and agencies and to integrate specific human rights goals by way of 'human rights action plans' into the wider, cross-government, capacity-building exercises in many developing countries.[15]

The second strand comprises the growing collaboration between public sector aid and private sector investment in developing economies. There have always been important private avenues of overseas aid, especially charitable organisations such as Oxfam, Médecins sans Frontières, Save the Children or World Vision, though these have usually operated independently of donor government aid agencies. There has also, of course, always been corporate investment (or FDI) in developing states, but this has traditionally been, if anything, even more removed from an association with state aid work. What has changed significantly since the mid 1990s has been both the nature of the relationship between corporate and state development oriented activities and, most dramatically, the enormous growth in FDI which has both spurred, and been spurred by, the growth in economic capacity of many developing countries and so-called 'emerging economies' (a sort of promising halfway house between developing and developed states). It was only just over a decade ago that William Meyer was able to argue for the importance of official foreign aid because of its 'sheer size . . . as compared to foreign investment'. Drawing on the work of David Lumsdaine, he calculated that the annual totals of official aid from all donor countries was, on average, double that of foreign direct investment in the forty years from 1949 to 1989.[16] Today the picture has changed entirely. The latest figures available (for 2007) show that worldwide FDI in developing states is now more than six times greater than that for total of ODA: that is, $500 billion for FDI,[17] against $73 billion for ODA.[18] The wider picture of financial flows into developing countries drives home still further the nature of the changed

---

15 HURIST's first phase (1999–2002) was dedicated to these objects; its second phase (2002–5) was concerned more with constructing and applying a human rights based approach to development programming, which I discuss later in this chapter. For a review of HURIST see *Human Rights Strengthening: HURIST (UNDP/OHCHR/UNOPS) – Evaluation Report (May–July 2005)*; also see www.undp.org/governance/programmes/hurist.htm.

16 William Meyer, *Human Rights and International Political Economy in Third World Nations* (Westport, CT: Praeger, 1998), pp. 113–14; Lumsdaine's work was published in *Moral Vision in International Politics: The Foreign Aid Regime 1949–1989* (Princeton: Princeton University Press, 1993).

17 UNCTAD, *World Investment Report 2008: Transnational Corporations and the Infrastructure Challenge* (New York and Geneva: UN, 2008), p. 3.

18 Extracted from the OECD statistics database. The ODA figure represents the total aid from OECD countries. http://stats.oecd.org/wbos/index.aspx.

circumstances of aid. Private giving (charitable donations and corporate philanthropy) from the US, the UK, France and Norway alone amounted to $37 billion in 2006[19] and remittances (effected by individuals from developing states working in developed states sending money home) had ballooned to $251 billion in 2007.[20]

To some extent the changes in the nature of the relationship between official aid agencies and private enterprise have been forced by the very scale of the latter's investment in developing states. Not only can such a level of investment – like the proverbial scale-breaking gorilla – not be ignored, there is also a growing body of opinion that this is an important opportunity to advance aid and development on another front. It was perhaps unsurprising, therefore, that one of the key issues raised by the Commission on the Private Sector and Development in its 2004 report *Unleashing Entrepreneurship* was to warn against overlooking this potential. '[M]any critical resources for private sector development are under the radar screen of development, since they are not carried out by traditional development players and do not occur under the explicit label of development',[21] it noted. Seeking, with varying degrees of success, to exploit these resources, there have emerged in recent years a wide variety of mechanisms by which partnerships between public aid agencies and private commercial enterprises in the field of development have been facilitated and encouraged.

The International Finance Corporation (IFC), the private sector arm of the World Bank, has grown enormously in size and scope since the late 1990s, as has the Multilateral Investment Guarantee Agency (MIGA), another arm of the Bank, which provides insurance against political risk for corporations investing in developing states.[22] National Export Credit Agencies (ECAs) are government bodies that perform the same service on behalf of individual states in respect of corporations registered in their jurisdictions investing in the developing world, and they too have recorded marked increases in business.[23] There has also been a marked

19 Centre for Global Prosperity, *The Index of Global Philanthropy 2008* (Washington, DC: Hudson Institute, 2008) p. 48.
20 Dilip Ratha *et al.*, 'Revisions to Remittance Trends 2007', Migration and Development Brief 5, 10 July 2008; for this Brief, and the latest World Bank figures on remittances, see www.worldbank.org/prospects/ migrationandremittances.
21 *Unleashing Entrepreneurship: Making Business Work for the Poor* (New York: UNDP, 2004), at p. 29.
22 As detailed and discussed below, pp. 137–39.
23 The global growth throughout the 1990s of ECAs is noted by Delio Gianturco, *Export Credit Agencies: The Unsung Giants of International Trade and Finance* (Westport, CT:

increase in the instances and sophistication of public–private partnerships developed by state aid agencies, led by initiatives initially in the energy and water supply sectors, and latterly in the provision of health services.[24]

Most dramatic of all, however, has been exponential growth of Bilateral Investment Treaties (BITs), now numbering more than 2,500 worldwide. These are agreements between states (predominantly between Western and developing states, but increasingly between developing states themselves) which govern the conditions under which private sector investment from the former is made in the latter, and especially what guarantees the investor demands from the recipient state, including in respect of the settlement of disputes.[25] The International Institute for Sustainable Development (IISD) monitors the negotiations that establish the BITs and seeks to address their implications for sustainable development. It notes the crucial fact that the international development agenda is now being driven 'at a dizzying pace' by such agreements,[26] in the absence of any modern multilateral framework for their regulation. Predictably, this unregulated environment has favoured the richer and more powerful investor states, with an overwhelming focus on 'just one aspect of the investment process: the protection of foreign capital and investments'.[27] The consequences for developing states that seek to implement any human rights initiatives that potentially contravene the terms of a BIT have been equally grave, *despite* the fact that the purported contravening action might itself be based on the need to meet obligations under international human rights law.[28] For example, there have been a number of arbitration cases brought by large corporations against the South African

Quorum Books, 2001), pp. 41–4. And Karyn Keenan, of Halifax Initiative Coalition notes that, according to data collected by the OECD, ECAs in OECD member states 'provided US$125 billion in credits, insurance, guarantees and interest support' in 2005; *Export Credit Agencies and the International Law of Human Rights* (January 2008), p. 1.

24 See, for example, *The Global Fund to Fight AIDS, Tuberculosis and Malaria* and the *Global Alliance for Vaccines and Immunization*, both of which are financial instruments rather than implementing entities, comprising multi-stakeholder partnerships of UN agencies, governments, civil society organisations, the private sector and philanthropic organisations.

25 BITs are discussed further in chapter 4 below.

26 See IISD's website, www.iisd.org/investment/bits.

27 This quotation is taken from the *IISD Model International Agreement on Investment for Sustainable Development* (Winnipeg: International Institute for Sustainable Development, 2005), p. x, which is a proposal designed to fill this regulatory hole.

28 Andrea Shemberg, *Stabilization Clauses and Human Rights* (11 March 2008), paper prepared for the IFC and the UN Secretary General's Special Representative on Business and Human Rights, paras. 33–6; available at www.ifc.org/ifcext/media.nsf/Content/Stabilization_Clauses_Human_Rights.

Government claiming that its black empowerment legislation imposes financial costs on them proscribed by relevant BITs signed by South Africa.[29] Evidently, therefore, the utilisation of the market for aid and development goals does have its limits. But within the broad context of development assistance, greater private sector engagement with the poorest of the poor – those at the 'bottom of the pyramid' of wealth – must generally be welcomed by the poor, corporations and development agencies alike. To be sure, propositions like C. K. Prahalad's assertion that there is a need to unlock the 'significant latent purchasing power'[30] of the estimated four billion poor at the bottom of the pyramid[31] are premised on the prospects of corporations making mighty profits.[32] But, at the same time, there can be no denying the potent force of parallel arguments that if corporations prove themselves to be sufficiently perceptive and innovative to garner the market, the poor that comprise the target market will not only want to participate, but understand and covet the developmental potential of so doing, as Prahalad argues.[33] It is noteworthy that in the pursuit of what he sees as the goal of 'the morphing of the pyramid into a diamond' (see Figure 4), Prahalad stresses that the market-based system he envisages comprises an array of public and private sector actors including corporations (of all sizes), informal traders, cooperatives, NGOs and state law enforcement agencies.[34]

So, the new world order of international aid and development sees a two-way insinuation between the private and state sectors. Going one way, the private sector – to the extent that it operates in the developing world (which is significant) – is being drawn into greater public gaze through the scrutiny and expectations that attend its operations, especially when those operations are associated with public development projects (via, for example, the Equator Principles),[35] be they state aid agencies or multilateral ones. The particular matter of the human rights

---

29 See further Luke Peterson, *South Africa's Bilateral Investment Treaties: Implications for Development and Human Rights*, Dialogue on Globalization Occasional Paper No. 26 (Geneva: Friedrich-Ebert-Stiftung, 2006). I discuss this case further, as well as other human rights related matters concerning corporations and BITs, in chapter 4.
30 C. K. Prahalad, *The Fortune at the Bottom of the Pyramid: Eradicating Poverty through Profits* (Upper Saddle River, NJ: Wharton School Publishing, 2005), p. 11.
31 Calculated as those having less than $1,500 p.a. purchasing power; *ibid.* p. 4.
32 Though this contention is now the subject of considerable and heated debate, see Mallen Baker, 'Is There Really a Fortune at the Bottom of the Pyramid?', *Ethical Corporation* (3 September 2006).
33 Prahalad, *The Fortune at the Bottom of the Pyramid*, chapter 3.
34 *Ibid.* pp. 63–6.   35 See further below, chapter 3, note 159.

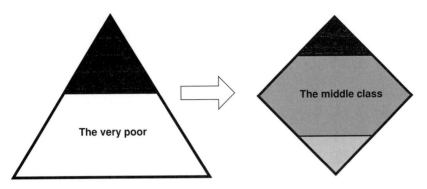

The very poor

The middle class

Fig. 4   The morphing of the pyramid into a diamond. *Source:* Prahalad, *The Fortune at the Bottom of the Pyramid* (2005), at p. 110.

implications of this dimension of the aid/commerce overlap will be analysed in the next chapter. What concerns me here, in this chapter, is the insinuation going the other way. That is, the accommodation by state aid of more private sector partnerships and practices, and what implications this has for human rights. The challenge this poses – especially given the rapidity and depth of the changes in the aid landscape catalogued above – can be encapsulated in the simply stated aim of how to exploit the new environment while, at the same time, avoiding being exploited by it.

Dani Rodrik frames this challenge in the broader terms of what impact globalisation (effected through the tremendous expansion of private enterprise through trade) has on the institutional capacity of states, and especially developing states. He argues that globalisation undercuts their ability 'to erect regulatory and redistributive institutions, and does so at the same time that it increases the premium on solid national institutions'.[36] This presents a serious dilemma to bilateral and multilateral aid agencies who are today trying to bolster such capacity, and to do so, at least in part, by way of the instrument of globalisation. This tension is a fine example of what Rodrik labels 'the central economic paradox of our time', namely:

> that 'development' is working while 'development policy' is not. On the one hand the last quarter century has witnessed a tremendous and historically unprecedented improvement in the material conditions of hundreds of millions of people living in some of the poorest parts of the world. On

36 Dani Rodrik, *One Economics, Many Recipes: Globalization, Institutions, and Economic Growth* (Princeton: Princeton University Press, 2007), p. 195.

the other hand, development policy as it is commonly understood and advocated by influential multilateral organizations, aid agencies, Northern academics, and Northern-trained technocrats has largely failed to live up to its promise.[37]

It might be, as some argue (but not Rodrik himself), that by adopting a human rights approach to development, greater clarity of purpose and process might be given to development policy. I consider these arguments and their counter-arguments later in this chapter, but first we need to delineate the precise nature of the link between poverty alleviation and human rights generally, and human rights law in particular.

Poverty alleviation and human rights

There are two important dimensions to the link between poverty allevia-tion and human rights: one moral, the other legal.

Moral and legal arguments

Thomas Pogge's challenging book *World Poverty and Human Rights*, which I referred to earlier, presents a most forthright set of arguments for why, morally, the link between poverty and human rights is important and what implications flow from it. He is concerned with deconstructing and rebutting the various defences that are raised against charges that the levels of abject poverty existing in the world today are morally repugnant, *and* that we who are not suffering so are to some degree morally responsible for the continuing plight of those who are. These are charges that Pogge essentially believes in.[38] Pogge accepts the part of these defences that asserts there is a morally significant difference between causing poverty and merely failing to reduce it. In this respect, he can be distinguished from Edmund Burke who famously held that 'all it takes for evil to triumph is for good men to do nothing'. However, Pogge then continues:

> And I grant at least for argument's sake that, notwithstanding the enor-mous complexity of modern economic interaction, such a distinction can be applied, at least roughly, to the global order. My argument conceives, then, both human rights and justice as involving solely negative duties: specific minimal constraints – more minimal in the case of human rights – on what harms persons may inflict on others . . .

---

37 *Ibid.* p. 85.
38 Thomas Pogge, *World Poverty and Human Rights* (Cambridge: Polity Press, 2002), pp. 11–15.

> I challenge the claim that the existing global order is not causing poverty, not harming the poor. This dispute is about the explanation of the persistence of severe poverty: why is global economic inequality increasing so rapidly that, despite an impressive rise in human affluence overall, hundreds of millions still barely survive from one day to the next?[39]

Moreover, Pogge adds, as the prevailing global institutional order is a product of, and driven by, *our* governments, then *we* – on whose behalf the governments act – 'bear primary responsibility' for the outcomes.[40] Pogge is right to challenge the complacency that is so often the response to accusations that the current global order may indeed be harming the poor as much as, or more than, helping them, and to rail against the absence of conclusive proof that it is *not* doing so. But equally he (like everyone else for that matter) is unable to demonstrate how, in fact, the current order *is* directly causing such damage; he also provides very little by way of comprehensive suggestions as to how the current order could be reformed or replaced to address poverty better.[41] The value of Pogge's critique, however, lies in its trenchant conscious-pricking assignment of the responsibility better to address poverty to we who are in a position to do something about it. By 'we' he means us as individuals, our governments and the global institutions, instruments and regimes they have created; and by 'doing something' he exhorts us to invoke 'the global moral force of human rights' as the object of global institutional change and the vivification of legal obligations to ensure human rights to all that would flow therefrom.[42]

This brings us, then, to the point where the legal dimension of the poverty/human rights relationship becomes apparent. It is a dimension that is fundamentally about 'the empowerment of the poor':[43] empowerment that stems from the rights that those in poverty are (or should be) able to claim against states, and the concomitant legal obligations placed on states (by international or domestic laws, or both) to meet those claims. The conditions of poverty that people are forced to live in violate many rights, such as those noted in the opening page of this chapter. As Nelson Mandela pronounces, 'overcoming poverty is not a gesture of charity. It

---

39 *Ibid.* p. 13.   40 *Ibid.* pp. 13, 15–20.
41 His suggestion of a 'Global Resources Dividend' for raising the necessary funds to tackle global poverty (his chapters 5–8) is short of any detailed consideration of the practicalities of how to ensure their appropriate distribution, application or sustainability. That said, Pogge might (fairly) argue that that is a next step for others to take.
42 *Ibid.* pp. 169–77.
43 As the UN's OHCHR puts it in its 2004 report, *Human Rights and Poverty Reduction: A Conceptual Framework*, p. 13.

is an act of justice. It is the protection of a fundamental human right, the right to dignity and a decent life. While poverty persists, there is no true freedom.'[44]

This much is incontrovertible, but there are nonetheless inherent limits to what international human rights *law* actually demands in this respect, as opposed to what we may fervently hope of it. For although there can be no question that human rights treaties mandate states to ensure the protection of all rights therein to all persons within their respective jurisdictions, international instruments are at best equivocal on what are the obligations of states to those beyond their borders whose human rights are being violated as a consequence of the poverty they must endure.

Certainly, to the extent that the situation threatens international peace, then there is some provision for the Security Council to take steps to address the problem, whether by force or by peaceable means. Further-more, post-Kosovo, a case has been made by some for egregious human-itarian need to be a valid ground for military intervention, in addition to the accepted ground of self-defence. But these are essentially vehicles for the short-term management of political crises rather than long-term strategies for dealing with human rights by alleviating poverty. The Inter-national Covenant on Economic, Social and Cultural Rights is more aspi-rational than directorial in this regard. The eponymous committee that oversees the Covenant has stressed 'the *potential* inherent in the articles of the Covenant that refer to "international cooperation" as a powerful basis for the Committee on which to base its work on globalisation and based on which states parties *could* contribute to creating a climate whereby economic globalisation does not lead to the violation of economic, social and cultural rights'.[45] The much discussed 'right to development' (RTD) remains unfinished business in terms of international law, marooned in a Declaration since 1986, its path to binding Covenant status hav-ing been effectively blocked by a combination of political opposition, textual uncertainty and purported impracticability of implementation and enforcement. Much of the dispute centres on the ambiguity of the allocation of development responsibilities and rights in the text of the

---

44 Nelson Mandela, Speech for the Make Poverty History campaign, Trafalgar Square, Lon-don, 3 February 2005, available at news.bbc.co.uk/2/hi/uk_news/politics/4232603.stm.

45 *Record of the Workshop on International Trade, Investment and Finance and Eco-nomic, Social and Cultural Rights*, 6 May 2000; www.unhchr.ch/tbs/doc.nsf/0/11d06750ac4e7acbc125691f002f01f0?Opendocument. The record refers specifically to Articles 2(1), 11, 15, 22 and 23 of the Covenant that themselves build upon the exhorta-tion for international cooperation in Articles 55 and 56 of the UN Charter.

Declaration itself. Articles 2 and 3 invest in individuals the status of an 'active participant and beneficiary of the right', while at the same time stipulating that 'all human beings have a responsibility for development', and that 'States have the right and the duty' and the 'primary responsibility' to advance development, as well as having the 'duty to co-operate with each other in ensuring development'. The capacity therein for confusion and argument over the expectations that might be made of the various parties – individuals, developing states and developed states – is manifest and has, predictably, been exploited to the full, especially in the confrontations between rich and poor states over whose responsibility development is. The situation has not been saved by the emphasis that Arjun Sengupta (the former UN Special Representative on the RTD) placed on the right being merely 'a process of development which leads to the realization of . . . human right[s]',[46] largely because such a characterisation does nothing to resolve the responsibility dilemma *between* states. And although a High Level Task Force on the Implementation of the Right to Development was established by the UN in 2004, which gained some impetus from linking the RTD to the achievement of the Millennium Development Goals by 2015,[47] it remains the case that, whatever value the RTD has today, it lies more in rhetorical argument than in any sense of legal entitlement or obligation.

Protestations, therefore, that assert that the international community has 'a clear legal obligation to provide assistance under international human rights law' to poor states, when in fact no effort is made to demonstrate any such clear obligation, are unhelpfully misleading, even if well intended.[48] The sentiment would be better situated in political and moral arguments about what ought to be done about the abomination that is egregious poverty. What is more, it may be that even the valiant efforts to construct such an unequivocal legal obligation may be a mistake. Smita Narula, for example, has produced a tightly argued case for the obligation of international cooperation to implement economic, social and cultural rights, based on Article 2(1) and – in respect of the right to food which is

---

46 Arjun Sengupta, 'On the Theory and Practice of the Right to Development' (2002) 24(4) *Human Rights Quarterly* 837, at 846.

47 See Sabine van Schorlemer, 'The Right to Development and the UN Development Goals: Critical Perspectives', in C. Raj Kumar and D. K. Srivastava (eds.), *Human Rights and Development* (Hong Kong: LexisNexis, 2006), pp. 253–69.

48 Kirsty Nowlan and Tim Costello, 'When Right Equals Rights: The International Obligation to Provide Assistance to Developing Countries' (2005) 30(4) *Alternative Law Journal* p. 159.

her particular interest – Article 11 of the ICESCR.[49] I am in agreement with Narula that economic and social rights are justiciable; they are certainly not rendered *non*-justiciable because they are equivocal (though that does make them more challenging for courts), but equivocal they are nonetheless. The nature of the states parties' obligations regarding the rights in the Covenant are that they have agreed to 'undertake to take steps, individually and through international assistance and co-operation . . . to the maximum of available resources, with a view to achieving progressively the full realization of the rights' (Article 2(1)). With such terms, legal certainty in answering what is in effect the core question of 'how much is enough?' is lost on the rough seas of political and economic argument. Narula herself appreciates the practical problems that one faces when striving to insist on states' 'aid-giving in legal obligation terms', suggesting instead that better results might come from focusing on 'the vehicles through which extraterritorial violations occur – namely, international financial institutions and transnational corporations',[50] and the *indirect* responsibilities on states that flow therefrom.

In the end, however, it must be accepted that human rights law cannot be relied upon to secure economic development, still less to 'solve' poverty alleviation. David Kennedy is right to talk of the deleterious distortions that result from framing such tasks in human rights language alone, or even primarily.[51] It is better to cajole and persuade all states, individually and collectively, to tackle development using all the persuasive resources to hand, including legal instruments, rather than to try to do battle on the narrow ledge of definitive legal interpretation alone. For these other persuasive resources – the moral, philosophical, political and economic imperatives to advance the development goals of peoples and countries – can be, in practice, no less compelling than legal prescription.

Politics and policies

The moral and legal dimensions of the association between poverty alleviation and human rights are, crucially, the key components that determine the levels of *political* determination that states possess to address the manifest problems of poverty, global and local. At present, that determination

---

49 Smita Narula, 'The Right to Food: Holding Global Actors Accountable under International Law' (2006) 44 *Columbia Journal of Transnational Law* 691, at 735–7.
50 *Ibid.* 737.
51 David Kennedy, 'The International Human Rights Movement: Part of the Problem?' (2002) 15 *Harvard Human Rights Journal* 101, 108–9.

– no matter the moral or legal arguments – is still lacking in comprehensive, concrete outcomes. Jeffrey Sachs's monumental analysis of the political and economic causes of global poverty has led him to conclude that '[t]he very hardest part of economic development is getting the first foothold on the ladder. Households and countries at the very bottom of the world's income distribution, in extreme poverty, tend to be stuck.' What, therefore, he sees as 'our generation's challenge' is that:

> we should ensure that the international rules of the game in economic management do not advertently or inadvertently set snares along the lower rungs of the ladder in the form of inadequate development assistance, protectionist trade barriers, destabilizing global financial practices, poorly designed rules for intellectual property, and the like, that prevent the low-income world from climbing up the rungs of development.[52]

Economists like Sachs essentially believe in the need for aid – albeit massively increased and its serious 'plumbing' problems sorted out (which issue is discussed in the final section of this chapter when I focus on the global institutional apparatus of aid). That is in contrast to economists like Martin Wolf. Wolf sees the aid goals of the World Bank as untenable and its problems as insurmountable,[53] and that promotion of the 'magic of the market' through free trade and commerce is the only sustainable way forward.[54] This may be considered somewhat extreme. There is no need to see aid on the one hand, and trade on the other, as mutually exclusive. The long-term sustainability of whatever development gains come from the provision of aid is only possible if viable commercial, trade, technological and governmental activities are established locally, thereby allowing the aid tap to be turned off. Above all else, the crucial role that aid plays is to provide the initial economic leg-up noted by Sachs, with the express intention then to engage more surely with the normal, self-sustaining features of a market economy.

All arms of the global economy recognise this leg-up role of aid and are, to varying extents, intersecting accordingly. We see this in respect of the alliances between private sector commerce and aid discussed earlier. The fortunes of both commerce and aid are closely linked to engendering thriving trade relations inside and especially outside the countries in question. The arguments made for development-oriented

52 Jeffrey Sachs, *The End of Poverty* (London: Penguin, 2005), pp. 24–5.
53 To this end Wolf quotes, approvingly, Montek Ahluwalia (a former senior IMF economist) once telling him that 'the Bank was a growing business in a dying industry'; Martin Wolf, *Why Globalization Works* (New Haven, CT: Yale University Press, 2004), p. xv.
54 *Ibid.* chapter 4.

trade as discussed in the last chapter, as well as initiatives such as 'aid for trade', preferential trade agreements for developing states and the Doha Round of trade talks itself, are all geared towards the integration of trade and aid goals (and amount to some 25 per cent of all aid),[55] even if their implementation in practice leaves much to be desired. It is true that there remains a lack of consensus among economists as to whether, to what extent and under what conditions more trade openness is good for the poor,[56] but that has not stopped a great deal of attention being trained on the possibilities and potential of such.

The World Bank, for example, directed no less that 8.1 per cent of its total budgetary commitments between 1987 and 2004 (some $38 billion) towards boosting freer trade in 117 poor countries, though with mixed success, according to a 2006 report by the Bank's own Independent Evaluation Group.[57] The UNDP has pursued a sustained interest in how to harness the undoubted development advantages of growth, while minimising the equally evident instances of disadvantage, such as the absence of measures to protect the vulnerable from trade liberalisation shocks, or the inadequacy of processes for the redistribution of trade gains. A detailed and intelligently argued report that it commissioned in 2003, for example, emphasised the importance of the two-way, mutually reinforcing, relationship between aid and trade, while highlighting that 'none of these benefits are guaranteed', and that, ultimately, it was essential that

---

55 'The average share of aid for trade in the total of all aid was 34% between 2002 and 2005, during which time commitments rose by 22% in real terms. The share fell slightly from 35% to 32% during that period, reflecting high levels of donors spending on social sectors, such as education and health': OECD and WTO, *Aid for Trade at a Glance 2007: First Global Review* (Paris: OECD and Geneva: WTO, 2007), p. 10, www.wto.org/english/tratop_e/devel_e/a4t_e/a4t_at_a_glance07_e.pdf. In late 2007, Pascal Lamy noted, following a conference of WTO members and heads of international organisations on the Aid for Trade Global Review, that 'donors have made commitments that would lead to $8 billion in new financing for Aid-for-Trade by 2010 and bring the total support to $30 billion'. Pascal Lamy, 'Aid for Trade Global Review', 3 December 2007, at www.ideas4development.org/aid-for-trade-global-review/en/.

56 See James Harrison, *The Human Rights Impact of the World Trade Organisation* (Portland, OR: Hart, 2007), p. 42.

57 World Bank Independent Evaluation Group, *Assessing World Bank Support for Trade, 1987–2004* (Washington, DC: World Bank, 2006). The IEG's Director-General, Vinod Thomas, summed up the tenor of the Report thus: 'The evaluation confirms that liberalizing trade alone is not enough to generate growth and fight poverty . . . The World Bank has done the right thing in promoting more open trade worldwide, but not necessarily done everything to help generate the desired payoffs.' See IEG Press Release, 'World Bank's Independent Evaluation Group Issues Report Assessing Two Decades of Global Trade Programs', 22 March 2006, available from http://go.worldbank.org/7QI0S4WU00.

'trade should be seen as a means to development rather than an end'.[58] Furthermore, in its 2005 *Human Development Report*, the UNDP pursued this line into the arena of the prevailing multilateral trade system by criticising what it sees as the system's bias in favour of rich nations and against the interests of the developing world, where rather than there being too much free trade, there is not enough. The selective protectionist measures of rich states that effectively lock out or restrict trade from developing states in such crucial markets as commodities and agriculture were identified as the key obstacles to the latter's exploitation of the development dividends of trade.[59]

The importance of the political question of what to do about poverty and the human rights abuses it occasions has also been represented in a number of specific initiatives that the developed world has signed up to in order to promote aid provided to the developing world. These are all somewhat grandly heralded and are directed at alleviating the consequences of poverty as a whole rather than to addressing human rights abuses per se, but in respect of the latter they nevertheless have important, usually indirect, impacts.

The shibboleth of the 0.7 per cent GNI target

There is always pressure on developed states to provide more aid to the developing states. The most conspicuous campaign in this respect has been the push for countries to agree to pledge 0.7 per cent of their gross national income (GNI) to aid, and then to fulfil the promise. The target, which has been touted for around fifty years, was originally based on a crude calculus of what amount of aid was needed to lift poor countries out of poverty. Whatever the concerns about its provenance, methodology and sufficiency – and there are plenty on all these fronts[60] – the target has obtained something of an iconic status: a '*cause célèbre* for aid activists . . . [that] has been accepted in many official quarters as the legitimate target

---

58 UNDP, *Making Global Trade Work for People* (London and Sterling, VA: Earthscan, 2003), pp. 24–6, 41.

59 UNDP, *Human Development Report 2005: International Cooperation at a Crossroads: Aid, Trade and Security in an Unequal World* (New York: UNDP, 2005), chapter 4.

60 For example Michael Clemens and Todd Moss, 'Ghost of 0.7%: Origins and Relevance of the International Aid Target', Centre for Global Development, Working Paper No. 68, September 2005, note, rather startlingly, that 'when we use essentially the same method used to arrive at 0.7% in the early 1960s and apply today's conditions, it yields an aid goal of just 0.01% of rich-country GDP for the poorest countries and *negative* aid flows to the developing world as a whole', at p. 2.

for aid budgets', as Michael Clemens and Todd Moss have put it.[61] The target was affirmed in a 1970 UN General Assembly Resolution,[62] and was agreed to by many states (including all major donors, as well as the World Bank, the IMF and the WTO) in the 2002 Monterrey Consensus.[63] And yet, even if we just take the figure to be merely a lobbying instrument (as was originally intended), to get rich states to increase their aid budgets, this apparently modest goal is achieved by only very few states – namely: Sweden, Luxemburg, Norway, the Netherlands and Denmark. Some countries (as figure 5 shows) fall well short of the target: Australia, Canada, Japan and the USA are all at 0.3 per cent GNI or below (the USA is the lowest, at just 0.16 per cent, though it is still by far the largest donor in dollar terms).

There are those who have calculated that the 'real aid' contributions of the donor countries is much lower (roughly 50 per cent lower) than even these figures. The methodology here is contentious, but the basic premise is that any aid that fails certain quality, effectiveness or poverty-focus standards is discounted from the final total. The sort of aid penalised in this way includes technical assistance; poorly coordinated projects or projects that impose unconscionably heavy administrative burdens on recipient countries; aid that is not focused on poverty alleviation; and also debt relief.[64] My own view is that not all of these aspects of modern aid should be regarded as equally lamentable; at least not when placed in context. As ActionAid – an especially trenchant critic of 'phantom aid' – rightly argues, development assistance needs to address the chronic failure to meet people's basic economic and social rights that comes with their impoverishment.[65] And for aid to do so, not only must its quantum be massively increased, but its quality too. The effectiveness of aid is, however, an especially difficult thing to measure. For while it is broadly agreed that aid cannot be focused only on short-term, damage control (providing immediate provision of food, water, clothing and shelter), it must also, to a substantial degree, facilitate long-term sustainability within the recipient state itself by securing all aspects of modern society: health services, education, power, transport, communications,

61 *Ibid.*   62 UN General Assembly Resolution 2626 (XXV), 24 October 1970, para. 43.
63 UN, *Report of the International Conference on Financing for Development: Monterrey, Mexico, 18–22 March 2002*, UN Doc. A/CONF.198/11 (New York: UN, 2002), pp. 9–10, para. 42.
64 See ActionAid, *Real Aid: An Agenda for Making Aid Work* (Johannesburg: ActionAid International, 2005), especially chapter 2.
65 *Ibid.*

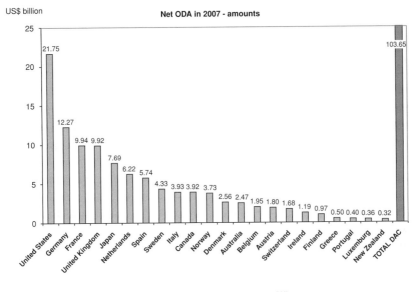

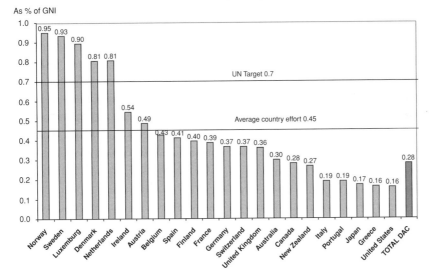

Fig. 5 Net official development assistance in 2007. *Source:* OECD Statistics Online, www.oecd.org/dataoecd/27/55/40381862.pdf.

governance, legal regulation and much else. Such services are only made possible when crippling burdens of servicing aid debts are removed or drastically reduced (thereby staunching 'money bleeding out of developing countries'[66] and reversing the perversity of situations in which more funds are flowing *from* poor countries *to* rich ones, than the other way around); technical assistance is rendered and technology transfers instigated; governmental structures are built or strengthened, and personnel trained. To be sure, these latter initiatives cannot be a *carte blanche* simply to siphon money back into the economies of the donors via the payment of consultants or mandated purchases from donor state firms, and to impose formulaic, burdensome and counter-productive accountability measures on recipient state agencies, but some significant degree of such assistance is necessary, and can and should be recognised as such.

Increasing aid and forgiving debt

Fundamentally, what is beyond doubt is that more – much more – aid is needed if there is to be any realistic hope of addressing the consequences of severe poverty including egregious human rights failures. Recently, there have been calls 'to go back to the future' in respect of providing more aid by way of simple, unadorned grants (often called budget support) that would allow state governments to build up their public sectors (and not just pin so much hope on the private sector) better to provide basic public services.[67] The nature of the apparently fast-growing size and spread of Chinese aid is very much in this traditional format, being more direct, with a particular focus for example on large infrastructure projects, and less conditional than has become the fashion in the West (though still with the usual expectations of strategic spin-offs that characterise all aid to greater or lesser extents, no matter who is the donor).[68] Also, during the first half

---

66 These are Joseph Stiglitz's words: *Making Globalization Work* (New York: W. W. Norton, 2006), p. 212. Stiglitz cites the example of Argentina's situation immediately before it defaulted on its foreign debts in 2002, when the country's foreign debt stood at nearly $150 billion, and the servicing of which amounted to a staggering $16 billion in 2001, comprising fully 10% of its total GDP for that year; *ibid.*

67 See Oxfam, *In the Public Interest: Health, Education, and Water and Sanitation for All* (Oxford: Oxfam International, 2006).

68 See for example Martyn Davies *et al.*, *How China Delivers Development Assistance to Africa* (Centre for Chinese Studies, University of Stellenbosch, 2008), a report prepared for the UK's Department for International Development. The qualifier of 'apparently' is necessary because China does not issue any official figures for its aid progamme; see *The Economist, Pocket World in Figures* (2008 edition), p. 45.

of 2008, the aid responses to the global food crisis that had seen the prices of staple foods such as rice and flour in many poor countries nearly double in price over the previous year were characteristically traditional in format. For example, the UN's World Food Programme was urging rich countries to provide immediate, large-scale injections of funds to supply food, and President Bush requested Congress to approve an extra $770 million for USAID 'to provide new emergency food assistance to those in need . . . [and to] help meet immediate needs in countries already experiencing food shortages and . . . target new food insecure populations'.[69]

There have also been sporadic efforts in recent years to address the ruinously destructive problem of massive foreign debts owed by some developing states. The West's overwhelming concern not to allow a situation of global moral hazard – in which the rich countries and international financial institutions fear that to forgive debt will send the wrong message to poor country borrowers that they can always, ultimately, rely on rich country lenders to write off the debt should they get into difficulties with their repayments – has been very hard to shake off. The IMF has been especially hard-headed on this point. Such that even when in 1996 a 'Highly Indebted Poor Countries' (HIPC) programme was established in order systematically to provide debt relief, the conditions imposed by the IMF, which was overseeing the initiative, were so onerous that only four countries (Uganda, Bolivia, Guyana and Mozambique) were granted relief by 2000. As public outcry mounted against what was widely perceived to be a scandalous myopia of the Fund, and the Jubilee 2000 Campaign was launched to lobby for wider and deeper debt relief, HIPC was expanded and liberalised somewhat, so that by 2005 twenty-eight countries had received some sort of dispensation on their debt repayments. Further, the leaders of the G8 countries agreed at their Gleneagles summit in the same year to provide 100 per cent debt relief for eighteen of the poorest and most indebted states (most of which were in Africa). Such 'deep' (i.e. complete) relief is considered to be fundamentally necessary for many heavily indebted states as 'any dollar spent in Washington or London or Bonn is a dollar not available for attacking poverty at home', as Joseph Stiglitz puts it.[70] And yet, even these gains are under threat from so-called 'vulture funds' – whose venal speciality is to feed off the carcass of a poor country's foreign indebtedness by purchasing it (that is paying off the

69 See USAID Press Release, 'USAID Stands Prepared To Increase Food Aid Efforts', 1 May 2008, www.usaid.gov/press/releases/2008/ps080501.html.
70 Stiglitz, *Making Globalization Work*, p. 227.

creditors) at a hugely discounted rate and then suing the poor states for the full balance of the outstanding debt. In late 2007, the IMF calculated that such legal actions worth nearly $2 billion worldwide were outstanding, and were being brought against some of the very countries that were party to the Gleneagles agreement.[71]

Whether inspired by immediate humanitarian concerns or a reform of aid philosophy or debt forgiveness, any designs to increase the flow of aid to developing countries should not be thwarted by what Jeffrey Sachs scathingly calls 'the current favorite explanation of donors for not doing more to help the poorest countries: the alleged lack of "absorptive capacity" to use more aid'.[72] Certainly, poor countries will have fairly limited abilities to utilise multiple, immediate and large injections of aid; such limitations are one of the reasons why they are poor and in need of aid in the first place. But with coordination (between donor and recipient states, and between donors themselves) and long-term planning, these limitations can be managed. My own experiences working with domestic human rights agencies in Indonesia and Vietnam, which were being festooned with aid offers from all quarters in the years immediately following the two countries' respective domestic reforms and international reintegration, bear this point out. What is needed to handle such situations must include medium- to long-range needs assessments conducted in close cooperation with the relevant recipient state agencies and incorporating the positions and expectations of the donor community.[73] 'Getting from here to there', as Sachs continues, 'is a matter of routine planning, not heroics.'[74]

The Millennium Development Goals (MDGs)

Of all the global initiatives launched to tackle poverty, the MDGs are the grandest of all. The UN's Millennium Declaration 2000 reiterated the central aims of the UN and its member states, and identified as key strategic concerns: international peace and security, global economic development and universal respect for human rights.[75] From the Declaration, the eight

---

71 Ashley Seager and James Lewis, 'Vulture Funds Devour Their Prey', *Guardian Weekly*, 26 October 2007, p. 16.
72 Sachs, *The End of Poverty*, p. 274.
73 For an example, see Inter-Agency Steering Committee/Ministry of Justice, 'Comprehensive Needs Assessment for the Development of Viet Nam's Legal System to the year 2010', Hanoi, 2002.
74 Sachs, *The End of Poverty*, p. 274.
75 UN General Assembly Resolution 55/2, 8 September 2000, UN Doc.A/RES/55/2. All of the then 189 member states of the UN signed the Declaration.

MDGs have been drawn, most of which are timetabled to be achieved by 2015. Collectively, the Goals are intended to address the main global development needs that face us today; they are:

Goal 1 – Eradicate extreme poverty and hunger
Goal 2 – Achieve universal primary education
Goal 3 – Promote gender equality and empower women
Goal 4 – Reduce child mortality
Goal 5 – Improve maternal health
Goal 6 – Combat HIV and AIDS, malaria and other diseases
Goal 7 – Ensure environmental sustainability
Goal 8 – Develop a global partnership for development

Each goal has specific internal targets to which progress indicators have been added: thus, for example, a specific target under Goal 1 is to halve, between 1990 and 2015, the proportion of people who suffer from hunger, and the progress indicators nominate specific sorts of data (the prevalence of underweight children under five years of age, and the proportion of population below minimum level of dietary energy consumption), and their sources (UNICEF-WHO and FAO, respectively).

The MDGs have succeeded in achieving a sort of totemic status within the development community – they are, for example, emblazoned on banners in the entrance hall of the World Bank headquarters on H Street in Washington DC – and they are regularly cited by states (in 'MDG National Plans') and multilateral organisations alike.[76] Their progress is monitored – officially by the UN's MDGs Monitor,[77] and unofficially by many NGOs. It is fair to say that progress has been patchy. Certainly, according to the 2007 MDGs Report,[78] there has been some success in combating the incidence of extreme poverty, women's participation in political processes has been growing (slowly),[79] child mortality rates have

76 Though not, 'amazingly', as Jeffrey Sachs remarks, by the Bush Administration, which 'refus[es] to use the phrase "Millennium Development Goals"'. Jeffrey Sachs, 'No Time To Waste', *Guardian Weekly*, 16–22 September 2005, Special Report on *Towards a Fairer World*, p. 2.
77 See www.mdgmonitor.org. Between 2002 and 2006 the Millennium Project, headed by Jeffrey Sachs, performed an advisory role to the UN Secretary-General; see www.un-millenniumproject.org.
78 See United Nations, *The Millennium Development Goals Report 2007* (New York: UN Department of Economic and Social Affairs, 2007).
79 Notably, at the time of writing, Rwanda was reported as being the first country ever to have a majority of women members sitting in its legislature (44 of 80 members); Barney Jopson, 'Rwandan Women Outnumber Men in Parliament', *Financial Times*, 18 September 2008.

been dropping, and more children are now in primary education globally. But on the other side of the ledger, the Report notes that over 500,000 women still die each year from treatable and preventable complications in pregnancy and childbirth, the decline in malnourished and underweight children is still woefully slow (especially in Sub-Saharan Africa), the numbers of people dying from AIDS is increasing rather than decreasing, and, of particular concern given its impact on so many aspects of poverty, half the population of the developing world lack basic sanitation. On this last point, the Report graphically notes the scale of the problem by stating that 'in order to meet the MDG target, an additional 1.6 billion people will need access to improved sanitation over the period 2005–2015. If trends since 1990 continue, the world is likely to miss the target by almost 600 million.'[80]

The lack of adequate progress is for many both morally and politically unacceptable. For some it is also economically reprehensible. For not only does the rich world possess the means to achieve the goals – 'rich countries can readily afford . . . to close the financing gap'[81] – but by addressing the fundamentals of poverty, the productivity and self-sustainability of the developing world will be lifted, and the prospects of greater global economic (and political) security better assured.

There is, evidently, an overlap or intersection between human rights objectives and the MDGs. The latter 'reflect a human rights agenda – rights to food, education, health care and decent living standards', as the UNDP's Human Development Report 2003 puts it.[82] The importance of the relationship cannot be denied, but it is implicit rather than explicit, and it is incomplete – civil and political rights hardly feature at all in the MDGs. As Philip Alston, the former Special Advisor to the UN High Commissioner for Human Rights on the MDGs, has counselled, there are differences between the MDGs and human rights which 'need to be acknowledged and strategies need to be identified for ensuring authentic compatibility'.[83] Alston's typically insightful analysis laments the lack of enthusiasm or conviction in either the development or human rights communities for better exploring, explaining or exploiting the

---

80 *Ibid.* p. 4.   81 Sachs, 'No Time To Waste'.
82 UNDP, *Human Development Report 2003: Millennium Development Goals: A Compact among Nations to End Human Poverty* (New York and Oxford: Oxford University Press, 2003), p. 29.
83 Philip Alston, 'Ships Passing in the Night: The Current State of the Human Rights and Development Debate as Seen through the Lens of the Millennium Development Goals' (2005) 27(3) *Human Rights Quarterly* 755, at 760.

linkages that do exist; 'the two agendas resemble ships passing in the night, even though they are both headed for very similar destinations', he concludes.[84]

The key to the communicating door between the two agendas is the accountability that a human rights framework – that is, especially one based in international law – brings to the practice of implementing the development goals. Many, including Alston, have stressed the significance of this feature in rendering mutually beneficial results for both agendas. The UN High Commissioner for Human Rights has argued that:

> the international human rights framework is essential for achieving the goals, as it increases the understanding of the policies and institutions required to achieve them, strengthens the national and international accountability framework necessary for making progress towards their achievement, and empowers individuals to claim their rights and take part in the decision-making processes that affect their lives.[85]

The use of a human rights approach to achieving the MDGs is part of a wider debate on whether and how a human rights based approach to development can be formulated and implemented in practice.

A Human Rights Based Approach (HRBA) to development

Development, we have established, is, at base, about poverty alleviation. Underpinning poverty there are certain causal structural factors that concern human rights: 'structural inequalities and discrimination – based on class, race, gender and other characteristics – within and between countries',[86] as a 2003 UN report puts it. So, it is argued, there is not just room to approach development objectives by way of human rights, there is an imperative to do so.

The so-called HRBA to development is in fact a range of arguments, some of which are better than others. All, however, insist on the relevance and utility not only of aligning the *substantive* goals of human rights with those of development, but also, crucially, of the *process* of

---

84 *Ibid.* 755.
85 Report of the High Commissioner for Human Rights, 'The Right to Development', UN Doc. E/CN.4/2005/24, 5 January 2005, para. 19. This necessary symbiosis has been stressed further, especially in respect of the potential for human rights to empower and enforce development goals, in the OHCHR's recent paper entitled *Claiming the Millennium Development Goals: A Human Rights Approach* (New York and Geneva: UN, 2008), chapter 2.
86 UNDP, *Making Global Trade Work for People*, p. 24.

human rights. Framed as they are in international and domestic laws, human rights bring with them a significant (if imperfect and incomplete) apparatus that identifies responsibilities, guides implementation and demands accountability.

Development and human rights are not, of course, the same,[87] nor are their ends coterminous, but their association can be mutually beneficial. The UNDP's Human Development Report 2000 described the linkage thus:

> Human development and human rights are close enough in motivation and concern to be compatible and congruous, and they are different enough in strategy and design to supplement each other fruitfully. A more integrated approach can thus bring significant rewards, and facilitate in practical ways the shared attempts to advance the dignity, well-being and freedom of individuals in general.[88]

In *Voices of the Poor*, an extensive survey of some 60,000 of the world's poor, the World Bank was able to draw up a list of what the poor themselves said were their primary needs to improve their lives.[89] The results (abbreviated in the box below) were surprising in respect of their congruity with human rights goals. As Mac Darrow and Amparo Tomas commented in their review of the survey's results:

> contrary to much of the orthodoxy, the interviewees perceived poverty not merely as the absence of commodities and services to meet basic needs, but rather as a question of disempowerment. When asked what was needed most to increase their freedom of choice and improve their lives, the answers read like the Universal Declaration of Human Rights.[90]

---

87 While accepting that convergence does exist, Hans-Otto Sano has characterised the differences between the two traditions thus: '[h]uman rights has as its subject norms, rules, and duties together with their institutional foundations, whereas development theory has general processes of change, resource control/conflict, and resource allocation at its core'; in 'Development and Human Rights: The Necessary, but Partial Integration of Human Rights and Development' (2000) 22 *Human Rights Quarterly* 734, at 741–2.

88 UNDP, *Human Development Report 2000: Human Rights and Human Development* (New York and Oxford: Oxford University Press, 2000) p. 19.

89 Deepa Narayan, Raj Patel, Kai Schafft, Anne Rademacher and Sarah Koch-Schulte, *Voices of the Poor: Can Anyone Hear Us?* (New York: Oxford University Press for the World Bank, 2000); Deepa Narayan, Robert Chambers, Meera Kaul Shah and Patti Petesch, *Voices of the Poor: Crying Out for Change* (New York: Oxford University Press for the World Bank, 2000); Deepa Narayan and Patti Petesch, *Voices of the Poor: From Many Lands* (New York: Oxford University Press for the World Bank, 2002).

90 Mac Darrow and Amparo Tomas, 'Power, Capture and Conflict: A Call for Human Rights Accountability in Development Cooperation' (2005) 27 *Human Rights Quarterly* 471, at 477–8.

'VOICES OF THE POOR': ASSETS AND CAPABILITY EXAMPLES
MENTIONED BY POOR PEOPLE TO INCREASE THEIR FREEDOM OF
CHOICE AND IMPROVE THEIR LIVES

Material assets – Employment; ownership of productive assets; land; house; boat; savings

Bodily health – Freedoms from hunger and disease; strong, healthy-looking bodies

Bodily integrity – Freedom from violence and abuse; sexual and reproductive choice; freedom of physical movement

Emotional integrity – Freedom from fear and anxiety; love

Respect and dignity – Self-respect; respect from others and the community

Social belonging – Belonging to a collective; honour, respect and trust within and across social groups

Cultural identity – Living in accordance with one's values; participation in rituals that give meaning; sense of cultural continuity

Imagination, inventiveness, information and education – Informed and educated decision making; literacy; entrepreneurship; problem solving capacity; expressive arts

Organisational capacity – Ability to organise and mobilise; participation in representative organisations

Political representation and accountability – Ability to influence those in power; accountability of those in power

Source: Darrow and Tomas, 'Power, Capture and Conflict', p. 478

The information in the box was compiled by the two authors drawing on the results of the World Bank study in order to highlight the 'ten "assets and capabilities" (or in human rights terms, constitutive and legally enforceable characteristics of human dignity and freedom) identified through these investigations'.[91]

What value is added by conceiving these needs as human rights is the key question we must ask of any advocate of a HRBA to development. Is it the rhetorical power of rights discourse; or the provision of a mechanism by which responsibility can be assigned and accountability extracted; or the assignment of legal means by which individuals can identify legitimate claims and have them enforced? The added value is in fact drawn from the answers to all of these questions, though to varying degrees depending on circumstances and perspective. The legal spine that the HRBA is said to

91 *Ibid.* 478.

insert into development policy-making and implementation is born of the express standards set by international human rights laws, the empowerment of individuals identified as rights-holders and states identified as the associated duty-bearers, and the establishment of mechanisms through which the parameters of the rights/duties relationship are set and disputes between their respective bearers settled.

The human rights approach has been held to be 'more fundamental' than social justice or welfare oriented approaches to development. André Frankovits and Patrick Earle take this line, arguing that 'it is not premised upon government largesse. It is not discretionary and it establishes a very different relationship between the individual or group and the state. A right confers power. A human right enables even the most marginalized and ostensibly powerless person or group to make a claim against the state.'[92] The UN thinks along similar lines. In 2003 it formulated a proposed 'common understanding' among UN agencies as to the human rights based approach to development cooperation. It pronounced that all development programmes should promote human rights objectives; that international human rights laws 'guide all development cooperation and programming in all sectors and in all phases of the programming process', and that development will enhance the capacities of the duty-bearers, as well as of the rights-holders.[93]

All that said, the efforts to promote the idea of a HRBA to development are still in their 'fledgling' stages,[94] though what they lack in maturity they make up for in vigour. This enthusiasm, however, has itself been problematic. Darrow and Tomas note that

> human rights-based approaches have proliferated in myriad forms and contexts, from community-based capacity development to the integration of human rights in macro-policy contexts and national development planning. But the rhetoric has so far not been matched by conceptual rigor, systematization of practice, or lessons-learning – shortcomings that threaten continuing support for such approaches.[95]

Peter Uvin concludes his frank and thought-provoking critique of the notion by noting that its 'great *potential* to alter profoundly the way

---

92 Human Rights Council of Australia, *The Rights Way to Development: A Human Rights Approach to Development Assistance, Policy and Practice* (Sydney: Human Rights Council of Australia, 2001), p. 28.
93 'The Human Rights Based Approach to Development Cooperation: Towards a Common Understanding among UN Agencies', available at www.undp.org/governance/docs/ HR_Guides_CommonUnderstanding.pdf., p. 2.
94 Alston, 'Ships Passing in the Night', 807.
95 Darrow and Tomas, 'Power, Capture, and Conflict', 472.

the development enterprise goes about its business' is something, as yet, unrealised in practice.[96]

Some development agencies such as UNESCO, UNICEF and (especially) the UNDP profess to follow a HRBA; the UNDP has indeed conducted a series of country programme reviews based on human rights criteria.[97] Some bilateral aid agencies – notably, those of Denmark (DANIDA), Sweden (SIDA) and the UK (DFID) – have also inserted human rights approaches into their strategic planning and in their implemented programmes. For example, DFID's rights based approach has been summarised as essentially a recognition of 'the centrality of the relationship between human rights and poverty reduction',[98] and further, a relatively recent government review of the role of conditionality in DFID's poverty reduction objectives declared that for its aid partnerships with recipient countries to be effective there must be a shared commitment to human rights (alongside achieving the MDGs and instituting domestic financial management and accountability).[99] Other national aid agencies, such as those of Australia (AusAID) and the US (USAID), abjure any adherence to a HRBA, but still engage in substantial human rights programmes, for example providing human rights training, addressing gender discrimination, treating HIV/AIDS sufferers, deploying anti-people-trafficking mechanisms, supporting community groups pursuing human rights initiatives of their own, and undertaking formalised, high-level human rights dialogues (which AusAID does with China and Vietnam).[100] In the case of the US, many of its human rights oriented initiatives have, since 2004, been driven and directed by the Millennium Challenge Corporation (MCC), which sits outside USAID. MCC funds are made available only to countries that meet certain standards grouped under the three broad categories of good governance ('ruling justly'), investment in

---

96 Peter Uvin, *Human Rights and Development* (Sterling, VA: Kumarian Press, 2004), p. 166.

97 See the *Human Rights-Based Reviews of UNDP Programmes: Working Guidelines* (June 2003). These Guidelines (and their updated version of 2005) were piloted in a number of states including Argentina, Bosnia, Ecuador, Macedonia and Kyrgyzstan; see *Human Rights Strengthening: HURIST (UNDP/OHCHR/UNOPS) – Evaluation Report (May–July 2005)*, pp. 29–31.

98 Laure-Hélène Piron, 'Learning from the UK Department for International Development's Rights-Based Approach to Development Assistance', Overseas Development Institute, July 2003, para. 3.1.1; www.odi.org.uk/RIGHTS/Publications/DFID%20RBA%20Final%20Doc%20July%202003.pdf.

99 *Partnerships for Poverty Reduction: Rethinking Conditionality – A UK Policy Paper* (London: DFID, 2005), para. 1.3.

100 See, for example, AusAID, *Human Rights and Australia's Aid Program*, at www.ausaid. gov.au/keyaid/humanrights.cfm.

people (meaning health, education and safety) and economic probity (liberalisation and sustainable growth). The first two of these are especially closely related to human rights protection.[101] The fact, however, that the funds are distributed on such an explicitly conditional basis inevitably courts controversy over the nature and composition of the conditions and the methods used to measure compliance, as well as the slowness of the distribution process.[102]

In practice I have to say that, from my own experiences working with and alongside a number of these agencies, the differences between those that expressly state human rights as primary goals and those that see them as derivatively important (that is derivations of successful poverty reduction and increased economic growth) are hard to discern.[103] What seems to be important is that they all see human rights protection as being a fundamentally necessary outcome of their efforts, whatever the precise processes. How aid agencies might *better* achieve this result is the key to what a HRBA to development seeks to offer.

Good governance and the rule of law

Running parallel to the whole HRBA debate, there has developed in aid circles a huge interest in the promotion of institutional and regulatory assistance driven by the long-term goals of self-sufficiency and sustainability, as well as an adaptation of the old proverb that it is better to help a man learn how to govern for a lifetime than simply to give him government for today. The heading I have given this sub-section refers to what are perhaps the most prominent of these parallel initiatives. In truth they are legion, ranging (in addition to good governance and the rule of law) from investments in education, health and housing, the empowerment of women, family planning and the protection of indigenous peoples, through anti-corruption, transparency and environmental protection, to participatory decision-making, humanitarian aid, food security and

---

101 See further, www.mca.gov/about/index.php.
102 For criticism of the conditions, and the methods of country selection, see Emma Mawdsley, 'The Millennium Challenge Account: Neo-liberalism, Poverty and Security' (2007) 14 *Review of International Political Economy* 487, and on the slowness point see Celia Dugger, 'US Agency's Slow Pace Endangers Foreign Aid', *New York Times*, 7 December 2007, p. A1.
103 Indeed, an Australian Parliamentary Committee reviewing AusAID's human rights programmes reached a similar conclusion. See Joint Standing Committee on Foreign Affairs, Defence and Trade, *The Link between Aid and Human Rights* (Canberra: Parliament of Australia, 2001), Appendix A, p. 34.

peace-building. As Philip Alston has noted: 'a careful review of a typical selection of development policy documents will yield a veritable thesaurus full of terms which might be considered to be adequate synonyms for human rights'.[104] The issues concerned stretch across economic, social and cultural as well as civil and political rights. The World Bank, no less, has made the point explicitly in a milestone policy paper written in 1998, in part to mark the fiftieth anniversary of the UDHR:

> The Bank contributes directly to the fulfillment of many rights articulated in the Universal Declaration. Through its support for primary education, health care and nutrition, sanitation, housing and the environment, the Bank has helped hundreds of millions of people attain crucial economic and social rights.[105]

There is no doubt that governance and human rights are intimately associated. A dramatic illustration of this can be found in a recent Oxfam study of what happens when governance is bad or non-existent. Oxfam has calculated that the economic costs of the conflicts that have plagued Africa since the end of the Cold War in 1990, rendering it almost governmentless at certain times and in certain places, amount to some $300 billion – roughly equivalent to the total of all the foreign aid Africa received over the same period.[106] The flow-on social and economic costs have, predictably, been horrendous: GDP per capita reduced by 63 per cent; 50 per cent more infant deaths; 15 per cent more undernourished people; life expectancy reduced by five years; 20 per cent more adult illiteracy; and 2.5 times fewer doctors per patient.[107] Conversely, as Todd Landman demonstrates in his study of seventeen Latin American countries between 1976 and 2000, when states free themselves from the scourge of conflict they experience human rights dividends which, if not necessarily universal and consistent, are nonetheless palpable.[108]

104 Philip Alston, 'What's in a Name: Does It Really Matter if Development Policies Refer to Goals, Ideals or Human Rights?', in H. Helmich (ed.), *Human Rights in Development Co-operation* (Utrecht: SIM, 1998), p. 95.
105 World Bank, *Development and Human Rights: The Role of the World Bank* (Washington, DC: World Bank, 1998), p. 3.
106 IANSA and Oxfam, *Africa's Missing Billions*, Oxfam Briefing Paper 107 (October 2007), www.oxfam.org/en/policy/bp107_africas_missing_billions.
107 *Ibid.* p. 6.
108 Todd Landman, 'Development, Democracy and Human Rights in Latin America, 1976–2000', in Janet Dine and Andrew Fagan (eds.), *Human Rights and Capitalism* (Cheltenham: Edward Elgar, 2006). In particular, Landman notes that while 'the raw pursuit of economic gain' will not necessarily deliver political freedoms and rights protection,

Closely aligned to governance is the notion of the rule of law – as distinct from the capriciousness-prone rule of man – which certainly has the potential to establish and promote order and justice. In his reflections on what it has and could bring to the Eastern European states formerly behind the Iron Curtain, Martin Krygier has, with typical panache, defined the notion as:

> when the law in general does not take you by surprise or keep you guessing, when it is as accessible to you as is the thought that you might use it, when legal institutions are relatively independent of other significant social actors but not of legal doctrine, and when the powerful forces in society, including the government, are required to act, and come in significant measure to think, within the law; when the limits of what we imagine our options to be are set in significant part by the law and where these limits are widely taken seriously – when the law has integrity and it matters what the law allows and what it forbids.[109]

But all that said, express recognition of the intimacy or surrogacy of human rights and governance/rule of law issues in development is not readily discernible among some agencies. The World Bank, for example, has had a history of awkwardness over this issue which I and many others have documented,[110] though that seems to be changing at least in respect of the Bank's rhetoric, if not practice (see more below). The IMF, on the other hand, has simply rejected any suggestion that it should be concerned with the human rights consequences of its actions; a position that has changed little despite the attention focused on it since the late 1990s (on which more below). The dim lights shone on human rights by the leading international financial institutions have further had the curious effect of dulling the use of human rights language by civil society organisations that criticise the Bank over the adverse social consequences of its operations. In a report on human rights criticisms of the Bank's private sector development projects that my colleague Tom Davis and

---

'political choices among elites combined with social mobilisation from below' (that includes the cessation of conflict) do appear to promote 'advances in democratization and rights protection'; *ibid.* at pp. 354–5.

109 Martin Krygier, 'The Quality of Civility: Post-Anti-Communist Thoughts on Civil Society and the Rule of Law', in Andras Sajo (ed.), *Out of and into Authoritarian Law* (The Hague and London: Kluwer Law International, 2003), p. 221.

110 See David Kinley, 'Human Rights and the World Bank: Practice, Politics and Law', in Caroline Sage and Michael Woolcock (eds.), *World Bank Legal Review*, Vol. II, *Law, Equity, and Development* (Washington, DC: The World Bank; The Hague: Martinus Nijhoff, 2006), p. 353, at pp. 359–66. See also the story I relate in the Preface to this book.

I were commissioned to write for the Bank in 2004, we were surprised to find a veritable dearth of appeals to breaches of human rights in the many and various criticisms made by NGOs.[111] The criticisms of large infrastructure projects over lack of adequate information for, and consultation with, communities; the suppression of dissent and restrictions on movement; environmental and health hazards; labour and workplace standards; access to clean water; and various problems associated with relocation of communities: all clearly provided the opportunity to add in a human rights angle, but it appeared that the critics either were unaware of the relevance of human rights standards, or considered that the employment of such language was less likely to be effective against the Bank than specifically economic, social or environmental criticisms, possibly because they anticipated resistance on the Bank's part to human rights arguments.[112]

Indeed at least since the late 1990s, international financial institutions generally, and the World Bank in particular, have engaged in a variety of activities that impact directly on human rights, as the above quote from the Bank illustrates. Herbert Morais – who has held senior legal counsel positions in the World Bank, the Asian Development Bank and the IMF – noted in an article in 2000 that these activities included:

> reform of the civil service, reform of public sector enterprises, legal and judicial reform, reform of local governments, land titling and registration reform, combating corruption, the rights of indigenous people and minorities, the rights of people displaced or resettled as a result of projects funded by international development banks, family planning, and enhancing the rights of women.[113]

In respect of the World Bank, this list remains representative today of its quasi-human rights activities, with the notable addition of operations combating environmental degradation and promoting environmental sustainability.

It is through good governance initiatives that development programmes come nearest to the express recognition of the relevance of

---

111 David Kinley and Tom Davis, *Human Rights Criticism of the World Bank's Private Sector Development and Privatization Projects*, Sydney Law School Research Paper No. 08/53, February 2004, available at http://papers.ssrn.com/sol3/papers.cfm?abstract_id=1133179.

112 *Ibid.* pp. 35–6.

113 Herbert Morais, 'The Globalization of Human Rights Law and the Role of International Financial Institutions in Promoting Human Rights' (2000) 33 *George Washington International Law Review* 71, at 90.

promoting human rights, for the adjective 'good' is, crucially, almost invariably taken to mean some form of democratic governance, and with democracy comes certain minimum civil and political rights, and through them the better servicing of economic and social rights. A prime example of this linkage is the EU's recently relaunched European Instrument for Democracy and Human Rights,[114] the mandate of which is to provide financial support to a wide range of bodies (from local authorities and chambers of commerce to small businesses, NGOs and universities) for the implementation of projects that enhance human rights, democratic reform and the rule of law.[115] The work of the World Bank Institute (the Bank's think-tank) has been especially influential in this area. Daniel Kaufmann and a number of colleagues have developed a sophisticated set of worldwide governance indicators that try to measure how 'good' the governance is in states as against criteria that reflect many international human rights standards.[116] In a paper analysing what the data collected show about the particular relationship between governance and human rights, Kaufmann concludes that while '[s]ome analysts have argued that there is a trade-off between liberties and development . . . we find the opposite evidence, that suppressing liberties is likely to be inimical to [development] project performance. This has obvious implications for development assistance.'[117] Such a conclusion drawn from extensive empirical evidence provides emphatic support for Amartya Sen's thesis that fundamental freedoms are essential ingredients to any meaningful pursuit and achievement of a state of development, as captured in his pithy remark that 'freedoms are not only the primary ends of development, they are among its principal means'.[118]

---

114 Formerly known as the *European Initiative for Democracy of Human Rights*. The subtleties of distinguishing an 'Instrument' from an 'Initiative' are not immediately (if at all) obvious!

115 See www.welcomeurope.com/default.asp?id=1110&idpgm=11816; the Instrument has been allocated a €1.1billion budget for the period 2007–13.

116 The indicators are broadly grouped under: voice and accountability; political stability; government effectiveness; regulatory quality; rule of law; and control of corruption. See www.govindicators.org; and for an analysis of the data collected between 1996 and 2006, see Daniel Kaufmann, Aart Kraay and Massimo Mastruzzi, *Governance Matters VI: Aggregate and Individual Governance Indicators: 1996–2006*, World Bank Policy Research Working Paper No. 4280 (July 2007); at http://papers.ssrn.com/sol3/papers.cfm?abstract_id=999979.

117 Daniel Kaufmann, 'Human Rights and Governance: The Empirical Challenge', in Alston and Robinson (eds.), *Human Rights and Development*, p. 352, at p. 365.

118 Amartya Sen, *Development as Freedom* (New York and Oxford: Oxford University Press, 1999), p. 10.

Human rights critiques of governance and rule of law programmes

It cannot be said, however, that every programme that promotes such ends is 'an unqualified human good'.[119] There is a tendency for example, as Frankovits and Earle have noted, for development programmes to overemphasise the importance of institution- or capacity-building and not to pay sufficient attention to what the institutions are being built for. 'We are not dismissing the need for efficient, well managed and effective institutions', they say, 'on the contrary, they are crucial. What we *are* saying is that the governance debate has got it back to front: the institutions are the instruments.'[120] Many argue that when conditionality, including human rights conditionality, constitutes a part of governance programmes it can be ineffective or even counterproductive. This is because 'conditionality by its very nature destroys the very domestic accountability and social transformation it seeks to achieve'.[121] Reflecting the consensus of the 2005 Paris Declaration on Aid Effectiveness,[122] multilateral and bilateral aid agencies are today much concerned with building 'partnerships' with developing states and ensuring their 'ownership' of the programmes (and results) that flow therefrom. For example, the new lending framework of the World Bank and IMF is now constructed through revamped Poverty Reduction Strategy Papers (PRSPs),[123] which are supposed to be more negotiated agreements between the donor institution and the recipient country than a didactic imposition of the views of the former onto the latter. Still, it cannot be said that these shifts in approach and alignment have been especially successful in practice. As Ngaire Woods notes, 'the result, however, is not the kind of "ownership"

119 To paraphrase the noted Marxist historian E. P. Thompson's infamous remark that 'the rule of law is an unqualified good', and was so even in eighteenth-century England. It was controversial because some thought that it effectively endorsed the many unjust laws of that time and of today, while others believed that it was perfectly consistent with the strongest criticism of such injustice; see Daniel Cole, 'An Unqualified Human Good: E. P. Thompson and the Rule of Law' (2001) 28(2) *Journal of Law and Society* 177.

120 Human Rights Council of Australia, *The Rights Way to Development*, p. 46.

121 Uvin, *Human Rights and Development*, p. 68.

122 The Declaration was signed by more than a hundred ministers, heads of agencies and senior officials from aid organisations, see www.oecd.org/document/18/0,2340,en_2649_3236398_35401554_1_1_1_1,00.html.

123 PRSPs are often framed as five- to ten-year country plans for achieving economic growth and reducing poverty. They are usually broadly focused and can, depending on the circumstances, contain explicit reference to human rights concerns. See, for instance, Afghanistan's *National Development Strategy 2008–13* (May 2008), at http://siteresources.worldbank.org/INTPRS1/Resources/Afghanistan_PRSP(May2008).pdf.

their [the Bank and the Fund] experience suggests is necessary. Lacking is any shift in responsibility, priority-setting, and choice which has been indicated by previous failures of conditionality.'[124]

There are also examples of development initiatives in which governance issues are deemed crucial and yet human rights concerns rate little or no mention. A topical illustration of this circumstance is the global food crisis that is unfolding as I write these words in the middle of 2008. The astronomical price rises for staple foods in many developing countries (rice, wheat, maize) require not only an effective short-term humanitarian response, but also better long-term management of global food supplies by the governments of developing and developed states, individually and together. Yet this crisis of governance has almost completely ignored its human rights dimension. In his report as the newly appointed UN Special Rapporteur on the right to food, Olivier de Schutter lamented,

> that neither in the policy responses to the current food crisis, nor in the exploration of long-term solutions to enhance food supply, is the human right to adequate food [ICESCR, Article 12] even mentioned – let alone, used as a guide for the implementation of international cooperation and national strategies. This constitutes a failure which the Special Rapporteur calls upon the Human Rights Council to remedy. In terms of improving accountability, monitoring and participation, and because it will lead to emphasize the dimension of non-discrimination, the reference to the human right to adequate food may constitute a significant contribution to the development of national strategies, and it can guide the identification of best practices.[125]

The slavish promotion of the rule of law is also not without serious complications. Law is, after all, merely an instrument of political, social and economic views on order and justice, not any guarantee of order and justice in and of itself. This applies to human rights law as much as to any other type. It is an instrument in the hands of tyrants and despots, as it is in the hands of the elected and virtuous. At its most basic, therefore, it can be used for good or ill; what are important are the motives and objectives that lie behind its use. David Kennedy has been especially critical of what he sees as too eager a desire within the development community to avoid

---

124 Ngaire Woods, *The Globalizers: The IMF, the World Bank and Their Borrowers* (Ithaca, NY: Cornell University Press, 2006), p. 190.

125 Olivier de Schutter, *Background Note: Analysis of the World Food Crisis by the UN Special Rapporteur on the Right to Food* (2 May 2008), p. 14, www2.ohchr.org/english/issues/food/docs/SRRTFnotefoodcrisis.pdf. Article 12 of the ICESCR provides for the 'the right of everyone to an adequate standard of living for himself and his family, including adequate food'.

making hard economic and political choices by preferring instead 'the softer – and often legal – vocabularies of ethics or human rights'.[126] He continues:

> the idea that building the 'rule of law' might *itself* be a development strategy encourages the hope that choosing law *in general* could substitute for all the perplexing political and economic choices which have been at the centre of development policy making for half a century. Although a legal regime offers an arena to contest the choices, it cannot substitute for them. The campaign to promote the rule of law as a development path has encouraged policy makers to forgo pragmatic analysis of the choices they make in building a legal regime – or to think that the choices embedded in the particular regime they graft onto a developing society represent the only possible alternative.[127]

The vagaries and virtues of the rule of law must be better understood within development circles, if the pitfalls of the former are to be avoided, and the latter more fully exploited. Lawyers and others who care to think more carefully on the issue are aware of this need. In one of Amartya Sen's forays into legal philosophy he rightly points to the limits of the law in respect of what we can reasonably expect it to achieve in protecting human rights, which depends so much on non-legal factors such as culture, religion, community consensus, political power and economics; and this is especially so in developing states where the legal apparatus is likely to be far less extensive and robust.[128] I have argued elsewhere that, within the context of globalisation, it is quite possible for the different aspects of the notion of the rule of law to be differently stressed by different global actors. Commercial or economic interests, for example, tend to be especially interested in the formal features of the promised certainty and predictability of the rule of law, while human rights advocates emphasise the substantive requirements that law must be representative, fair and just if it is to be considered law at all.[129] Far from being preordained then, the mixing and matching of these (and other) perspectives of the rule of law is an ongoing challenge for development specialists.

126 David Kennedy, 'The Rule of Law as a Strategy for Economic Development', in his *The Dark Sides of Virtue* (Princeton: Princeton University Press, 2004), p. 152.
127 *Ibid.* p. 151.
128 Amartya Sen, 'Human Rights and the Limits of the Law' (2006) 27(6) *Cardozo Law Review* 2913.
129 David Kinley, 'Human Rights, Globalization and the Rule of Law: Friends, Foes or Family' (2002) *University of California, Los Angeles Journal of International Law and Foreign Affairs* 239.

'The Globalisers'[130] – development agencies and human rights

Whether, how and to what extent human rights will be better protected and promoted through aid and development programmes is, to a large degree, dependent on the quality of the ideas that inform such programmes and of their implementation. In both those respects the institutions most directly and comprehensively concerned with generating ideas about development and putting them into practice will play a vital role. That being so, I conclude this chapter by looking more closely at the critiques of the roles that international public and private development bodies play, and *should* play, in the promotion and protection of human rights.

I will here focus largely on the World Bank and the IMF (and the role of states in their functioning), but the category also includes the states in their own rights, the regional development banks (in Africa, Asia, South America and Europe),[131] and multilateral agencies such as the UNDP and UNICEF. I also include large private bodies such as globally active development NGOs and institutionalised corporate philanthropy such as the Gates Foundation and the Helú Foundation, as well as the older Carnegie, Ford and Rockefeller Foundations, whose funding of development projects has, collectively, increased markedly in recent years, especially in such human rights related areas as education and health.[132]

Engaging with human rights

Reflecting its people's respect for past tragedies, it is sometimes said that the history of Ireland is written on its tombstones. You might fairly say that the histories of the Bank's and the Fund's relationships with human rights have been determined by the words etched out of the stone of their

---

130 A label borrowed from Ngaire Wood's book of that title.
131 It is perhaps worth noting in passing that these are not necessarily marginal organisations with only limited finances. For example, the European Investment Bank's (EIB) budget is significantly larger than that of the World Bank, divesting around $300 billion in loans between 2003 and 2007, as against just over $20 billion per year for the World Bank; see Heather Stewart, 'A Bank Shrouded in Mystery', *Guardian Weekly*, 28 March 2008, p. 42. However, its objects are really very different from the World Bank and the other regional development banks, for although the EIB does invest considerable sums in developing countries (especially in Africa), it does so with the express aim to further the economic, social and political interests of the member states of the European Union, see www.eib.org/about/index.htm.
132 See Paul Maidment, 'Billionaires Who Give It Away' (Forbes.com), March 2008; at http://money.ninemsn.com.au/article.aspx?id=390627.

respective Articles of Agreement (AA). In both cases it has been a story of narrow legal interpretation that has restricted their engagement with human rights.

The AAs of the two institutions make clear their broad economic purposes – to promote long-term economic growth through increasing productivity, international trade and foreign investment, and thereby to promote employment, real income and standards of living.[133] The principal differences between the two lie in the instruments and methods they use to achieve these ends. The IMF is primarily concerned with the macro-economic issue of international monetary cooperation and stability, which it seeks to manage by manipulating the monetary policies of states in return for the loans it provides them, regarding, in particular, money supply, exchange and interest rates, inflation and fiscal rectitude. It normally steps in only at times of financial crises, or when trying to avert them when they appear imminent. It is, in other words, an international lender of last resort. The World Bank, on the other hand, is more focused on micro-economic matters and its activities are much broader and ongoing.[134] The World Bank Group comprises five institutions[135] which separately and together sponsor the development and maintenance of essential services in developing economies, such as power, water, health, transport, communications, government, and environmental protection. It does so by way of a range of facilities including grants, loans, private sector partnerships, insurance guarantees and dispute settlement services. The interlinks and distinctions between the two institutions are explained in part by the fact that they were established simultaneously at a conference of forty-four states parties at the Mount Washington Hotel in the

---

133 See Article 1 of both the AAs of the International Bank for Reconstruction and Development (http://go.worldbank.org/7H3J47PV51) and the IMF (www.imf.org/external/pubs/ft/aa/index.htm).

134 The relative sizes and locations of their staff reflect these differences: the Bank has almost 10,000 staff situated in offices all over the world as well as in Washington DC, whereas the IMF has fewer than 3,000 (and at the time of writing (mid 2008) it was set to make very substantial staff cuts to address its budgetary difficulties born of a drop in countries requiring its services), the vast majority of whom are stationed in the Fund's Washington DC headquarters.

135 The Bank itself comprises the International Bank for Reconstruction and Development (IBRD) and the International Development Association (IDA), and then there are in addition three affiliates that make up the full complement of the World Bank Group, namely, the International Finance Corporation (IFC), the Multi-lateral Investment Guarantee Agency (MIGA) and the International Centre for Settlement of Investment Disputes (ICSID).

New Hampshire resort town of Bretton Woods in 1944. There, the delegates sought to create global mechanisms by which to minimise future economic shock and turmoil, and maximise economic growth and stability. This emphasis on economic development and management is an important point to grasp, for it was intended that the handling of the social and humanitarian concerns of the post-war world would be addressed by another multilateral organisation, namely the UN, to be established the following year, together with the pre-existing International Labour Organisation (ILO) focusing on the specific issues of labour rights, workplace relations, health and safety.

It is the rigidity with which this global division of responsibilities was and is maintained that has given rise to so much of the debate and disquiet concerning the relationship of the Bretton Woods institutions with human rights. There are a number of provisions within the Bank's AAs that appear to underscore the division by stressing that 'the Bank and its officers shall not interfere in the political affairs of any member' and that 'only economic considerations shall be relevant to their decisions' (International Bank of Reconstruction and Development (IBRD, Article IV, section 10)).[136] Curiously, no such express provisions are made in the AAs of the Fund, and yet in practice and philosophical inclination the Fund has been far less amenable to any arguments as to the relevance of human rights to its work. The constitutional basis for such a stance appears to rely on what the Articles do say about the narrowness of the Fund's mandate. Such disclaimers regarding political considerations and human rights have, as Mac Darrow, in his seminal work on this question, succinctly puts it, 'usually relied on more foundational assertions of mandate specificity and technical specialisation'.[137] To a degree, one can understand (if not necessarily endorse) the Fund's attitude in this regard – its mandate, capacity, competence and expertise are all geared towards the pulling of macro-economic levers, rather than overtly political or social ones, still less specifically human rights ones. However, from the human rights perspective, one of the most frustrating aspects of the Fund's attitude in this regard is its refusal to see the human rights implications of its actions, and to dismiss any such derivation as beyond its remit and

136 Further prohibitions against considerations of political or 'non-economic considerations' are also made in respect of the IBRD concerning its loan arrangements (Article 3(5)), and similar provisions also exist in the Articles of Agreement of the International Development Agency.
137 Mac Darrow, *Between Light and Shadow: The World Bank, the IMF, and International Human Rights Law* (Oxford and Portland, OR: Hart, 2003), p. 114.

therefore responsibility. There are some at the Fund who recognise this as a legitimate concern, even if they are not able to see an easy way to fix the problem. But, certainly in my experience, many Fund officials are either ignorant of the issue altogether or dismissive (often condescendingly so) of any suggestions that there is a question of responsibility here that is at least worth considering. I am not alone in this regard, as there is no shortage of critics of the Fund and its officers regarding the adverse social (as well as economic) consequences of its activities. Economists such as Stiglitz (who once acidly remarked that the Fund was full of third rate economists from first rate universities) laments the Fund's exacerbation of the economic and social crises in Indonesia in the late 1990s and Argentina in 2002;[138] Woods relates how ineffective the Fund's structural adjustment programmes were in alleviating poverty in Sub-Saharan Africa in the 1980s;[139] and Sachs tells a similarly sorry story about the IMF's inflexibility in the face of manifest deprivation in Ethiopia in 2003–4.[140] Human rights commentators and lawyers such as Sigrun Skogly and Mac Darrow have also, separately, criticised the Fund's 'command and control' management structure which when coupled with the disciplinary homogeneity of its staff strongly mitigates consideration of matters outside the purview of macro-economics.[141] Allied to this, Margot Salomon has argued for the Fund to reverse its current reading of the recurring instruction in its AAs – that it 'shall pay due regard to the circumstances of members' – which has typically been interpreted not only as an interdiction against domestic interference, but apparently as a reason not to take into account *any* political or social matters (including human rights) in its deliberations. As she points out, there are in fact greater reasons to interpret this provision to require doing just that, than there are in support of the currently preferred understanding.[142] There are, further, a number of vociferous, informed and skilful NGOs such as the Bretton Woods Project and the Bank Information Centre,[143] which have long histories of trenchant criticism of the Fund's studied disengagement with human rights.

138 Joseph Stiglitz, *Globalization and its Discontents* (New York and London: W. W. Norton, 2002), pp. 77, 117, and *Making Globalization Work*, pp. 222–4, respectively.
139 Woods, *The Globalizers*, pp. 158–9.   140 Sachs, *The End of Poverty*, pp. 267–8.
141 Darrow, *Between Light and Shadow*, p. 201; and Sigrun Skogly, *Human Rights Obligations of the World Bank and the IMF* (London: Cavendish Publishing, 2001), pp. 19–23.
142 Margot Salomon, 'International Economic Governance and Human Rights Accountability', LSE Legal Studies Working Paper No. 9/2007 (September 2007), p. 12; at http://ssrn.com/abstract=1013505.
143 See http://brettonwoodsproject.org and www.bicusa.org/en/index.aspx, respectively.

The Bank too has been on the receiving end of many criticisms regarding its reluctance both to engage with human rights concerns within its scope of operations and to acknowledge the human rights impact of its economic footprints. As Siobhán McInerney-Lankford – a lawyer working in the Legal Vice-Presidency of the Bank – has written, 'these are challenges which have either not been acknowledged, or the significance of which has not fully been appreciated'.[144] Still, it has to be said that, within parts of the Bank's establishment and operationally, there have been signs of a greater openness to the idea that human rights concerns do have a role, even an important role, to play in the fulfilment of the Bank's objectives.

The task before those who are amenable to this line is nevertheless limited by the AA provisions noted above. McInerney-Lankford is right to say that the many 'calls for drastic policy changes' of the Bank are naïve in thinking that these provisions can simply be overlooked, for they have not only some textual meaning, but also what she calls 'normative significance'.[145] The latter is especially important within the traditional thinking of the Bank and of the member states themselves, and provides a considerable political obstacle, though not one, in my view, that is insurmountable. The point about the limitations of textual meaning, however, is less convincing. After all, as Mac Darrow reminds us, legal interpretation (especially in the arena of international law) is more art than science, even if 'it is a characteristic or part of the art to disguise it as a science'.[146] Indeed confirmation of the evident open-endedness of such terms as 'political affairs' and 'economic considerations' comes from McInerney-Lankford herself, later in her article, as well as from her boss, Roberto Dañino, when he was still General Counsel of the Bank, who pronounced that in his view 'there is no stark distinction between economic and political considerations', and therefore 'it is consistent with the Articles that the decision-making processes of the Bank [should] incorporate social, political, and any other relevant factors which may have an impact on its economic decisions'.[147]

---

144 Siobhán McInerney-Lankford, 'Human Rights and Development: Some Institutional Perspectives' (2007) 25(3) *Netherlands Quarterly of Human Rights* 459, at 461.

145 *Ibid.* p. 491.

146 Darrow, *Between Light and Shadow*, p. 115; Darrow is, as he notes, here borrowing from Robert Jennings's famous epithet on this point.

147 Roberto Dañino, 'The Legal Aspects of the World Bank's Work on Human Rights: Some Preliminary Thoughts', in Sage and Woolcock (eds.), *World Bank Legal Review*, Vol. II, *Law, Equity, and Development*, p. 295, at p. 305.

In point of fact, this whole matter has been a case of theory catching up with practice, for in the field it has always been well-nigh impossible for the Bank to avoid involvement in human rights matters. Laurence Boisson de Chazournes (a former senior counsel in the Bank) has shown how, during the 1970s and 1980s, the Bank was inevitably drawn into political imbroglios with overtly human rights concerns, such as with Apartheid South Africa, Portugal's colonial repression in Angola and Mozambique, the military Junta in Myanmar, Iran's theocratic repression, and Mobutu's genocidal mania in Zaïre; and the Bank's 'non-economic' impacts in these circumstances applied just as much when it withheld aid as when it provided aid.[148] Since these times, the insinuation of human rights matters in the planning and operational mandates of the Bank has, as noted earlier, become more apparent, even if not always explicitly labelled as such. Human rights have also become of increasing concern to the Bank's private sector development projects, especially in respect of the work of its associate agencies, the IFC and MIGA. Indeed, Peter Woicke, the former Executive Vice-President of the IFC, referred to the agency's task of 'navigat[ing] a path through human rights, as one of the burning issues of our day'.[149] The exponential growth of the Bank's involvement in private sector development projects is reflected in the expansion of the IFC's work in facilitating joint Bank–corporate initiatives in developing countries and in the size of the IFC's project funding, which has quadrupled in the last five years.[150] It is also apparent from the dollar amounts being underwritten by MIGA against the frustration of private sector projects caused by political circumstances in developing countries, which have risen tenfold from the early 1990s to today.[151] Both agencies have been criticised for their involvement in backing corporate initiatives

148 Laurence Boisson de Chazournes, 'The Bretton Woods Institutions and Human Rights Converging Tendencies', in Wolfgang Benedek et al. (eds.), Economic Globalisation and Human Rights (Cambridge: Cambridge University Press, 2007), pp. 213–18.

149 Peter Woicke, 'Putting Human Rights Principles into Development Practice through Finance: The Experience of the International Finance Corporation', in Alston and Robinson (eds.), Human Rights and Development p. 327, at p. 351.

150 Funding has risen from $2.6 billion in 2003 to 8.2 billion in 2007, and 'commitments in FY08 are expected to be in the range of $10.5 to $12.5 billion'; see IFC, FY09–11, Business Plan and Budget (26 June 2008), para. 1.6 and graph 6.1 on p. 43.

151 That is, from less than $200 million in 1990 to nearly $2 billion in 2008. See Independent Evaluation Group–MIGA, 2008 Annual Report: Evaluating MIGA's FY05–08 Strategic Directions (15 April 2008), fig. 2.1 at p. 26. Notwithstanding such growth, the Report notes that MIGA's share of the political risk industry has declined in recent years, from 6 per cent in 2004 to 4 per cent in 2007, which 'reflects increased supply of political risk Insurance', ibid.

that have caused serious and well-documented human rights problems. These have included accusations of breaches of land rights, health and clean environment rights, rights to water, and indigenous rights regarding the building of two huge pulp mills by European firms on the River Plate border between Uruguay and Argentina;[152] restrictions on rights to free expression, participation and assembly, and to remedies, as well as endangering the right to health and safe working conditions in respect of the 1,000 km Chad–Cameroon pipeline;[153] and complicity in crimes against humanity by an Australian mining corporation in its operations in the Democratic Republic of Congo.[154]

Both MIGA and the IFC have responded to these criticisms in various ways including, in MIGA's case, engaging specialists in assessing the social (as well as the environmental) implications of the activities of the corporations they work with, and entering into dialogues with its critics by responding to criticisms.[155] The IFC has also reacted by professing that it has 'learnt lessons' from its experiences.[156] It has also engaged in more proactive efforts to reform its policies and practices. In 2005 it undertook a review of its safeguard policies (against which the performance of projects was measured to try to 'safeguard' against their adverse impacts) with a view to embracing more substantial and explicit social standards including human rights and labour conditions. But following pressure from within the Bank proper and some of the member states,

152 Projects backed by both the IFC and MIGA; see Jorge Daniel Taillant, 'International Development Finance and Global Governance: Human Rights and Sustainable Development' (2007), paper obtainable from CEDHA (www.cedha.org.ar).

153 The IFC invested in and worked with the consortium of oil giants, ExxonMobil, Petronas and Chevron, who built the pipeline; see Amnesty International, *Contracting Out of Human Rights: The Chad–Cameroon Pipeline Project* (London: Amnesty International UK, 2005).

154 Tricia Feeney from the UK-based NGO Rights and Accountability in Development (RAID) has been especially effective in exposing these atrocities and lobbying the Bank to take appropriate action; see her correspondence with the then Bank President, Paul Wolfowitz, appended to the Bank's Compliance Advisor/Ombudsman's Report: *CAO Audit of MIGA's Due Diligence of the Dikulushi Copper-Silver Mining Project in The Democratic Republic of the Congo* (November 2005), an audit that Feeney's letter helped instigate; www.cao-ombudsman.org/html-english/documents/DikulushiDRCfinalversion02-01-06.pdf.

155 See MIGA's July and September 2001 responses to the Friends of the Earth Report: 'Risky Business: How the World Bank's Insurance Arm Fails the Poor and Harms the Environment' (July 2001); www.miga.org and www.foe.org, respectively.

156 See the two *Lessons of Experience* reports it launched in October 2006 on the Chad–Cameroon pipeline and the Baku–Tiblisi–Ceyhan pipeline, www.ifc.org/ifcext/media.nsf/Content/LOE_BTC_Chad.

the resultant new Performance Standards were diluted so as to focus largely on environmental concerns, with the muted 'human rights' component represented mainly in surrogate provisions covering consultation and disclosure, labour conditions, community health and the protection for indigenous peoples. It is notable that throughout the whole thirty-four-page document, there is not a single mention of the term human rights.[157]

Still, it should be recognised that in the activities of the IFC and (to a lesser extent) MIGA, the Bank is potentially able to exert leverage over private sector partners in respect of human rights. Mac Darrow, for example, believes that 'the leveraging of the Bank's [and IFC's] social safeguard policies through relatively modest contributions (in financial terms) to joint ventures with private actors represents an important and emerging area of Bank influence'.[158] Notably, the World Bank's Inspection Panel in its consideration of the Chad–Cameroon pipeline case[159] has iterated the importance of human rights to the decision-making processes that the Bank must take not only in such public–private partnerships as this, but also, by extension, in all Bank activities where human rights issues arise. Notably, the IFC has also directly influenced related initiatives in the (pure) private sector. The Equator Principles, for example, which comprise 'a financial industry benchmark for determining, assessing and managing social and environmental risk in project financing', were established as a private sector off-shoot of the IFC's safeguard policies/performance standards.[160]

Real obstacles to the more meaningful integration of human rights in the Bank's strategic thinking, policy-planning and project implementation are still very evident. Politically, the views of some member states, as channelled through the Bank's Boards (both of Executive Directors and

---

157 IFC's Performance Standards on Social and Environmental Sustainability (2006), available at www.ifc.org/ifcext/sustainability.nsf/Content/EnvSocStandards.

158 Darrow, *Between Light and Shadow*, p. 217. Currently there are eleven World Bank environmental and social safeguard policies (each of which comprises combinations of Operational Policies (OPs) and Bank Procedures (BPs)). The most relevant to human rights are those covering the preservation of natural habitats, involuntary settlements and the protection of indigenous peoples. See http://go.worldbank.org/WTA1ODE7T0.

159 The Inspection Panel, *Investigation Report: Chad–Cameroon Petroleum and Pipeline Project* (2002), paras. 212–14, available at http://siteresources.worldbank.org/EXTINSPECTIONPANEL/Resources/ChadInvestigationReporFinal.pdf.

160 The Equator Principles have been adopted by more than sixty private banks and other financial institutions; see www.equator-principles.com/principles.shtml.

of Governors),[161] are equivocal, if not hostile in some cases, to the notion entering the Bank's core domain. One of Galit Sarfaty's conclusions to her extensive empirical study of World Bank culture is that the impasse between the members of the Board of Executive Directors regarding the role of human rights in the Bank's operations has 'simply resulted in inaction' on the part of the Board, prompting management to make 'incremental changes in operations' that pass ' "under the radar" of member states'.[162] However, as evidenced by their uptake of those human rights related programmes that the World Bank does administer, the poorest and neediest states that constitute the Bank's clientele can and do welcome human rights matters being taken into account, provided they comprise part of a wider consideration of their social needs, and provided that they do not crystallise into unyielding conditionality. This, then, constitutes yet another reason for the need to push ahead with reforming the governance structures of both the Bank and the Fund. Naigre Woods notes ruefully that:

> more than three-quarters of the members of each of the IMF and the World Bank are not directly represented on the Board of Executive Directors. Nor are they represented in the senior management of either institution. Many have virtually no nationals working on the staff. These are the countries who are most deeply affected by each of the institutions.[163]

There is also the obstacle of bureaucratic intransigence. Born of a combination of a maligned 'approvals culture' (emphasising and rewarding getting projects started and completed rather than necessarily their substantive merits or efficacy), lack of relevant expertise, and an innate reluctance to take on anything new (the pervasive curse of all bureaucracies), any significant and lasting incorporation of human rights considerations into the work of the Bank faces an uphill battle.[164] This is so

161 The Board of Governors comprises representatives from every member state. The Board of Executive Directors, to which nearly all power is delegated by the Board of Governors, comprises only twenty-four, including seats reserved for the biggest shareholder (i.e. financier) states; the voting system is also weighted in their favour. See http://go.worldbank.org/UVCJX4BN00.
162 Galit Sarfaty, 'Why Culture Matters in International Institutions: The Marginality of Human Rights at the World Bank' (2009, forthcoming) *American Journal of International Law*, at 15 (of draft). She notes, in particular, the implacable opposition of countries such as China and Saudi Arabia, the transaction costs concerns of states like Brazil and India, and the disagreements between those Western states who broadly support greater account being taken of human rights as to how that should be effected.
163 Woods, *The Globalizers*, p. 190.
164 See Kinley and Davis, *Human Rights Criticism of the World Bank's Private Sector Development and Privatization Projects*, pp. 85–102.

even when the word comes from the very top, as occurred when James Wolfensohn was President. Wolfensohn, who once said that dealing with the Bank's bureaucracy was 'like grappling with an octopus',[165] sought to reform it by, among other measures, attempting to inject the rhetoric of human rights into the veins of the monster. The Bank's 1998 report on Development and Human Rights, previously mentioned, was a case in point, proclaiming that:

> The World Bank believes that creating the conditions for the attainment of human rights is a central and irreducible goal of development. By placing the dignity of every human being – especially the poorest – at the very foundation of its approach to development, the Bank helps people in every part of the world build lives of purpose and hope.[166]

More than ten years on it cannot be said that these words have been followed through in practice to the extent of their promise.

Fixing the plumbing and other ways forward

At the centre of Jeffrey Sachs's prescriptions for ending global poverty there lies the need to 'fix the plumbing' through which development funding flows.[167] It is no good turning on the taps of more funding (the other great need at the heart of the Sachs vision), if the pipes are blocked or don't service the right places. Multilateral institutions like the IMF and the World Bank, as well as state aid agencies, development NGOs and private sector development projects, need, to varying degrees, to be more innovative (like the Grameen Bank's development of micro-financing, and the 'One Laptop per Child' campaign),[168] more flexible (fashioning programmes to meet demand and need rather than imposing 'one size fits all' programmes that are held in stock), and more aware of the social consequences of their economic footprints, whereby not only should institutions abide by the principle of 'do no harm' in their operations,[169] they should actively promote recognition of human rights concerns in their mainstream activities.[170]

---

165 As quoted by Sebastian Mallaby, *The World's Banker* (Sydney: UNSW Press, 2004), p. 148.
166 World Bank, *Development and Human Rights*, p. 2.
167 *The End of Poverty*, pp. 269–70.   168 See http://laptop.org/vision/index.shtml.
169 As advocated, for example, by the OECD, Development Assistance Committee, *Action-Oriented Policy Paper on Human Rights and Development*, DCD/DAC(2007)15/FINAL (23 February 2007), at p. 15.
170 As employed by a number of UN and bilateral development agencies in the particular sectors of women's and children's rights, the rights of minorities and indigenous peoples,

In terms specifically of human rights I think the biggest problem facing their intersection with development, and the as yet elusive goal of their mutual reinforcement, is the matter of how human rights are perceived by many economists, development specialists and aid agencies. There is a tendency to view them as definitive, unyieldingly prescriptive, and mandatory. This is to over-stretch the legal dimension of human rights. To be sure, human rights are more often than not expressed in legal terms, but those terms are not imbued with the characteristics listed. Few laws are. But laws that seek to regulate such fundamental principles of individual and social existence as human rights are certainly more open-textured than many suppose. I have written about this both in broad philosophical and political contexts,[171] and in the particular respect of the World Bank,[172] arguing for a more nuanced approach to the presentation and interpretation of human rights standards. This is not only to reflect what is, in fact, the reality and practice of human rights. It is also, quite deliberately, to countermand what so many who resist engaging with human rights, including those in the development community, see as the malign rigidity of human rights laws. To reassure and persuade them, as it were, that while human rights laws typically do bring with them compliance expectations and accountability mechanisms, the substance of human rights is in many respects open to subtle differences in interpretation (necessarily so if their quest to be universal is to mean anything) and their goals are not only broadly similar to those of development, they are constitutive of its full realisation.

> Human rights and human rights laws are not above politics, but rather immersed in it; they are, indeed, the very stuff of politics in the broadest sense, concerned with how and on what basis states treat those within their jurisdiction... The implication of disaggregating the notion of international human rights in this way is that it provides the opportunity, if not the requirement, to rethink... attitude[s] towards human rights.[173]

It remains the case that, at the level of international law, responsibility for the protection and promotion of human rights lies with states, and indeed it is, generally speaking, the states, not international institutions, that

---

health and education; see accounts compiled by OECD, *Integrating Human Rights into Development: Donor Approaches, Experiences and Challenges* (Paris: OECD, 2006), at pp. 44–51.

171 David Kinley, 'Human Rights Fundamentalisms' (2007) 29(4) *Sydney Law Review* 545.
172 Kinley, 'Human Rights and the World Bank', pp. 367–75.   173 *Ibid.* pp. 370–1.

have the established means to meet these obligations, whether individually, or collectively acting through such international bodies. This does not, of course, absolve organisations like the IMF or the World Bank from taking human rights seriously. It is, rather, to stress that their role should be seen as aiding states – both rich and poor – to meet their human rights obligations at home and, where relevant, abroad.[174]

Conclusion

The question of how development policies and practices can better aid the efforts to fulfil the human rights of the poorest and most marginalised on our planet ultimately centres on how well we design them. Our efforts thus far cannot be said to be satisfactory. Far from it. William Easterly, in his polemic *The White Man's Burden*, calculates that the West has spent $2.3 trillion on foreign aid over the past 50 years and yet has not managed to address many of the most basic and persistent problems of extreme poverty, disease and preventable deaths to anything like the level that one might fairly expect of such a sum.[175] Put this way, the record is lamentable. But if we are to be serious about raising the standards in which the poorest live and thereby to accord to them even the barest minimum respect for their human rights, what are needed are better plans, not no plans at all, as Easterly advocates.[176] Certainly, he is correct to criticise the formulaic and unresponsive attitudes of development 'planners' (as he calls them) when the results of their plans are so abjectly ineffective. But not all development policies have been, or are so, as the discussion in this chapter illustrates, and as Easterly himself admits. Leaving it wholly to the market place of adaptable and responsive 'searchers' to eek out the most effective and efficient means to address the many and varied development problems is not only fanciful,[177] it would lead to results just as reprehensible as

---

174 An important ancillary role stressed by the 'Tilburg Guiding Principles on World Bank, IMF and Human Rights', in Willem van Genugten, Paul Hunt and Susan Mathews (eds.), *World Bank, IMF and Human Rights* (Nijmegen: Wolf Legal Publishers, 2003), p. 247, at paras. 23–7.

175 William Easterly, *The White Man's Burden* (New York: Penguin, 2006), p. 4.

176 *Ibid.* p. 5.

177 Not even Fredrick Hayek, the doyen of laissez-faire liberalism, advocated such a free market; see Simon Deakin, 'Social Rights in a Globalized Economy', in Philip Alston (ed.), *Labour Rights as Human Rights* (Oxford and New York: Oxford University Press, 2005), pp. 52–5, in which he quotes Hayek's acceptance of a role for 'the provision by government of certain services which are of special importance to some unfortunate minorities, the weak or those unable to provide for themselves'.

the world's score-card on poverty alleviation thus far.[178] The market fails; searchers/entrepreneurs are not always looking in the places of most need; and such responses that there are may not be interested in long-term sustainability. One need only consider the consequences in development and human rights terms of those situations such as Myanmar, North Korea and Zimbabwe, in which Western aid programmes are almost non-existent,[179] to realise how the 'aid market' can fail to deliver.

For these reasons any development strategy must entail state-based intervention through planning, regulation, incentive and sanction. The structure and objects of international human rights regimes – in their political and legal guises – have been developed with the same needs in mind. The challenge is to design and implement plans that integrate the developmental and human rights needs of the poor, and thereby better serve them.

This must be done conceptually through institutional recognition of the interdependency of the human rights and global economy relationship in the context of economic aid, and in practice by an acceptance of the need to design and implement the means to leverage the relationship for the benefit of human rights ends, especially in respect of the world's poor. These are themes and arguments as to consequences and responsibilities that I return to in the final chapter, when I integrate all three dimensions of the global economy – aid, trade and commerce – to consider how best they can, collectively, advance the protection and promotion of human rights.

---

178 See Amartya Sen's critique of Easterly's book: 'The Man without a Plan', *Foreign Affairs*, March/April 2006, p. 171.

179 Excepting the humanitarian aid rendered to Myanmar in the extraordinary circumstances following the devastation of Cyclone Nargis in May 2008. The International Crisis Group (ICG) has been damning about such disengagement, the dire consequences of which the aftermath of Nargis graphically exposed. In the ICG's view, 'in its attempt to defeat the regime by isolating it, the West has sacrificed opportunities to promote economic reform, strengthen social services and empower local communities. Despite the fact Myanmar is prone to natural calamities, very little has been done to support disaster prevention and preparedness'; *Burma/Myanmar after Nargis: Time To Normalise Aid Relations*, Asia Report No. 161 (October 2008), p. 16, available at www.crisisgroup.org.

4

Commerce and human rights

Introduction

In the year of this book's publication, the worst corporate calamity of modern times will mark its twenty-fifth anniversary. Around midnight on 2–3 December 1984, a dense cloud of 40 tons of highly poisonous methyl isocyanate (MIC) gas drenched the Indian city of Bhopal, after a catastrophic chemical reaction occurred in a holding tank at the nearby pesticide plant operated by the Indian subsidiary of the US firm Union Carbide. More than 3,000 people died in the immediate aftermath, according to official figures (though many civil society organisations put the figure at almost three times that number), and more than 50,000 people were permanently disabled. In the following weeks a further 15,000 died as a direct consequence of the leak, and it has been estimated that since then approximately the same number have died for reasons that included exposure to the gas, drinking contaminated water or consuming produce from contaminated soil.[1] Recent reports on the medical consequences of the disaster show an intergenerational impact with clear evidence of birth and developmental abnormalities that correlate to those who, though exposed to the gas, survived, and have since had children.[2]

Despite the intense worldwide media interest in the tragedy, and the string of court cases it spawned, it remains unclear precisely what caused the water to enter the holding tank that set off the chain of events leading to the gas leak, but many believe it was due to the chronic disrepair

---

1 See Amnesty International, *Clouds of Injustice: Bhopal Disaster 20 Years On* (London: Amnesty International UK, 2004).
2 Nishant Ranjan, Satinath Sarangi, V. T. Padmanabhan, Steve Holleran, Rajasekhar Ramakrishnan and Daya Varma, 'Methyl Isocyanate Exposure and Growth Patterns of Adolescents in Bhopal' (2003) 290(14) *Journal of the American Medical Association* 1856, at 1857, and Randeep Ramesh, 'Bhopal Gas Victims Are Still Being Born', *Guardian Weekly*, 9 May 2008, p. 10. In fact, owing to the lack of thorough follow-up medical research (the curtailment of which is itself the matter of enormous controversy), it is difficult to ascertain the full extent of consequences throughout the local population.

of the plant's infrastructure, while the company claims it might have been the work of a saboteur. What cannot be disputed, however, are the many public notices and reports that document the long-term deterioration of safety standards at the plant, including in respect of installations, management procedures and staff training. The relevant holding tank, for example, was filled with MIC to between 73 and 87 per cent of capacity on the night of the accident, despite safety regulations stipulating that tanks be filled to no more than 50 per cent capacity in order to allow sufficient space to accommodate the adding of dilutants in emergencies. Accusations abound over Union Carbide's cost-cutting carelessness regarding safety, and the double standards tolerated by the US parent company in respect of the poor operational and safety protocols being followed (or not followed) at its Indian subsidiary.[3] Even if not all of these claims were accurate, the company's categorical rebuttal of them was overblown (for example, its claim that safety at Union Carbide 'was a deeply ingrained commitment that involved every employee worldwide'),[4] and compromised, as evidenced by it own admissions and actions in the litigation that ensued.

Allegations as to negligence regarding safety procedures, and the responsibilities under civil and criminal law that flow therefrom, constituted the basis of the actions pursued in both the American and the Indian courts. The Indian Government initially sought unspecified damages against Union Carbide in a negligence suit filed in the Federal Court in New York, but the company successfully argued in its defence that the court was not the appropriate jurisdiction in which to hear the dispute (that is, *forum non conveniens*), and the case was dismissed.[5] Clearly, New York was not the forum in which the incident occurred, and the operating corporation was indeed Union Carbide India Ltd (UCIL), not the defendant Union Carbine Corporation (US) (UCC), but the plaintiffs had argued that through the latter's 51 per cent ownership of the former, it maintained effective control of, and therefore responsibility for, operations at Bhopal. The court's dismissal was, however, conditional on the

---

3 See, for example, Alfred de Grazia, *A Cloud over Bhopal* (Bombay: Kalos Foundation, 1985), pp. 65–102.

4 As stated by Jackson Browning, Union Carbide's former Vice-President of Health, Safety and Environmental Programs, 'Union Carbide: Disaster at Bhopal', in Jack Gottshalck (ed.), *Crisis Response: Inside Stories on Managing Image under Siege* (Detroit: Visible Ink Press, 1993), p. 367.

5 *In Re Union Carbide Corporation Gas Plant Disaster at Bhopal* 634 F.Supp. 842 (SDNY 1986) at 850–1.

company submitting itself to the jurisdiction of the Indian courts, but clearly the loss of the opportunity to argue the case before the American courts, and with it the possibility of obtaining significant damages and setting an important legal precedent in the American courts, was a blow to the victims of the Bhopal disaster. Negligence suits were pursued in the Indian courts and the case was eventually settled out of court in 1989 when UCC agreed to pay $470 million in compensation to the victims. By 2004 only one quarter of that amount had been distributed by the Indian Government which held the compensation fund despite the patent need. Following an enforcement ruling of the Indian Supreme Court the Government has made undertakings to distribute the remainder, though now it is clear that the breadth and depth of the need is much greater than the amount initially settled on.[6] Warren Anderson, the CEO of UCC at the time, was declared a fugitive from justice by a magistrate court in Bhopal in 1992 for failing to appear in court to face charges of manslaughter. Neither the Indian nor the US Government has shown any inclination to activate extradition proceedings against Anderson, who continues to live in the US. The gas plant at Bhopal was abandoned after the disaster and UCIL was sold to another chemical manufacturer in 1994. The site itself and adjoining lands are yet to be properly cleaned up by Dow Chemical Company, which took over UCC in 2001.[7]

The scale of the Bhopal incident together with its legal ramifications represents a watershed in the recent history of business's relations with the community on two fronts. First, the episode graphically exposed the nature of a corporate culture that permitted such horrific consequences and that spurred subsequent efforts to avoid being held responsible. And second, it revealed the inadequacies of the legal regimes that governed the corporation both before and after the disaster; that is, in regulating against its occurrence, and in the provision of remedies for the loss and suffering it caused. As I argue throughout this chapter, these two factors are emblematic of the key concerns that occupy the field of corporate social responsibility as a whole, and the question of human rights responsibilities

6 A further class action suit was filed in the US against Union Carbide in 1999, most of which was dismissed on the same grounds as the 1986 case, save in respect of claimed damage to property which had not been argued before, but these claims too were finally dismissed by the Second Circuit Court of Appeals in New York in 2006; see *Bano v. Union Carbide Corporation* 198 Fed.Appx. 32 (2nd Cir. 2006).

7 For the chronology of the continuing saga, see the Bhopal Information Centre, at www.bhopal.com/chrono.htm.

of corporations in particular. At issue in respect of both the general and the specific is the extent to which law can, should and does have a role to play.

Defining the territory

There is a considerable degree of ecumenicalism within the commerce and human rights relationship, with respect, in particular, to the impact of corporations as the driving force of commercial enterprise. Rights and responsibilities are asserted in legal and non-legal terms (and in respect of the former, in hard and soft law varieties). Allegations of abuses of human rights, as well as proclamations of their advancement, are regularly aired in a wide range of arenas: legal, political, social and economic. Though the human rights themselves are sometimes expressly referred to as such, often they are not, even when their relevance is manifest (as in the case of Bhopal). Instead, one finds that surrogate terms are widely used, such as environmental damage, social consequences, legal breaches and unethical behaviour. The whole gamut of human rights standards are, in fact, relevant: economic, social and cultural rights, as well as civil and political rights. Reflecting on a review of more than 300 reports of alleged human rights abuses by corporations, John Ruggie, the UN Secretary General's Special Representative on the Issue of Human Rights and Transnational Corporations and other Business Enterprises (henceforth 'SGSR'), has concluded that 'there are few if any internationally recognized rights business cannot impact – or be perceived to impact – in some manner'.[8] That said, the most prevalent are: labour rights (workplace relations, conditions of employment and occupational health and safety); health related rights (especially concerning environmental conditions, access to water and food security); free speech rights (that is both to receive information, as well as to impart it); rights to fair trial and to an effective remedy (that is when individuals or groups are involved in litigation with corporations in home or host states); physical security (concerning, in particular, the actions of law enforcement agencies working for or with corporations); rights to land, housing and living standards (often affected in situations of forced or voluntary relocations); and the rights of

---

8 Report of the Special Representative of the Secretary-General on the issue of human rights and transnational corporations and other business enterprises, John Ruggie, 'Protect, Respect and Remedy: A Framework for Business and Human Rights', UN Doc. A/HRC/8/5, 7 April 2008, para. 52.

indigenous peoples (regarding culture, land, movement and non-discrimination).[9]

The circumstances in which corporate abuses of these rights occur, as well as the size, type and format of the corporations involved, are many and varied. Corporations can be large or small; be engaged in just about any type of business (from financial and professional services, through manufacturing and agriculture to extractive industries); be operating in developed or developing states (or both), or in circumstances of peace and order, or conflict and chaos; be subject to heavy or light (or no) legal regulation. The abuses may be caused by ignorance, neglect, carelessness, mendacity or even design. But, at the broadest level, it is possible to see some dominant tendencies and trends emerging from the matrices of these different factors. Major corporations (almost invariably transnational corporations (TNCs)) that have an image or brand to protect are especially heavily scrutinised for transgressions, in particular regarding their operations in developing countries. Together, the extractive industries (oil, gas and minerals), apparel and footwear manufacturing, timber and logging, power generation, protective services, pharmaceutical products, and the financial services sector (notably banks that fund impugned projects), account for the vast majority of human rights claims made against corporations, with the first two mentioned sectors predominating.

Legal regulation is manifold and stringent in most developed states, it is inconsistent and patchy in many developing states, and it is almost non-existent at the level of international law. There is also some cross-over between these categories, as highlighted, for example, by such extra-territorial legal devices as universal jurisdiction in respect of grave criminal offences, legislation with extra-territorial reach (as with certain criminal laws, and the US's *Alien Torts Claims Act*) and *forum non conveniens* disputes. Of the causes of human rights infringements by corporations, carelessness and neglect are by far the most common. Ignorance of the existence of pertinent human rights standards and their application in any given circumstance is also common, though this is nearly always associated with a corporation's lack of care or its

---

9 See David Kinley and Junko Tadaki, 'From Talk to Walk: The Emergence of Human Rights Responsibilities for Corporations at International Law' (2004) 44 *Virginia Journal of International Law* 931, at 966–93; and also see a report by Human Rights Watch and the Center for Human Rights and Global Justice, NYU School of Law, *On the Margins of Profit: Rights at Risk in the Global Economy*, Vol. 20, No. 3(G) (February 2008), which usefully categorises the principal rights at risk and the nature of their abuse. Available at hrw.org/reports/2008/bhr0208.

negligence. In the West, at least, it is now rare to find corporations setting out intentionally and knowingly to infringe human rights. Rather,
infringements are usually the indirect consequence of the corporation's
blinkered pursuit of its commercial objectives – which all, ultimately,
reduce to profit. This is so even in the most striking examples. Thus, in a
review of Edwin Black's book *IBM and the Holocaust*, Richard Bernstein
considers that IBM's continuation of commercial relations with Hitler's
Germany (in particular its sale of a new system for managing data that
assisted in the orchestration of the Holocaust) demonstrated 'the utter
amorality of the profit motive and its indifference to consequences'.[10] IBM
was not alone in this case, or in respect of corporate involvement in any
number of tyrannical regimes, before and after Nazi Germany. The blindness of corporations in such situations is often wilful and reprehensible,
as well as culpable, and it shows how, no matter what the circumstances,
there will always be corporations that carry on 'business as usual'.[11]

Changing landscapes and mindsets

I should stress that while these are readily observable tendencies and
trends, they do not account for the whole picture of the intersection
between human rights, corporations and commerce. Even aside from the
fact that I am, for the moment, focusing only on human rights abuses
(I redress the balance by stressing how and in what circumstances commerce benefits human rights in the section that follows this one), there is a
crucial dimension to this relationship that must be added. This is the need
to appreciate the deeper nature of global corporate enterprise, the changes
it is undergoing, and how these factors affect the evolving relationship
between commerce and human rights. Within, between and around the
edges of the above trends there are a clutch of important emerging issues
that must be accounted for in any assessment of the current situation
and in any prognosis of future developments. Together they form a dense
matrix of complicating factors, all of which intertwine at some level or
other.

One such issue concerns corporations that are not transnational, or do
not have a brand name or public image to protect. These firms are just as

10 Richard Bernstein, 'IBM's Sales to the Nazis: Assessing the Culpability', *New York Times*
    (7 March 2001), at p. E8, as quoted by Beth Stephens, 'The Amorality of Profit: Transna-
    tional Corporations and Human Rights' (2002) 20 *Berkeley Journal of International
    Law* 45.
11 Stephens, 'The Amorality of Profit', at 46.

liable, if not more so, to care little for human rights standards, whether they are regulated or not. It has been acknowledged, for example, that many human rights infractions in the footwear and apparel industries occur in anonymous factories situated down the supply chain. The pressure on such big, branded corporations as Nike, Adidas and Gap at the top of these supply chains has resulted in these corporations making greater efforts not only to formulate and enforce human rights protecting policies and practices in their own operations, but to apply them to their suppliers as well. But still, questions remain as to how far down the chain (that is, the supplier's suppliers, and their suppliers in turn, etc.) such pressure can be meaningfully applied, and the fact that nearly all such policies apply only to the formal sector, by-passing altogether the plight of home workers in the informal sector.[12]

The complexion of the global face of TNCs is also changing. Of particular note is the rise of globally powerful and increasingly expansive corporate players from new or emerging economies, such as India's Tata (motor vehicles), Mittal (steel) and Infosys (information technology), China's Sinopec (oil), ICBC (banking) and Chery (cars), Brazil's Sadia (foodstuffs), Embraer (aeronautics) and Vale (mining), Russia's Gazprom (oil and gas), Mexico's Cemex (concrete), and Malaysia's Petronas (oil and gas).[13] Sixty-two of the world's biggest companies in the *Fortune 500* list are now from emerging economies, up from thirty-one in 2003.[14] In 2007, almost 13 per cent of the world's total foreign direct investment was coming from corporations located in developing economies, and more than 10 per cent of all cross-border mergers and acquisition spending in that year was also sourced from developing states.[15] Few of these corporations, let alone all those smaller than them, have anything like the domestic or even international pressure to conform to human rights standards as do many Western corporations. This does not mean to say that none of them pays any heed to such standards – as I mentioned in chapter 1, Tata, for example, is very explicit about the value it puts on

12 See Rachelle Jackson, 'The New Supply Chain Standards: FTSE4Good Enough?', *Ethical Corporation*, 3 January 2005, at www.ethicalcorp.com/content.asp?ContentID=3345.

13 For discussion of the phenomenon, and especially the impact of South–South FDI flows in which corporations such as these are instrumental, see Dilek Aykut and Andrea Goldstein, *Developing Country Multinationals: South–South Investments Comes of Age*, OECD Development Centre, Working Paper No. 257 (December 2006).

14 See 'A Bigger World', Special Report on Globalisation, *The Economist*, 20 September 2008, p. 3.

15 UNCTAD, *World Investment Report 2008: Transnational Corporations and the Infrastructure Challenge* (New York and Geneva: UN, 2008), p. 37, at p. 272.

observing its social and human rights responsibilities;[16] and nor does it mean to say, of course, that Western corporations are all good corporate citizens in this regard. Rather, it is to point to the fact that differences in corporate culture, domestic regulatory frameworks, consumer attitudes, and social and political expectations will necessarily lead to variegated levels of human rights observance by corporations.

Another emerging factor is the increasing porosity of the public/private divide in economic relations. This is evidenced in the enormous global movement towards privatisation of all sorts of public utilities (from water and power, through telecommunications and banking, to security and detention), and the massive growth in the incidence, scope and size of so-called public–private partnerships (PPPs) in commercial dealings. Both these phenomena are having an impact on the protection and promotion of human rights, not least as regards the task of determining whether, and to what extent, the state is *indirectly* responsible under international law for the actions of a privatised body, alongside its *direct* responsibility to ensure human rights protection to all within its jurisdiction which endures no matter what the level of privatisation.[17] A particular concern regarding the privatisation of essential services is the impact of replacing 'need' as the rationale of the service in question, for 'efficiency and profit'. In consequence, unprofitable sectors of society (often poor or remote communities, or ones that are infrequent or light users) are at risk of having their service provision depleted or cut off altogether. A report on *Human Rights, Trade and Investment* by the UN High Commissioner for Human Rights notes, in respect of privatisation and the right to water, that:

> while promoting investment through private sector participation in the water and sanitation sector might be a possible strategy to upgrade the sector, there is concern that private sector participation might threaten the goal of basic service provision for all, particularly the poor, and transform water from being an essential life source to primarily an economic good.[18]

---

16 Thus, Clause 17 of Tata Code of Conduct covering ethical conduct provides that 'every employee of a Tata company shall preserve the human rights of every individual and shall strive to honour commitments'; available at www.tatainteractive.com/pdf/ TIS_TCOC.pdf.

17 See Adam McBeth, 'Privatising Human Rights: What Happens to a State's Human Rights Duties when Services are Privatised?' (2004) 5 *Melbourne Journal of International Law* 133.

18 Report of the UN High Commissioner of Human Rights, 'Human Rights, Trade and Investment', UN Doc. E/CN.4/Sub.2/2003/9 (2 July 2003), para. 47.

The usual response to such fears, of course, is to ensure that there is an appropriate degree of public intervention and oversight, by way of stipulations made in the privatisation agreement itself as to the range of service delivery and permissible charges, and through the establishment of a regulator with powers of enforcement. Thereby the sharper edges of private sector management of a public resource can be dulled in order to secure such wider goals as social welfare and human rights protection. Public–private partnerships are a particular device that may be employed for just these ends. They are essentially agreements to employ private capital to secure an asset or service that remains in, or is controlled or administered by, the public sector domain. The partnership details vary greatly, as, indeed, do perceptions of their impact on the efficiency, effectiveness, scope and fairness of service delivery in social and economic terms.[19]

The final point I wish to make in this list of emerging trend-setting issues concerns the matter of the motivations behind corporate abuses of human rights. It needs to be stressed here that the circumstances in which corporations operate today have changed – or at least, so it is perceived – regarding the relevance of human rights concerns. As I said before, instances in which corporations *intend*, knowingly and deliberately, to act in ways that breach human rights standards (as opposed to not knowing or caring about the human rights consequences of their actions) are the exception rather than the rule. Typically, corporate transgressions born of such 'inadvertency' range from unpardonable ignorance (including both 'head-in-the-sand' ineptitude and wilful neglect), to sincere practical or policy dilemmas, which have the virtue, at least, of being more understandable, if not exactly pardonable. A graphic illustration of the former attitude is displayed in the following excerpt from the transcript of a television documentary in which the CEO of Anvil Mining, Bill Turner, was interviewed about allegations that Anvil's employees took part, and Anvil's vehicles and plant were used, in a murderous, government-backed military campaign in the town of Kilwa in the Democratic Republic of Congo in October 2004:

> SALLY NEIGHBOUR [*journalist, Australian Broadcasting Corporation*]: And what about all the civilians who were killed?
> BILL TURNER: I don't know – I don't know – I don't know. We were not part of this. This was a military action conducted by the legitimate

---

19 See Michael Likosky's excellent case-study analyses of the human rights risks related to the establishment and delivery of public–private partnerships: *Law, Infrastructure and Human Rights* (Cambridge: Cambridge University Press, 2006), especially chapter 3.

army of the legitimate government of the country. We helped the military get to Kilwa and then we were gone. Whatever they did there, that's an internal issue. It's got nothing to do with Anvil. It's an internal government issue. How they handle that is up to them. No involvement of us, absolutely.

SALLY NEIGHBOUR: Well, except that they used your vehicles to move their troops in.

BILL TURNER: So what? So what?

SALLY NEIGHBOUR: To move their troops around.

BILL TURNER: So what?[20]

This exchange also reveals the ready appeal to corporations of seeking refuge behind the complication of political necessity; that is, where the political circumstances of the host state are such that the corporation makes out that it has little or no choice but to comply with local rules, regulations or requests, even if they lead to human rights abuses. This was effectively the reasoning initially relied upon by the corporations in such celebrated cases as Shell in Nigeria (when the company was accused of complicity by sponsoring the Nigerian military in its brutal suppression of peaceful protests against Shell's alleged environmental pollution by the local Ogoni people, through killings, rape and detention without trial),[21] and Unocal in Myanmar (when the company was accused of complicity in human rights abuses because it engaged Myanmar soldiers to protect its Yadana gas pipeline while knowing of the military's record of murder, rape, forced labour and forced relocation).[22]

Regarding the less culpable (if no less damaging and intractable) problem of human rights abuses that flow from genuine practical dilemmas, I might here recall a story told to me in Indonesia by the operations manager of a Unocal (as it then was) oil-rig situated some miles off the coast of East Kalimantan. The presence of the oil-rig had attracted local fisherman who were able greatly to extend their range of accessible fishing grounds by tying up overnight to the platform's legs, rather than having

20 ABC, *Four Corners*, 'The Kilwa Incident', 6 June 2005; at www.abc.net.au/4corners/content/2005/s1386467.htm.

21 *Wiwa v. Royal Dutch Petroleum Co.*, 96 Civ. 8386 (KMW), 2002 U.S. Dist. LEXIS 3293 (S.D.N.Y. 22 February 2002). More than ten years after the filing of the original lawsuit, the case awaits resolution, having been delayed by discovery disputes and other ancillary motions; see Centre for Constitutional Rights, *Wiwa v. Royal Dutch Petroleum, Wiwa v. Anderson* and *Wiwa v. Shell Petroleum Development Company*, at http://ccrjustice.org/ourcases/current-cases/wiwa-v.-royal-dutch-petroleum,-wiwa-v.-anderson-and-wiwa-v.-shell-petroleum-d.

22 *Doe v. Unocal* 403 F.3d 708 (9th Cir. 2005). The case was settled in 2005; see further discussion below, at p. 192.

to return to port each night. This was enormously beneficial to the many local communities that relied heavily on fishing for their livelihoods. The manager was well aware of this fact, but equally he was very conscious of the safety implications of such a practice (for rig personnel as well as the fishermen), and the rules prohibiting such trespass. It genuinely troubled him to do so, but he felt he had no choice but to enforce the rig's exclusion zone boundaries in respect of the fishermen. This sort of dilemma is not an uncommon problem that corporations, especially in the extractive industry, have to deal with. Companies that are involved in voluntary relocation programmes often face similar difficulties when they must ensure that compensation packages are fair not only in absolute terms, but also relative to pre-existing community differences and distinctions. And there are many other examples of such practical and ethical difficulties.

From the perspective of the victims of human rights abuse, of course, it hardly matters what was the perpetrator's motivation, but in terms of finding ways to address the problem, motivation is crucially important.[23] There is some leverage to be had when breaches are inadvertent. Levels of awareness can be raised and consciences can be pricked, dialogue, debate and argument can be pursued, and remedial and preventive action can be taken. Few, if any, of these ploys would find much purchase where a corporation considers human rights to be irrelevant and inapplicable to its objects and operations. The vast majority of corporations, however, cannot afford to be so chronically myopic. True, their attention may be so focused on their operational efficiency, market share and profit that they neither consider the human rights implications of their actions, nor fully appreciate their relevance once such implications are pointed out to them. But, through a combination of public and private exposure of the issues, engagement with stakeholders, and an eye and an ear cast to the newly emerging expectations made of corporations regarding their social, environmental and human rights footprints, corporations are increasingly less and less able to ignore or dismiss the matter.

In practice, one finds that many corporate executives and managers, at least in the West, are open to discussion on the topic. More often than not, they are frank about the causes of any alleged abuse, and increasingly

23 In this respect I find myself in direct disagreement with Onora O'Neill's view that 'unclarity about the motivation of TNCs does not matter much, given that we have few practical reasons for trying to assess the quality of TNC motivation'; Onora O'Neill, 'Agents of Justice', in Andrew Kuper (ed.), *Global Responsibilities: Who Must Deliver on Human Rights?* (New York: Routledge, 2005), p. 50.

willing to take appropriate action of some kind. There can be no denying that some are sceptical participants in such discussion and action, while others are clearly reluctant; but few simply refuse to engage in any way at all. Even when such 'engagement' is litigious, or takes some other combative stance, that too, as I amplify later, can lead to improvements in the corporation's future attitude and behaviour regarding human rights. 'Reputation risk' is an enormously powerful force in this context. Successful corporate branding is the holy grail of the modern corporate enterprise. The phenomenal potential of modern communications has been ably harnessed by corporations to make Coca-Cola's labels, Nike's 'swoosh' and David Beckham's (or Christiano Ronaldo's) No.7 Manchester United shirt readily recognisable in almost every corner of the Earth. But, as every senior executive of a big brand corporation is painfully aware, there exists an equal and opposite potential for global communications to besmirch and degrade. The inimitable Warren Buffet put it succinctly when, on becoming chairman of Salomon Brothers (a prominent Wall Street investment bank) in 1991, he told the staff: 'lose money for the firm and I will be understanding; lose a shred of reputation for the firm, and I will be ruthless'.[24]

In terms of unwanted and damaging headlines, there is nothing quite like the linking of a corporation with accusations of human rights abuses.[25] So, even if only for the reason of self-interest, human rights are now gaining entry into many corporate board rooms, just as environmental matters began to do (with similar ambivalent reception) in the early 1990s. The position is now such that, during a recent speech about his Final Report of his first mandate to the UN Human Rights Council, the SRSG John Ruggie could say with confidence that the notion that corporations possess human rights responsibilities (albeit not necessarily legal ones) is not today seriously demurred from.[26] At the same time, in

---

24 'Berkshire Pays the Price for Buffett's Secrecy', *The Age*, Business section, 4 June 2005.
25 Two of the criteria used in the Reputation Institute's *Global Pulse Study 2008* of the world's most respected companies are 'governance' and 'citizenship'. The Survey's results indicated that consumers saw these two combined as amounting to more than 30 per cent of a company's reputation. 'This', commented Anthony Johndrow, the Institute's Managing Director, 'makes it critical for companies worldwide to communicate how they support good causes, protect the environment, behave ethically and act openly and transparently about the way they do business'; Media Release, 5 June 2008; at http://reputationinstitute.com/events/Global_Pulse_2008_Results.pdf.
26 John Ruggie, 'Business and Human Rights: A Political Scientist's Guide to Survival in a Domain where Lawyers and Activists Reign', Speech at the Annual Conference of the International Law Association (British Branch), London, 17 May 2008.

a report on the human rights tensions surrounding the involvement of such corporations as Nike and Coca-Cola in the Beijing Olympics, *The Economist* – a self-declared, arch-sceptic of corporate social responsibility – concedes that today we have what is, in effect, a new corporate order in which the 'striking' feature is 'how often [human rights] activists, big firms and governments are now all in agreement about the importance of human rights, and are working together to advance them'.[27] And even when they are not, or at least not initially, mindsets, including corporate, can change. Thus, for example, Global Solutions Limited (GSL), a transnational logistics and security company, was willing publicly to record its admitted changes in attitude and perspective regarding the 'understanding of our human rights obligations and, no less important, of how best these can be achieved' that followed its participation in the process dealing with a complaint brought against GSL under the OECD Guidelines for Multinational Enterprises concerning its management of immigration detention centres in Australia.[28]

All that said, much work needs to be done. Human rights abuses by corporations have been occurring since the institution of incorporation as the pre-eminent legal vehicle through which to do business, through to the manner and form of their operations today in the modern (post-1945) age of international human rights standards. We are today made more aware of the substance and scale of the abuses and the consequences that follow by the vigilance of NGOs and activists and the reach and penetrative capacity of modern communications. How to address, attenuate and remedy these abuses, and how to devise means to prevent their occurrence, are important matters with which this chapter is concerned, but, nonetheless, they are matters that must be seen within the broader context of the capacity of corporations to do good as well as bad for human rights.

Transnational corporations and their powers to do good and bad for human rights

No discussion of the corporate/human rights relationship can be taken seriously unless it also recognises the benefits commerce and corporations bring to individuals and to societies. Understanding what are the

<hr>

27 'Beyond the "Genocide Olympics"', *The Economist*, 26 April 2008, p. 81.
28 See *Australian National Contact Point's Evaluation of the GSL Specific Instance Process*, and correspondence attached thereto from Tim Hall, Director of Public Affairs, GSL, 6 October 2006; available at www.oecd.org/dataoecd/42/52/37616212.pdf.

relative merits and demerits of corporations in terms of their promotion of the ends of human rights is an essential first step towards meeting the fundamental challenge of how to preserve and enhance the positive human rights features of commercial enterprise while minimising its negative consequences. This is a challenge both analogous to, and interlinked with, the challenges that exist in respect of the relations between trade and aid with human rights that I tackled in the previous two chapters.

In typically admonitory and trenchant fashion, Aldous Huxley warned that 'facts do not cease to exist because they are ignored'.[29] Shining light on the facts of the damage corporations do to the well-being of individuals and communities must be balanced against what benefits they bring. As the key drivers of today's global economy, corporations have enormous capacity to create wealth, jobs and income; the taxes they pay finance public goods; the competition they generate accelerates innovation and development in almost every walk of life, from medicines and food production, to communications, transport and power generation; they propagate the transfer of technological and intellectual know-how; and by way of the interdependency of their commercial operations they can contribute to the establishment and maintenance of domestic social and economic order, as well as international peace and stability. They do so, what is more, not only in developing as well as developed countries, but across a range of socio-political circumstances: capitalist liberal democracies (old and new); free market socialism (viz. China and Vietnam); quasi free market theocracies (such as Saudi Arabia and Iran); post-colonial and post-dictatorship liberal economies (as in much of South and South East Asia, South America and, increasingly, Sub-Saharan Africa) and neo-communist autocracies (such as Russia and most of the other former Soviet states that today comprise the Commonwealth of Independent States) – albeit to significantly varying degrees.

Together, these features of corporate commercial enterprise provide the means by which human rights standards can be enhanced or better protected – what Mary Robinson has referred to as 'an enabling environment for the enjoyment of human rights'.[30] Such enablement is important to all states, but is especially crucial to poor or weakly governed ones where the scope for benign (as well as malign) influence is greatest. Onora O'Neill classifies TNCs as potential 'agents of justice' when they pursue policies that go 'beyond compliance' with local host (or even home) state laws

29 Aldous Huxley, *Proper Studies* (London: Chatto & Windus, 1927), p. 205.
30 Mary Robinson, 'Foreword', in Business Leaders Initiative on Human Rights, *Report 3: Towards a 'Common Framework' on Business and Human Rights: Identifying Components* (London: BLIHR, 2006), p. 1.

governing, for example, environmental, employment or anti-corruption standards.[31] In conflict and post-conflict situations some commentators, like Peter Davis, have noted that corporations can promote economic, social and even political stabilisation and reconstruction by assisting (but not replacing) failing or nascent governments in building infrastructure, providing basic health, education and communication services, and in technological and financial investment.[32]

In truth, we should expect all this to be so. Corporations, after all, are products of society, ultimately beholden to and regulated by it through the apparatus of the state. The sage words of that most red-blooded of progressives, Theodore Roosevelt, spoken more than a hundred years ago, remain apposite today: 'I believe in corporations . . . They are indispensable instruments of our modern civilization; but I believe that they should be so supervised and so regulated that they shall act for the interests of the community as a whole.'[33] Capitalism's laissez-faire is a normative principle, not a description of practice. State laws and attendant enforcement mechanisms govern not only the process of corporate creation (incorporation), but also just about all aspects of corporate conduct, from general business, investment, accounting and fiscal practices, directors duties, ownership conditions and shareholder rights, to workplace relations, labour rights, health, safety and environmental standards, product safety, purchasing and sales, and customer relations. Clearly, corporations still have much room to manoeuvre, but crucially their conduct is, and can be, regulated in respect of their human rights impacts as with any other matter deemed to be in the public interest. In short, we are all, to some extent, responsible for the corporations that we have. Our criticism of poor corporate conduct may be accurate, fair and appropriate, but it is too easily dispensed when we do not at the same time recognise the power we have to make things better. Corporate law specialist Janet Dine argues forcefully on this point when she talks of a

> moral deflection device [that] comes into play when we vilify companies for their behaviour. This gives us the high moral ground while still living comfortably because of the benefits they provide. Moral indignation at the terrible behaviour of some corporations . . . must not be allowed to obscure the fact that companies are designed by societies and their profits

31 O'Neill, 'Agents of Justice', pp. 49–50.
32 Peter Davis, 'Post Conflict Development – Successful Companies Learn from Wider Debates', *Ethical Corporation*, 13 May 2008, at www.ethicalcorp.com/content.asp?ContentID=5908.
33 As quoted by John Micklethwait and Adrian Wooldridge, *The Company* (London: Weidenfeld & Nicolson, 2003), p. 174.

underpin much of our wealth. So when they strike bargains with evil
regimes, repatriate their profits and sell us goods produced at low prices
because of sweated or slave labour, this is not because of the inherent evil
of the people that work in corporations but as a direct result of the legal
design of corporations and the operation of the international legal system
which provides them with many opportunities yet fails to regulate.[34]

Nonetheless, there is clearly some distance between statement and fact.
For in saying we have the authority and (perhaps) the power to reign in
corporate excesses while at the same time enhancing the advantages they
bring, this does not mean that such directed and effective intervention
will result.

The Realpolitik of corporate power

For a start, we need to remember, of course, that state intervention in
respect of corporate activity is not always human rights friendly, let alone
motivated by concerns of human rights promotion at all. State inter-
dictions may be driven by self-generated government policies or by the
lobbied interests of corporate sectors, or a mixture of both. In this regard
it matters little that, under international human rights law, the obligations to meet the stipulated standards are directed towards states parties
when the state deems it politic to breach or ignore those standards, or
feels comfortable doing so, or is simply unaware of or unable to fulfil its
obligations properly, if at all. Numerous examples of this phenomenon
exist. I here briefly mention three different cases of corporate rights violations induced by state inadequacy, desperation or aggression. Together
they demonstrate how we really only get as good or bad corporations as
our governments allow or insist upon. Corporations may be ignorant,
indifferent or resistant towards human rights but, whatever their stance,
it is not unaffected – for good or ill – by the regulatory environments in
which they operate.

Consider first a poor state like Papua New Guinea, faced with the
prospect of losing the Australian mining giant BHP (now BHP Billiton)
as a major corporate investor in the country after the company was sued
for negligence in the Australian courts. It was alleged that the company was
responsible for the ongoing discharge of dangerous substances, including
ore-tailings and waste, from its Ok Tedi copper mine that poisoned huge
swathes of the Ok Tedi and Fly rivers in the country's western province,

34 Janet Dine, *Companies, International Trade and Human Rights* (Cambridge: Cambridge
University Press, 2005), p. 44.

destroying the livelihoods of thousands of people who lived along and depended on the river.[35] The corporation's conduct before, during and after the fiasco was so intensely, publicly and damagingly criticised that BHP decided effectively to cut its losses and abandon the project. The Ok Tedi copper mine – then one of largest copper mines in the world – generated approximately 20 per cent of PNG's exports and yielded royalties worth something in the region of 10 per cent of PNG's gross domestic product.[36] The Government was so concerned to keep the mine functioning that it was willing to advertise the fact in a television interview that it would – as it had already done with BHP[37] – indemnify any corporation interested in taking over the mine from any legal actions taken in its courts for breaches of local environmental or criminal laws.

Clearly, the PNG Government's invidious position may to some degree explain (if not justify) its actions. But my concern in the present context is merely to demonstrate how and why a desperate state can take desperate action that can facilitate and even encourage corporate breaches of human rights within its borders.

Aside from such desperation, a state's laws may simply be non-existent or inadequate to meet its obligations to protect human rights or related environmental standards. This common occurrence provides the basis for my second example of the constrictions of state/corporate relations. One of the arguments raised by Chevron in its defence to allegations that it was responsible for massive pollution of land and waterways in Ecuador, caused by the dumping of billions of gallons of crude oil waste over more

35 *Dagi v. Broken Hill Proprietary Co Ltd (No 2)* [1997] 1 VR 428 (judgment of 22 September 1995). The case was settled out of court in June 1996; however, a subsequent claim was brought in 2000 regarding the terms of, and BHP's compliance with, the settlement. The plaintiffs claimed that BHP was under an obligation to implement 'any technical and economically feasible tailings retention scheme' as recommended by an independent inquiry into tailings disposal announced by the Papua New Guinea Government. The inquiry never took place, so BHP claimed it did not need to implement any mitigatory management system for the 100,000 tonnes of tailings that were entering the river system daily, and would continue to do so for the life of the mine. See *Dagi v. Broken Hill Proprietary Co Ltd; Gagarimabu v. Broken Hill Proprietary Co Ltd* [2000] VSC 486 (unreported), Supreme Court of Victoria, 22 November 2000.

36 As estimated by Dr Roger Higgins, then the Managing Director of Ok Tedi Mining Ltd; see ABC TV, '7:30 Report', 12 August 1999, at www.abc.net.au/7.30/stories/s43531.htm.

37 The Papua New Guinea Parliament had enacted the *Ok Tedi Mine Continuation Act 2001* which indemnified the corporation from damages for environmental pollution emanating from the mine. Australian Associated Press, *Passes Law Indemnifying BHP Billiton*, 12 December 2001. The existence of this statutory protection in PNG was one of the reasons why the original *Dagi* case (see above) had been pursued in the Victorian Supreme Court in Melbourne.

than twenty years by Texaco (bought by Chevron in 2001), is not only
that the company abided by the (woefully inadequate) environmental
standards existing at the time,[38] but that it considers itself released from
further liability following a \$40 million remediation settlement with the
Ecuadorian Government in the 1990s. The company is presently being
sued for between \$7 billion and \$16 billion in the Ecuadorian courts,
following the assessment of damages by a court-appointed independent
assessor.[39]

And finally, consider circumstances in which the state aggressively pur-
sues human rights infringing policies such as in the celebrated instances of
internet censorship by Google, Yahoo! and Microsoft of the services they
provide in China. As with all internet service providers in China, these
three companies are subject to various Chinese criminal, anti-sedition
and national security laws imposed on all media outlets, on- and off-line.
China has one of the most sophisticated and expensive internet filtering
systems in the world (dubbed the 'Great Firewall of China') that identifies
and filters out such undesirable material posted in blogs or websites or
sent by emails that promotes democracy, human rights, Tibetan independence or just about anything critical of the government or the Communist Party. Internet providers the world over are, of course, subject to
certain content restrictions, typically with respect to criminal activities
such as terrorism, extreme hate speech, fraud or child pornography. The
difference with the Chinese censorship is its transparently political motivation. This has posed dilemmas both for media corporations working
in China and for observers or critics of their conduct. Should Yahoo!
have handed over the contact details of a journalist email client whom
the Chinese authorities suspected was disseminating information about
repressive government conduct and human rights violations to overseas
correspondents?[40] Should Microsoft have acceded to demands that it
close down a pro-democracy blog it hosted?[41] And should not Google
have resisted the Government's proscription of access to YouTube inside

38 See Lucy Siegle, 'The Secrets of Sour Lake', *Observer*, 7 October 2007, p. 46.
39 See Alison Frankel, 'Chevron Lawyers Indicted in Ecuador', *The Legal Intelligences*, 16 September 2008, p. 4.
40 See BBC News, 'Yahoo Helped Jail China Writer', 7 September 2005; news.bbc.co.uk/2/hi/asia-pacific/4221538.stm. It was in fact Yahoo Holdings (Hong Kong) that supplied the details to the authorities, which raises questions as to the nature of its relationship with the parent company and the accompanying lines of responsibility.
41 David Barboza and Tom Zeller, 'Microsoft Shuts Blog's Site after Complaints by Beijing', *New York Times*, 6 January 2006, available at www.nytimes.com.

China after hundreds of images were posted on the site of the Tibetan unrest and the army's brutal responses in March 2008?[42]

It might be argued that all of these are short-term prices worth paying in order to ensure the presence of foreign internet providers in China, which in the long run will assist in the development of free speech in the country. Alternatively, some will argue that such craven attitudes on the part of these corporations are an abomination, more concerned to secure market presence and boost market share than with any thought of free speech rights or morality. 'While technologically and financially you are giants, morally you are pygmies', is how Tom Lantos, Chairman of the US House of Representatives Foreign Affairs Committee, witheringly put it to Yahoo! executives appearing before a Committee hearing on corporate complicity in media censorship in China in November 2007. The Chinese Government relies heavily on the cooperation of the internet companies in its efforts to police the internet; what Justine Nolan ironically labels 'state-induced self-censorship'.[43] Yet, countering such aggressively pursued human rights breaches by a state from the outside is not only difficult in practice, but controversial in design. Draft legislation introduced into the US Congress in 2006 which sought by measures both persuasive and coercive to have US corporations resist such overtures of foreign governments to limit freedom of expression failed to be enacted, in part because not only were the media corporations themselves sceptical about its practicability, but so were free speech NGOs, including the redoubtable Reporters Sans Frontières.[44]

The power of corporations is often a matter of some controversy. Are they really able to resist or influence states, or even to take on state functions (and their attendant responsibilities)? And if so, what are their features that allow them to do so? These are important – indeed vital – questions in the whole commerce and human rights debate, bearing directly on how we identify and conceive the relevant debatable issues, how we mark out their boundaries, and what options we have to deal with the problems they entail.

---

42 Jane Spencer and Kevin Delaney, 'YouTube Unplugged', *Wall Street Journal*, 21 March 2008, at online.wsj.com/public/article_print/SB120605651500353307.html.
43 Justine Nolan, 'The China Dilemma: Internet Sponsorship and Corporate Responsibility' (2009) 4 *Asian Journal of Comparative Law* (online, article 3), p. 3.
44 For discussion of the promise and problems of the mooted *Global Online Freedom Act*, see Surya Deva, 'Corporate Complicity in Internet Censorship in China: Who Cares for the Global Compact or the Global Online Freedom Act?' (2007) 39 *George Washington International Law Review* 255.

Much has been made and unmade of the claims as to the financial clout of corporations, especially in terms of how they stack up against states and what implications can be drawn from such a comparison. A commonly quoted statistic is that, of the top hundred global 'economies', fifty-one are corporations.[45] Such a crude statistic could never be anything other than a very broad indication that some TNCs are indeed very large and very global, and have very large amounts of capital flow through their hands – hardly Damascan revelations. And yet TNC critics, sceptics and advocates alike have engaged in a *dialogue de sourdes* over the methodology employed in making these calculations and what are the consequences of corporate power (whatever its quantum). Unsurprisingly, economists have latched onto what is for them the comfortable domain of econometric measurement to lambaste those naïve enough to compare a state's GDP with a corporation's gross sales. Martin Wolf[46] and Jagdish Bhagwati[47] are right to point out the fallacy of this classic case of comparing apples with pears, although it has to be said that in Wolf's case he labours the point to an extent that lands him in precisely the methodological hot water that he so ridicules.[48]

Of greater significance are the differences of opinion on whether corporate power matters in terms of the promotion and protection of human rights. Regardless of definitional and measurement disputes, no one seriously denies that corporations are extremely powerful players in the global economy and thereby have, as the examples already discussed in this

45 Sarah Anderson and John Cavenaugh, 'Top 200: The Rise of Corporate Global Power', Institute for Policy Studies, Washington, DC, December 2000, at www.willison.ca/home.jsp_files/top200text.htm. Adopting a different calculus, this figure was substantially deflated to 29 out of 100 in an UNCTAD study in 2002: *Are Transnationals Bigger than Countries?* See Press release TAD/INF/PR/47 12/08/02; available at www.unctad.org/Templates/webflyer.asp?docid=2426&intItemID=2079&lang=1. I am grateful to Karin Buhmann for sharing with me the fruits of her own research on this matter.
46 Martin Wolf, *Why Globalization Works* (New Haven and London: Yale University Press, 2004), pp. 221–6.
47 Jagdish Bhagwati, *In Defense of Globalization* (New York: Oxford University Press, 2004), p. 166.
48 He replaces *gross* sales on the corporate side of the calculation with the 'value added' by corporations at the point of sale, which reduces the corporate figures dramatically. *The Economist* has also made the same argument – see Simon Cox (ed.), *Economics: Making Sense of the Modern Economy* (London: The Economist; Profile Books, 2nd edn 2006), pp. 26–7. However neither Wolf nor *The Economist* explains how this alternative indicator is any closer to GDP than is gross sales. Both are surely inadequate comparators to an indicator based on national consumption, investment, spending and trade balance as is GDP.

chapter show, very significant direct and indirect effects on our social and individual welfare. 'Big business', as Woodrow Wilson once remarked, 'is not dangerous today because it is big, but because its bigness is an unwholesome inflation created by privileges and exemptions which it ought not to enjoy.'[49] That said, such power – even political power – is not to be confused with the sovereign authority of states. Critics are correct to point out that corporations 'are not here to build a fairer society'; that is indeed 'the job of governments'.[50] However, this demarcation neither explains nor relieves corporations from legitimate expectations both that they must not impede such building work (the 'do no harm' principle), and that they should be encouraged or obliged to assist the state in protecting human rights. In fact, typically, it is the case that nearly all non-state entities – that is, legal persons such as individuals, corporations, community groups, trade unions, etc. – are already required to 'assist' the state in this regard. The so-called 'horizontal' human rights laws and policies of states that regulate private individual-to-individual relations (including corporations) operate alongside 'vertical' laws and policies that govern public state-to-individual relations (also including corporations). As such, a measure of accountability is not only expected of companies in relation to human rights, it is already imposed on them in certain important respects.[51] The significance of this situation has become all the more important as corporations increasingly take on functions and powers of public utilities and services, thereby blurring divisions not only of legal status, but also of legal responsibility.[52]

Proponents of the notion that with corporate power there comes corporate responsibility, in terms of human rights matters as with much else, draw directly on these circumstances. Yet too often those who criticise such a stance appear, inexplicably, to overlook or misunderstand the whole matter of accountability. Take, for example, Martin Wolf again. In

49 Woodrow Wilson, speech accepting the Democratic Party nomination to run for President of the US in 1912; as cited by Scott James, *Presidents, Parties and the State* (New York: Cambridge University Press, 2006), p. 156.
50 'The Acceptable Face of Capitalism', *The Economist*, 14 December 2002, p. 65.
51 As discussed in more detail later in this chapter, see pp. 187–8.
52 Thus, the International Law Commission's *Articles on the Responsibility of States for Internationally Wrongful Acts* (2001), Article 5 provides: 'The conduct of a person or entity which is not an organ of the State . . . but which is empowered by the law of that State to exercise elements of the governmental authority shall be considered an act of the State under international law, provided the person or entity is acting in that capacity in the particular instance.'

his book *Why Globalization Works*, Wolf dedicates a chapter to debunking what he claims are the principal propositions advanced by critics of corporations. Quite remarkably, not one of the five he nominates[53] relates to concerns over accountability gaps that exist at both domestic and international law regarding corporate infractions of human rights standards. Perhaps Wolf was concerned only to deal with the more extreme views – he characterises critics as 'detest[ing] corporations', engaged in 'collective hysteria' and being 'populists, Marxists and anarchists' (he appears to credit no one involved in this side of the debate as 'professional participants and analysts', as he expressly does so regarding parallel debates on the role of trade and finance).[54] Indeed, in his ensuing arguments Wolf invests in a fair amount of hyperbole of his own. His painting of companies like Shell as weak and defenceless against the blackmailing might of NGOs such as Greenpeace is quite a masterpiece in surrealism, given that if Shell's decision not to dump the Brent Spar oil platform at sea was taken because it was so concerned to protect its brand image, that says much more about Shell's business priorities than it does about Greenpeace's leverage![55] If Wolf is only concerned with point-scoring at this level (much of which, incidentally, I agree with), he is missing the most important point of all. Nobody worth listening to is saying that corporations are wholly unaccountable, operating free from legal regulation and restriction. But pointing out that businesses are subject to the demands of the market, consumers and certain corporations laws does not mean that in terms of the protection of human rights such demands are sufficient.

My final remark regarding the *Realpolitik* of corporate power concerns the interplay between what might be referred to as the primary and secondary inclinations of corporations. That is, where the corporate id to maximise profit is tempered by the ego not to do so at any cost. Few

---

53 These are: (1) corporations are more powerful than states; (2) brands give corporations power over customers; (3) FDI impoverishes developing countries and (4) their workers; and (5) corporations subvert democracy by controlling states; Wolf, *Why Globalization Works*, p. 221.

54 *Ibid.* pp. 220–1. Greenpeace, among others, had campaigned vociferously, and ultimately successfully, against Shell's initial decision to dump the decommissioned oil platform and storage buoy in the UK's territorial waters in the mid 1990s. There were in fact no environmentally risk-free options available to Shell in disposing of the facility, but the manner in which it and its opponents (and the UK Government) conducted themselves in the ensuing imbroglio is now considered a textbook example of risk communication gone wrong.

55 *Ibid.* p. 228.

corporations can afford reputationally (and therefore financially) to sub-scribe to the unalloyed 'greed is good' mantra of Gordon Gekko.[56] As we have established, reputation and brand image matter to corporations, and a whole professional industry has emerged to service the need to protect and preserve them. Whether for this reason or for broader, more altruistic reasons, corporations do consider their actions to be concerned with more than just profit. A *McKinsey Quarterly* survey in December 2005 of 4,238 global business executives recorded 84 per cent of respon-dents as agreeing with the statement that the role of large corporations is to 'generate high returns to investors, but balance[d] with contributions to the broader public good'.[57] This should not be surprising. TNCs that operate in the public gaze are often keen to stress how they act in ways that are not necessarily (at least not immediately) directly oriented towards profit. For example, Neville Isdell, the outspoken CEO of Coca-Cola, maintains that it is his 'core conviction that business is a force for good in the world. Business, when done right, strengthens communities, builds capacity, raises living standards and in the process helps drive social and environmental improvement.'[58] Some firms have even entered into what might be strictly regarded as the political domain, such as when in 2000 the UK firm Premier Oil used the leverage it gained from its operations in Myanmar to facilitate the Junta's release of a British activist held there for more than a year in solitary confinement (he had seventeen more years to serve), for daring to distribute pro-democracy pamphlets on the steps of Yangon's City Hall.[59] Whatever the merits and motivation of such endeav-ours, they raise the very significant question of whether, from a human rights perspective, we want to encourage corporate engagement of this

---

56 In Oliver Stone's 1987 film *Wall Street*. Together with some of Gekko's other choice epithets, such as 'what's worth doing, is worth doing for money' and 'lunch is for wimps', he is still flattered by imitation in the money markets, even if, by force of circumstance, today's traders are a little less brazenly avaricious. Stanley Weiser and Oliver Stone, 'Wall Street', Screenplay, 1987, at www.imsdb.com/scripts/Wall-Street.html.

57 'Global Survey of Business Executives', *McKinsey Quarterly*, January 2006, Exhibit 5: Role of Business in Society, p. 5. Only 16 per cent of respondents agreed with the Milton Friedman inspired statement that large corporations should 'focus solely on providing the highest possible returns to investors while obeying all laws and regulations'; *ibid.*

58 See Neville Isdell, 'Remarks at the WWF Annual Conference', Beijing, 5 June 2007, www.thecoca-colacompany.com/presscenter/viewpoints_isdell_wwf.html.

59 See Carl Mortishead, 'Oil Firm's Secret Deal on Burma Prisoner', *The Times*, 7 December 2000, p. 1; and see further Halina Ward, *Corporate Citizenship: Exploring the New Pos-sibilities*, Royal Institute of International Affairs, Conference Report, July 2001, p. 4, at www.chathamhouse.org.uk/files/3027_corp_citz_report.pdf.

sort, for clearly such action could be very broad-ranging, unaccountable and even counter-productive.[60]

Certainly, companies are increasingly keen to claim that they see human rights as a business issue, at least in so far as their breach can represent a serious business risk. At the time of writing, the incomparable Business and Human Rights website resource[61] lists no fewer than 213 major corporations that have express human rights policy statements.[62] These may take the form of strategy papers, operational programmes or performance standards, or they may be public proclamations, but in any event many are quite explicit in intent. Take, for example, Exxon-Mobil's statement in its 2007 Corporate Citizenship Report that 'we are... committed to promoting respect for human rights and to serving as a positive influence in the communities where we operate. It is the right and responsible thing to do, and doing so promotes stable and constructive business environments.'[63] The UN's Global Compact (which comprises ten briefly stated principles covering environmental protection, anti-corruption, labour rights and 'human rights' (howsoever the last two differ)) has now amassed more than 4,000 signatory corporations, which, though hardly a taxing commitment on their part, is nonetheless an indication of the breadth of interest in the issue.[64] The group of

60 See for example caveats to this end issued by Carl Mortishead (in relation to the Premier Oil case), 'Ethical Mantle Falls on Company Shoulders', *The Times*, 8 December 2000; and Bhagwati (regarding the general principle), *In Defense of Globalization*, p. 169.

61 www.business-humanrights.org.

62 As of September 2008. Further, in a 2006 study conducted by the SRSG of the human rights policies of 102 Fortune Global 500 companies, 91 per cent indicated that they possessed an explicit set of human rights principles; 62 per cent said that in those principles they refer expressly to the UDHR; and 36 per cent responded that they routinely undertake human rights impact assessments. See *Human Rights Policies and Management Practices of Fortune Global 500 Firms: Results of a Survey*, table 1, p. 10, at www.reports-and-materials.org/Ruggie-survey-Fortune-Global-500.pdf. Though these figures are impressive, it is hard to know what store to set by them given that the respondent firms were self-selected, and in many cases no doubt predisposed to answering the survey questions precisely because of their existing supportive stances on human rights.

63 ExxonMobil, *2007 Corporate Citizenship Report*, p. 40; www.exxonmobil.com/Corporate/files/Corporate/community_ccr_2007.pdf.

64 See www.unglobalcompact.org/AboutTheGC/index.html. To comply, corporations need only submit annually a brief 'communication of progress' report. Those companies that fail to do so are named (with the hope of being shamed) on the Global Compact (GC) website, but only if they fail to submit a report within three years of joining, and two years thereafter, or if they fail to engage in dialogue with the GC secretariat within three months following the raising of an 'integrity matter' with the corporation. There are currently almost 1,000 participant corporations (nearly one quarter of the total) so named in the GC's 'Non-Communicating' and 'Inactive' categories.

fourteen prominent TNCs that comprised the Business Leaders Initiative on Human Rights (BLIHR) (which completed its work in March 2009) were perhaps most actively engaged in building consensus and formulating policy towards the mainstreaming of human rights in business by devising 'practical ways of applying the aspirations of the Universal Declaration on Human Rights within a business context and to inspire other businesses to do likewise'.[65]

FDI and human rights

Perhaps the single most significant feature of corporate impacts on human rights is (as noted in the previous chapter) the increasingly substantial vehicle of FDI by which corporations, mostly from developed states, invest in developing states. FDI is considered especially important on account of its particular nature, it being physical investment – in the sense of plant, infrastructure, employment, etc. – rather than simply financial (typically, in respect of investment in stocks or currency speculation). As such, it contributes more directly to the domestic economy in terms of both input and output, and indirectly to the social goods that an expanded economy then has the potential to deliver. As an OECD report on the development implications of FDI has noted:

> Given the appropriate host-country policies and a basic level of development, a preponderance of studies shows that FDI triggers technology spillovers, assists human capital formation, contributes to international trade integration, helps create a more competitive business environment and enhances enterprise development. All of these contribute to higher economic growth, which is the most potent tool for alleviating poverty in developing countries. Moreover, beyond the strictly economic benefits, FDI may help improve environmental and social conditions in the host country by, for example, transferring 'cleaner' technologies and leading to more socially responsible corporate policies.[66]

It is then, to reiterate a constant theme throughout this book, this derivate potential of the economy that human rights protagonists are (and more ought to be) interested in exploiting. The task of profitable exploitation in this way is a matter easier said than done, but it is one whose vital importance cannot be overlooked.

---

65 See www.blihr.org.
66 OECD, *Foreign Direct Investment for Development: Maximising Benefits, Minimising Costs* (Paris: OECD, 2002), p. 5.

As a function of market demand or opportunity, FDI does not always go to the places of most need. Countries with more to offer in terms of raw materials, suitable workforce (in terms of training, skills and cost), existing infrastructure, and adequate banking and finance mechanisms, and governance and legal structures, generally present the best opportunities-to-risk profile and therefore tend to attract the bulk of investment. In recent years the developing or transitional states that best fulfil one or more of these criteria include Brazil, China, Mexico, India, Indonesia, South Africa and Vietnam. FDI contributes to the virtuous circle of such emerging economies, as it itself begets further strengthening of economic, social, political and legal factors, and so attracts further FDI. In contrast, countries that satisfy none or few of the above criteria are almost invariably the poorest and weakest states, which suffer from the vicious cycle of receiving little FDI in the first place and thereby further hindered in their chances of attracting any in the future. This group of countries has for many years comprised many African (especially Sub-Saharan) states, though this situation is changing, leading some at least to stretch the Asian economic 'tigers' metaphor to talk of the emergence of African 'lion cubs'.[67] According to UNCTAD's figures, annual FDI inflows into Africa doubled between 2004 and 2006 to $36 billion (almost a quarter of which was accounted for by Least Developed Countries (LDCs) – a slight rise on 2005), though this still represents a tiny fraction of the global total for 2006 of $1,306 billion.[68] The trend continued into 2007 according to the IMF,[69] largely on the back of oil, and some other mineral exploration (mainly by Australian, Canadian and Chinese firms),[70] though also of significant investments by European, Middle Eastern and African telecommunications companies (further fuelling Africa's extraordinary leapfrog from a situation of almost no private phones, straight over mass fixed-line phone networks, to substantial mobile phone penetration). In addition, the IMF report notes the improved financial management in many African countries, with strengthened central banks, improved fiscal regimes and greater accumulation of foreign currency reserves, which appear to be sufficiently attractive off-sets against endemic corruption and still weak legal systems for corporate investors.[71]

67 See, for example, 'Lion Cubs', *The Economist*, 19 April 2008, p. 87.
68 UNCTAD, *World Investment Report 2007*, pp. xv and xvii.
69 IMF, *Regional Economic Outlook: Sub-Saharan Africa* (Washington, DC: International Monetary Fund, 2008). Using slightly different calculations, the Fund puts the total of private capital flows to Sub-Saharan Africa at $53 billion in 2007, at p. 45.
70 UNCTAD, *World Investment Report 2007*, p. 36.
71 IMF, *Regional Economic Outlook: Sub-Saharan Africa*, p. 48 *et seq.*

It may be, therefore, that the economies of some Sub-Saharan Africa states have got their foot onto the first rung on the ladder out of poverty, but the trend must continue through the current food crises and fuel price hikes (though that should also benefit oil-producing countries like Sudan and Nigeria), and the fall-out of the global financial crisis, if there is to be any chance of improved economic conditions being translated into sustained improvements in social conditions and greater respect and protection of human rights.

However important FDI is to enabling such social enhancement, it is neither sufficient nor always necessarily beneficial. The very same political, administrative and legal factors stipulated above as vital to attracting FDI in the first place are also critical to the domestic process of making the economy work for social and human rights ends. Just as important as these consequential considerations are the conditions under which capital is raised, and what rights and obligations are attached to it once secured. Specifically, we need to know to what extent human rights concerns are taken into account in the drawing up of the financing contracts at the outset, and during the project cycle itself. In recent years, this previously largely overlooked area of corporate activity has attracted a great deal more attention. In many ways it has been a natural progression from scrutiny of the actions of corporations in the field, to asking questions about how, from whom and under what terms they raised the capital to finance their actions.

From the human rights perspective, concerns over the mechanics of FDI have shifted from outright dismissal by investors that they had any responsibilities at all in this regard. Acceptance – or at least acknowledgement – of their relevance is now widespread, even if full comprehension of their implications is not. As already noted, major corporations (which are also often the biggest users of development finance) now commonly stipulate their adherence to human rights standards to be a matter of company policy. Many of the biggest banks that provide the majority of such project finance have signed up to the Equator Principles (EPs) which, by focusing on the associated risk concerns, require lenders to consider the environmental and social implications (including some that bear on human rights issues)[72] of any proposed investment. Since

---

72 Mainly regarding disclosure and consultation (the right to freedom of expression comprises both receiving and imparting information), and grievance procedures (right to a fair trial, which encompasses the raising of grievances through to their fair conclusion, whether outside or, ultimately, inside the court system). Principle 3, regarding the assessment of project finance located in developing countries, expressly refers to use of the IFC

coming into force in 2003, the EPs have achieved some success in what is admittedly a niche market. As Toby Webb, writing in *Ethical Corporation*, has put it:

> although small in global finance flow terms, project finance is a high profile business for both the banks that arrange the money, and the companies who set up the deals and run the projects on the ground. While the economic and political risks of oil, gas and mining projects around the world have always been significant, in modern times NGO campaigns have added real reputational risk to the financing mix.[73]

Generally, throughout the financial services sector, whether focused on developed or developing economies, there is growing recognition of non-financial roles and responsibilities. The UN's 2006 Principles for Responsible Investment (PRI), aimed at all types of financial institutions, exhort signatories to be more aware of environmental, social and governance issues in financial management. According to Donald MacDonald, the Chair of the PRI Initiative, in his 2007 Progress Report, 'the most important contribution the PRI has made is to reinforce and promote the paradigm that environmental, social and corporate governance issues matter to the financial performance of companies, and that mainstream investors have a responsibility to take these issues seriously and, where appropriate, act to address them'.[74]

The position of the commerce/human rights relationship today has been characterised by Sheldon Leader as being concerned with a different 'danger', namely one that 'arises from the way in which the two domains are being brought together. The collision that threatens is not over *whether*, but over *how* commercial imperatives are to be integrated with this branch of social justice.'[75] Even the modest achievements of the EPs must be put in context in this regard – they are unenforceable, do not

---

Performance Standards in the assessment process, which as I discussed in the last chapter have some, but still limited, human rights coverage.

73 Toby Webb, 'Strategy & Management: The Equator Principles: A Toddler Finds its Feet, but Still Takes an Occasional Tumble', *Ethical Corporation*, 14 November 2007, www.ethicalcorp.com/content.asp?contentid=5518. Interestingly, Webb reports one prominent critic from 'Bank Track', Johan Frijns, not only exposing continuing problem cases with EPs-signatory Banks, but also voicing his concern with NGO myopia in focusing only on such cases and not on the evident cases of best practice which have resulted in beneficial outcomes; *ibid*.

74 PRI Initiative, *PRI Report on Progress 2007: Implementation, Assessment and Guidance* (July 2007), p. 5; at www.unpri.org/report07/PRIReportOnProgress2007.pdf.

75 Sheldon Leader, 'Human Rights, Risks, and New Strategies for Global Investment' (2006) 9(3) *Journal of International Economic Law* 657 (emphasis added).

themselves prevent corporate malpractice, and do not cover other sources from which project finance is raised (not least from a corporation's own cash reserves).[76]

The terms upon which major investments are made in developing states are significant not only in respect of the lender/investor relations, but also in respect of the specific arrangements drawn up between investors and the host institutions. Increasingly, such arrangements are being governed by overarching Bilateral Investment Treaties (BITs) which, though concluded between states, are concerned with establishing the basic legal relations that are to apply in respect of all future investment agreements made between private and/or state entities of the states parties. Nearly all BITs adhere to the same essential formula; that is, they seek to protect the interests of the foreign investor under national law at least to the extent of protection enjoyed by domestic investors, as well as prohibiting expropriation except on just terms. In his illuminating report on the legal issues concerning international investment agreements and human rights, Howard Mann notes further that, increasingly, BITs (as well as relevant investment chapters within general trade treaties) specifically require steps to be taken to liberalise the host state's financial services sector, especially when 'associated with ongoing privatization programs in public services, such as water, energy, health or sanitation'.[77]

While BITs are increasingly being drawn up between developing countries, it remains the case that the largest proportion are concluded between developed and developing states.[78] This is significant in terms of the impact they can have on human rights. To begin with, there is the crucial matter of what happens when there is a dispute between the investor and a host state authority or corporation. Almost invariably today, all types of international investment agreements (IIAs), including BITs, contain dispute settlement provisions which allow, as Mann notes,

---

76 Webb, 'The Equator Principles'.
77 Howard Mann, *International Investment Agreements, Business and Human Rights: Key Issues and Opportunities* (February 2008), p. 4. The report is published by the International Institute for Sustainable Development, for whom Mann works as the Senior International Law Adviser; it is available at www.iisd.org/pdf/2008/iia_business_human_rights.pdf.
78 By the end of 2006, just over one quarter of all BITs were between developing states; 40 per cent were between developed and developing states; the remainder were between developed states. See UNCTAD, *Recent Developments in International Investment Agreements (2006 – June 2007)*, IIA Monitor No. 3 (2007), p. 5, available at www.unctad.org/en/docs/webiteiia20076_en.pdf.

foreign investors the right to initiate international arbitrations directly against the host state for alleged breaches of the IIA rights they obtain. Many of these arbitrations take place in a completely confidential setting, a fact that raises its own human rights issues [specifically in respect of access to information and rights to a fair trial] . . . To date, approximately 300 arbitrations under this process are known to have been initiated, with no way to know the exact number due to the confidentiality rules applied in many cases. It may be noted here that only private foreign investors can initiate these arbitrations, as the foreign investors have no obligations under the IIAs to be enforced against them through the dispute settlement process.[79]

The very fact that the process can be initiated by a private corporation – which, as we saw in chapter 2, is categorically not the case regarding disputes under the WTO dispute settlement process – provides the corporation with considerable leverage against the host state. As Mann continues:

It allows a broad range of issues to materialize that may not have if only states had the ability to initiate the process. To date, the range of issues raised by foreign investors under this process has included taxation measures, environmental measures, changes in banking and radio and television laws, alterations of royalties in the resource sectors, and many others.[80]

An area which, until recently, was not a feature on this list was that of human rights. But two cases in particular have illustrated how significant the impact of BITs can be on human rights, not so much by hammering home what we already knew or suspected, but rather by revealing how little we knew about this question. For while express mention of human rights issues are hardly ever part of a BIT, the protection of human rights in a host state may nonetheless be affected greatly by so-called 'stabilisation clauses', routinely built into BITs. These clauses, which are typically concerned with protecting foreign investors from such sovereign risks as the expropriation or nationalisation of their assets, owing to a host country's changed political, economic or social circumstances, 'may also', as Andrea Shemberg notes, 'be designed to insulate investors from environmental and social legislation, [which is] a matter of growing economic significance to investors'.[81]

---

79 Mann, *International Investment Agreements, Business and Human Rights*, p. 4.
80 *Ibid.* p. 5.
81 Andrea Shemberg, *Stabilization Clauses and Human Rights* (11 March 2008), paper prepared for the IFC and the UN Secretary General's Special Representative on Business and Human Rights, at p. vii; available at www.ifc.org/ifcext/media.nsf/Content/Stabilization_Clauses_Human_Rights. For a description of the various types of stabilisation clauses

The first case concerned a consortium of oil corporations led by BP and the stabilisation clauses in the 'host government agreements' (a type of investment contract) that had been drawn up between the consortium and the governments of Azerbaijan, Georgia and Turkey, regarding the construction of the Baku–Tbilisi–Ceyhan (BTC) oil pipeline that linked the Caspian sea in the east, to the Mediterranean coast in the west. Upon making public these provisions in 2003, BP came under intense criticism for their radical scope. The stipulation that any 'disruption to the economic equilibrium of the project' would require the state to pay compensation to the consortium was condemned for effectively limiting the states' capacities to meet their obligations actively to promote and protect human rights under international law.[82] The fact that, as a major development project many multilateral and bilateral development agencies (including the World Bank and the IFC) were involved in funding the project added points of leverage for the critics. In the end, to its credit, BP responded to the furore by amending the host government agreements by inserting a 'Human Rights Undertaking' in their terms, recognising the requirements made of states under international labour and human rights treaties, and stating that the consortium would not make any claims under the 'economic equilibrium', or like clauses in the agreements, following enactments of regulations by the states parties pursuant to any 'reasonable' interpretation of these treaties.[83]

The second case involves the use of just the sort of above-mentioned arbitration provision in an investment agreement that ostensibly protects economic interests against a state's human rights laws. In 2007, the Italian owners of two mining companies operating in South Africa unsuccessfully sought compensation from the South African Government for losses they claim they had incurred and will further incur as a consequence of the country's so-called 'black economic empowerment' laws. These laws require, inter alia, all mining companies working in South Africa to have at least a 26% 'historically disadvantaged South African' ownership by

and an analysis of their potential impact on human rights, see pp. 5–9 and 35–8 of the report, respectively.

82 See Amnesty International, *Human Rights on the Line: The Baku–Tbilisi–Ceyhan Pipeline Project* (London: Amnesty International UK, 2003). Similar concerns were also raised in respect of the Chad–Cameroon Pipeline, see Amnesty International, *Contracting Out of Human Rights: The Chad–Cameroon Pipeline Project* (London: Amnesty International UK, 2005).

83 See Baku–Tiblisi–Ceyhan Pipeline Company, *BTC Human Rights Undertaking*, 22 September 2003, at http://subsites.bp.com/caspian/Human%20Rights%20Undertaking.pdf.

2012.[84] For many mining firms (including the two in this case) this will require them to sell off stock in order to comply with the legislation. Invoking the terms of the Italian, Belgian and Luxemburgian BITs with South Africa, the Italian owners have initiated compulsory arbitration proceedings before the International Centre for Settlement of Investment Disputes (ICSID), which at the time of writing are yet to be resolved.[85] The black economic empowerment laws were introduced in an attempt to correct some of the economic, social and human rights injustices of Apartheid. According to Peter Leon, a lawyer representing the Italian owners, such objectives are not what his clients are objecting to. Rather, as they purchased the mining operations in question in 1994, after Apartheid had ended, they 'never benefited from the apartheid system, [so] why are they subject to this form of redress?', Mr Leon is reported as saying.[86]

The result in the first of these two cases is widely recognised as industry best practice, while the second is indicative of the potential scope within international investment agreements to pitch economic interests against human rights in a way that favours the former. That said, we need to be careful not to set up the two objects as diametrically opposed; the whole tenor of this chapter and this book is that they are in fact interrelated and interdependent. It is how we regulate the relationship – specifically, how to ensure that the economy contributes to, and does not detract from, the fuller enjoyment of human rights – that is key. The UN's High Commissioner for Human Rights accurately characterises the situation as one in which,

> [i]nvestors' rights are instrumental rights. In other words, investors' rights are defined in order to meet some wider goal such as sustainable human development, economic growth, stability, indeed the promotion and protection of human rights. The conditional nature of investors' rights suggests that they should be balanced with corresponding checks, balances and obligations – towards individuals, the State or the environment.[87]

---

84 See the South African *Broad-Based Black Economic Empowerment Act*, 2003 (Act No. 53 of 2003) (Government Gazette No. 25899, 9 January 2004) and the *Broad-Based Socio-Economic Empowerment Charter for the South African Mining Industry* (2002) available at the South African Department of Minerals and Energy: www.dme.gov.za/minerals/mining_charter.stm.

85 *Piero Foresti, Laura De Carli and others v. Republic of South Africa* (ICSID Case No. ARB (AF)/07/1).

86 Eric Onstad, 'Italian Firms Sue S. Africa over Black Mining Law', *Reuters*, 9 March 2007, available at www.reuters.com.

87 Report of the UN High Commissioner of Human Rights, 'Human Rights, Trade and Investment', UN Doc. E/CN.4/Sub.2/2003/9 (2 July 2003), para. 37.

In terms of BITs in general, and stabilisation clauses in particular, it has to be said that the governments of many developing states are far more keen to secure international investment contracts than they are about aggressively pursuing a human rights legislative agenda, especially if the latter compromises the former. As is so often the case in these circumstances, it is a matter of balance. Certainly, to restate the point, the long-term effects of sustained or increasing FDI can be of great social and human rights benefit, so it ought to be encouraged. At the same time, logically and (one hopes) politically, that goal cannot constitute the basis for the state or investors arguing against making any efforts in the short term to protect and promote human rights.

Making power responsible: regulating the relationship between corporations and human rights

Throughout this chapter we have repeatedly come up against the twin problems of how to address corporate abuses of human rights, and how best to encourage corporate support for human rights. In this final section of the chapter, I turn to the question of the regulation of corporations in the specific circumstance of their relations to human rights, to look at what has been and is being done, what might be done better or done for the first time, and what are the various formats in which regulation takes place – formal and informal, as well as domestic and international.

At the most basic level, the regulatory problems posed by corporate abuses of human rights stem from what the SRSG presciently argues is a:

> fundamental institutional misalignment . . . between the scope and impact of economic forces and actors, on the one hand, and the capacity of societies to manage their adverse consequences, on the other. This misalignment creates the permissive environment within which blameworthy acts by corporations may occur without adequate sanctioning or separation. For the sake of the victims of abuse, and to sustain globalization as a positive force, this must be fixed.[88]

Such 'misalignment' and resulting 'permissiveness' are precisely the challenges that lie at the heart of my comments about the dilemma of FDI at the end of the last section. The dissonance between economic and human

---

88 Report of the SRSG on the issue of human rights and transnational corporations and other business enterprises, John Ruggie, 'Business and Human Rights: Mapping International Standards of Responsibility and Accountability for Corporate Acts', UN Doc. A/HRC/4/35 (19 February 2007), para. 3.

rights imperatives, what is more, can occur whether there is appropriate regulation in place or not. Corporate pressures – direct and indirect – can be brought to bear on governments to curtail or dilute any inclination they have towards enacting human rights related regulations that negatively affect business, or when they seek to implement or enforce existing provisions. When regulatory tools are neutered in this way, the situation can appear somewhat hopeless. When corporations are intent on acting *only* in their best commercial interests, the task to impose other obligations on them can be 'like painting on clouds'. This was how an official from the Indonesian Environment Ministry was reported as putting it, in reference to his government's abject failure to enforce environmental laws against the mining giant Freeport-McMoran in respect of its alleged poisoning of hundreds of miles of the pristine Aghawagon river basin in West Papua by dumping nearly 1 billion tons of mine waste from the Grasberg copper and gold mine, operated by one of Freeport's subsidiary companies, into the river's headwaters.[89]

Legal regulation of human rights protection, as, indeed, with all subject-matters, is all about allocating responsibility and enforcing accountability. Law is an important and useful tool in the task of bringing corporations to account for their misdemeanours and pressing them to avoid their repetition. But its success depends heavily on social and economic circumstances, administrative capacity and political will, as well as legal pronouncement, whether in domestic or international law, or both. This context needs to be borne in mind by lawyers and non-lawyers alike in the whole debate about corporations and human rights. Human rights themselves are, as this book stands testimony to, multifaceted constructs with many dimensions besides law.[90] Moreover, the making, implementation and enforcement of laws are processes that are intensely political. Melissa Lane, writing about the moral dimension of corporate accountability, notes that, 'in an imperfect world, legal accountability of corporations leaves gaping holes not only in weak states, but also in mature democracies'.[91] By this she means that powerful special interests (including those of business) are nearly always pleaded in respect of laws being

---

89 Jane Perlez and Raymond Bonner, 'Controversial US Goldmine a Law unto Itself', *Sydney Morning Herald*, 28 December 2005, p. 13.

90 I have argued this point more broadly and philosophically in 'The Legal Dimension of Human Rights', in David Kinley (ed.), *Human Rights in Australian Law: Principles, Practice and Potential* (Leichhardt, NSW: The Federation Press, 1998), p. 2.

91 Melissa Lane, 'The Moral Dimension of Corporate Accountability', in Andrew Kuper (ed.), *Global Responsibilities: Who Must Deliver on Human Rights?* (New York: Routledge, 2005), p. 233.

made (or not made); laws can be, and in some places often are, out of date or inadequate, allowing corporations to exploit weaknesses; and when corporations decide to challenge the enactment laws or their interpretation, they can muster enormous legal and financial (and sometimes political) resources to their cause that rival and often surpass those of the state. Lane concludes by noting that '[f]or all these reasons, legal accountability alone – despite its virtues of clarity and sanction – all too often falls short of the expectations for control of corporations so prominent in popular discourse today'.[92]

It is true that such expectations may be set too high to be realistically achievable, though it cannot be denied that more can and must be done to curtail human rights abuses by corporations. But legal regulation cannot be thought of as a sort of morally pure (still less, value-free) knight in shining armour, come to slay, or at least tame, the wickedness of corporations. If bolstered by the parallel policies and practices of governments, civil society, international organisations, commentators, community opinion and corporations themselves, then our legal knight is more likely to succeed. It is to the relative merits of the legal and non-legal aspects of corporate regulation on human rights matters, and especially on how the two aspects interrelate, that I dedicate the remainder of this chapter.

Corporate social responsibility (CSR) and human rights

The general, non-law context in which sits the contestation over corporations and human rights is the rather amorphous but significant notion of corporate social responsibility (CSR).[93] It is amorphous because, since the late 1990s, its boundaries have been continuously stretched, its contents defined and redefined and its manifestations in practice multiplied unendingly. Yet, despite this (or perhaps precisely because of it), CSR has increasingly gained purchase in the minds and actions of critics, commentators and corporate leaders alike. As part of an earlier research project on corporations and human rights,[94] I recall interviewing a World Bank Official working in the Bank's Corporate Governance Unit in 2003, whose interpretation of corporate governance left no room whatsoever

---

92 *Ibid.*
93 The term is so commonly and elastically used that it defies any precise definition that is 'all-embracing'; see Marcel van Marrewijk, 'Concepts and Definitions of CSR and Corporate Sustainability: Between Agency and Communion' (2003) 44 *Journal of Business Ethics* 95, at 96.
94 With former colleagues at the Castan Centre for Human Rights Law, Monash University, see www.law.monash.edu.au/castancentre/projects/mchr/.

for any non-financial considerations, including – and especially – human rights.[95] This was astounding to me then (many large corporations that we had also interviewed in the project were then aware of, if not fully conversant with, the importance of such wider stakeholder interests to their governance structures), but it is quite clear that today few corporations of any size can afford – financially or otherwise – to ignore CSR in deliberations about their governance. In this atmosphere of 'new governance', many major corporations now dedicate sizeable resources and executive effort towards building CSR into their business values or principles. Somewhat ironically, it is the irregularities and skullduggery in the domain of corporate finance, as much as in the domains of social and environmental responsibility, that have provided the impetus for greater regulatory scrutiny of all aspects of corporate behaviour. The enactment of the US's Sarbanes-Oxley Act in 2002, in response to the immense corporate scandals that engulfed Enron and Worldcom, was principally a regulatory insistence on better fiscal and financial management and accountability,[96] but it was also seen by corporations and commentators alike as medicine for a cultural malaise that afflicted corporations in their attitudes towards the concerns of the societies and environments in which they operated.[97]

There now exists a vast array of codes, principles, guidelines and standards which corporations can sign up to or have their performance measured against. Phillip Rudolph, an experienced corporate lawyer who has worked for, and with, many TNCs on this topic, reports that there are at least 1,000 codes of conduct in existence,[98] with more being developed

---

95 Emphasising the point, see the paper by two other officials from the same Corporate Governance Unit, Olivier Fremond and Mierta Capaul, entitled 'The State of Corporate Governance: Experience from Country Assessments', World Bank Policy Research Working Paper No. 2858 (June 2002), at http://ssrn.com/abstract=636222, in which the authors expressly exclude the CSR 'agenda' from their analysis, p. 1.

96 Section 406 of the statute stipulates that issuers (of securities), including public and private corporations, must adopt 'a code of ethics for senior financial officers'.

97 A sense captured most succinctly by Elliot Schrage's melodramatic but memorable line that 'it's only a matter of time before some company becomes the Enron of human rights abuse'; 'Emerging Threat: Human Rights Claims' (2003) 81(8) *Harvard Business Review* 16 ('Memorandum').

98 Phillip Rudolph, 'The History, Variations, Impact and Future of Self-Regulation', in Ramon Mullerat (ed.), *Corporate Social Responsibility: The Corporate Governance of the 21st Century* (The Hague: Kluwer Law International, 2005), p. 367; the figure of 1,000 is taken from an estimate in a World Bank publication by Gare Smith and Dan Feldman, *Company Codes of Conduct and International Standards: An Analytical Comparison (Part I)* (Washington, DC: World Bank, 2003), p. 2.

all the time, such as in respect of corporate media censorship following the internet provider scandal in China, discussed earlier. These codes range across six main categories:[99] (i) model codes, developed by inter-governmental bodies (e.g. the UN Global Compact); (ii) intergovernmental codes, concluded between governments (e.g. the OECD's Guidelines for Multinational Enterprises); (iii) multi-stakeholder codes, which are negotiated agreements often involving corporations, labour representatives, NGOs and governments (e.g. the UK Government's Ethical Trading Initiative Base Code); (iv) industry codes (nearly all major industries have such codes, including, for example, banking with the Equator Principles); (v) company codes, which many companies (and certainly all major ones) now possess, reflecting not only the standards set by whichever of the above types of code they subscribe to, but also their own particular CSR values, and which may cover strategic direction, employee and community relations, investment protocols, complaint handling, compliance monitoring, and supply-chain management; and finally (vi) compliance and verification codes, which are tools developed to assist corporations in assessing their CSR performances (e.g. Social Accountability 8000,[100] the Global Reporting Initiative Guidelines,[101] and the forthcoming (in 2010) ISO 26000 guidelines for Social Responsibility).[102]

It can be fairly said that many of these codes incorporate some human rights values, usually embedded within avowedly social and environmental standards, but few are explicitly and centrally concerned with corporate abuses, and/or promotion, of human rights. Those that are include: the Voluntary Principles on Security and Human Rights, drawn up between a number of large mining and exploration corporations, prominent human rights NGOs, and the governments of the Netherlands, Norway, the UK and the US, which are intended 'to guide companies in balancing the needs for safety while respecting human rights and fundamental freedoms';[103] Amnesty International's Human Rights Guidelines for Companies; and the UN Norms on the Responsibilities of Transnational Corporations and other Business Enterprises with Regard to Human Rights (henceforth, the 'UN Norms'), which I discuss in detail below.

---

99 Drawing directly on Rudolph's typology for the first five listed categories; *ibid.* See also Josep Lozano and María Prandi, 'Corporate Social Responsibility and Human Rights', in Mullerat, *Corporate Social Responsibility*, p. 183.

100 www.sa-intl.org.   101 www.globalreporting.org.

102 www.iso.org/sr.   103 See www.voluntaryprinciples.org.

The position today is that even arch-critics of CSR – like Clive Crook, the former deputy editor of *The Economist* – accept that 'today, corporate social responsibility, if it is nothing else, is the tribute that capitalism everywhere pays to virtue'.[104] Though somewhat sardonically put, Crook's words highlight what has, in effect, been a long 'love/hate' relationship with the principles of CSR, if not (at least not until more recently) the formalised term itself. In terms of process, CSR has been about trying to take issues that have been traditionally seen as outside the purview of business and move them into the sphere of what business is, or ought to be, concerned with. In terms of substance, the field has had many contenders, from the earliest days of making corporations treat their workforces as human beings rather than merely a commodity, through matters of product safety and consumer protection, to more recent concerns over environmental protection, disclosure and transparency, ethical business practices and investment, local community welfare, and human rights, including both civil and political, and economic, social and cultural rights. The stakeholders that may express these concerns about a business now stretch beyond merely its shareholders (and even they are now much less the homogenous, dividend-seeking bloc that they were once assumed to be), to include employees, governments, local communities, civil society, project financiers and international organisations. Claire Moore Dickerson even goes so far as to assert that 'the source of this different understanding of corporate social responsibility . . . is a general change in perception, which increasingly conforms to norms of the East and South, and which is reflected in the evolving human rights norms'.[105]

That said, corporations are, generally, disinclined to take on board such a varied array of interests, actors and objects that are seen as, at best, on the periphery of their core business. This is the 'hate' dimension of the relationship, and it is what fuels CSR critics who see that such distractions from a corporation's core concerns (centrally, to make a profit in whatever they do) is neither good for business nor legitimate.[106] On the other hand, capitalism and corporations are nothing if not enterprising and opportunistic. This is the basis for the 'love' dimension. It did not take long for many corporations to appreciate that if this is what stakeholders really want (and they are, after all, potential consumers, financiers, regulators,

104 Clive Crook, 'The Good Company', *The Economist*, 20 January 2005, p. 4.
105 Claire Moore Dickerson, 'Human Rights: The Emerging Norm of Corporate Social Responsibility' (2001–2) 76 *Tulane Law Review* 1431, at 1433.
106 Martin Wolf, 'Sleep-walking with the Enemy', *Financial Times*, 16 May 2001, p. 21.

opinion-makers), then that is what they should deliver, provided, crucially, that in the process they continue to make profits. 'Enlightened
self-interest' is how some have put it,[107] which, as exemplified by the
highly successful 'Fair Trade Certification' programme, aims to secure
labour, social and environmental standards for producers, at the same
time as making profits for retailers.[108]

For a time, terms such as 'triple bottom line' (that is: profit, society and
environment) held sway, but thankfully this particular tag is now hardly
ever heard, having been consigned to the oxymoronic dustbin (profit is the
only *bottom* line, the other two are just – quite rightly – conditions that are
imposed on how that profit is generated).[109] Companies now frequently
refer to needing to earn their 'social licence to operate',[110] which, at least
at one level of interpretation, is not at all a new concept. As discussed
earlier, corporations are entirely products of society in the sense that it is
society, through the state, that both facilitates and regulates the existence
of corporations and what it is they can and cannot do. However, today
there is usually more invested in the label. Some in the corporate world see
the whole CSR enterprise to be something largely outside (and typically
trying to ward off) state regulation. According to this view, CSR entails no
more than a voluntary adherence to principles that are seen as reflections
of community expectations, whatever the law might actually demand.
Examples of this include the setting of social and/or environmental targets
that are 'beyond compliance'; investing in local communities (it is now not
uncommon for extractive industry corporations working in developing
states to assist in providing health care, school education, transport or
communication facilities); and institutionalised corporate philanthropy
(as discussed below).

In part, of course, this is just good risk management; avoiding community 'outrage', as my colleague Katherine Teh-White calls it, over corporate insensitivity to, or contempt towards, social or environmental

---

107 See the report of the Australian Parliamentary Joint Committee on Corporations and
    Financial Services, *Corporate Responsibility: Managing Risks and Creating Value* (Can-
    berra: Parliamentary Joint Committee on Corporations and Financial Services, 2006),
    at para. 4.76; and 'Just Good Business: A Special Report on Corporate Social Responsi-
    bility', *The Economist*, 19 January 2008, p. 21.
108 See www.fairtrade.net.
109 This is the point I was making in chapter 1 concerning Milton Friedman's notorious
    remarks on the subject of corporate objectives.
110 For example, mining giant Anglo American's *Report to Society 2006*, which talks of
    'maintaining a social license to operate'; available at www.investis.com/aa/development/
    sdreports/gr/2007gr/sc-engagement.htm.

standards.[111] There can be little doubt that personal vanity and ambition also play their powerful parts in corporate decision-making in this regard. This may be taken too far at times, with fanciful claims being made of corporate intentions. For example, it is surely somewhat gauche at best for Indra Nooyi, the Chairperson and CEO of PepsiCo, to prescribe that alongside financial results, 'large companies' must also 'ensur[e] that their products contribute positively and responsibly to sustaining human civilization'.[112] But Geoff Brennan and Philip Pettit (economist and philosopher, respectively) are on to something in their thought-provoking book *The Economy of Esteem*, when they argue that in addition to the two celebrated drivers of economic and social order – the 'invisible hand' of the market and the 'iron hand' of the state – there is a third, the 'intangible hand' of esteem, which today is far less studied and understood in the social sciences.[113] Brennan and Pettit associate the desires of individuals to secure personal esteem (directly, or indirectly through that bestowed on institutions with which they are intimately connected) with the social phenomenon of community expectations of, and pronouncements on, who or what deserves to be held in esteem.[114] Business leaders fit neatly into this framework, where their actions, or the actions of the corporations they run, have the potential to attract esteem or disesteem, by way of good or bad publicity, respectively. For businesses today – certainly for those of any size or prominence – publicity is something they have to expect. For them, they simply cannot be 'confident that the things [they] do will be unobserved', especially, one might add, in the field of human rights.[115] For many corporations and their CEOs, therefore, rather than shun publicity regarding human rights specifically, and their CSR profile generally, they have learnt to accept and even embrace it. Corporate executives are increasingly keen to assure public gatherings that, when they gaze into the proverbial bathroom mirror in the morning, they really do want to be able to say, without blinking, that they are proud, or at least have a clear conscience, about what it is their company does and how it does it. Not all of them, at all times, can

111 See www.futureye.com/team_katherine.php; Teh-White is the Managing Director of
     Futureye.
112 Indra Nooyi, 'The Responsible Company', in *The World in 2008* (London: The
     Economist, 2007), p. 143.
113 Geoff Brennan and Philip Pettit, *The Economy of Esteem: An Essay on Civil and Political
     Society* (Oxford and New York: Oxford University Press, 2004), pp. 4–5.
114 Referring to the latter as 'civil society', *ibid.* p. 5.   115 *Ibid.* p. 185.

do so with such candour, of course, but the sentiment is clear: business leaders care about their corporation's image and their own reputation and self-esteem.

A singularly clear manifestation of this concern is the phenomenon of institutionalised corporate philanthropy. From Rockefeller and Ford, through to Buffett and Gates, the tradition has been built, especially in the United States.[116] There can be no doubt that for these corporate and individual giants, and, on much smaller scales, for many other executives, their concerns stem from what they consider to be their social responsibilities that lie alongside their commercial obligations. Thus, for Bill and Melinda Gates, the fundamental reason why they established their foundation was because, as they say, 'we benefited from great schools, great health care, and a vibrant economic system. That is why we feel a tremendous responsibility to give back to society.'[117] Though, no matter how big the pay-back – and the Gates Foundation's is unquestionably impressive[118] – such philanthropy does not beatify; 'philanthropy no more canonises the good businessman than it exculpates the bad', as *The Economist* tartly observes.[119]

Important though it is, focusing too intently on the business case for CSR undermines its rationale (it is concerned with business 'responsibility' not 'opportunity'), and it leaves the enterprise open to abuse. Such a 'limited form of CSR', as Tom Campbell points out in characteristically prescient fashion, 'amounts to little more than intelligent business practice that enhances long-term profitability, to the virtual exclusion of responsibilities that are not just justifiable in terms of the economic interests of the corporations in question'.[120] Campbell argues that 'the real

116 It might be noted that the manifestation of corporate philanthropy as a matter of CSR appears to be a particular Anglo-American phenomenon; see 'Corporate Social Responsibility: In a Global Context', in Andrew Crane, Dirk Matten and Laura J. Spence (eds.), *Corporate Social Responsibility: Readings and Cases in a Global Context* (New York: Routledge, 2008), p. 3, at p. 13. I am grateful to Karin Buhmann for raising this point with me.

117 'Letter from Bill and Melinda Gates', at www.gatesfoundation.org/AboutUs/OurValues/GatesLetter/default.htm.

118 According to its 2007 Annual Report, the Foundation has $38.7 billion in assets; had given away $3 billion in 2007, and had already approved a further $4.4 billion for disbursement in 2008; see www.gatesfoundation.org/nr/public/media/annualreports/annualreport07/AR2007Financials.html.

119 'The Meaning of Bill Gates', *The Economist*, 28 June 2008, p. 16.

120 Tom Campbell, 'The Normative Grounding of the Corporate Social Responsibility: A Human Rights Approach', in Doreen McBarnet, Aurora Voiculescu and Tom Campbell

crunch questions in CSR concern what to do when the business case does not hold because it is not economically wise for a particular economic unit or business sector to "do the right thing".[121] There are two answers to this proposition. The first is that in reality, after all other things are taken into consideration, corporations will still opt for the least bad of the economic choices before them, so in that sense these will have made a business case for their actions, however unpalatable these might be in absolute terms. The second is that Campbell's observation effectively marks the boundary between that which can reasonably be expected of voluntary CSR, and that which has to be mandated by law.

The voluntarism of CSR has its critics as well as its supporters, but the debate and practice have now reached a stage of maturity such that CSR can no longer (if ever it could) be seen as a law-free domain. Not least, this is due to the fact that, as Phillip Rudolph says, '[l]awyers typically represent the front lines in the development of documents and tools intended to embed these [CSR] expectations into commercial relationships. More and more deals are requiring, as part of the due diligence process, an assessment of CSR-related activities and risks.'[122] But it is also due to the dawning realisation that it is not necessarily true that 'you can never have too much of a good thing'. For in so far as CSR initiatives can, broadly, be seen as good things, the facts of their multiplication and their kaleidoscopic coverage and format have provided fertile grounds for confusion, and evasion. This is the salutary message that John Conley and Cynthia Williams draw from their empirical study of the implications (including for human rights) of CSR practices in mainly UK and US corporations. So apparent to them was the skill and stealth with which many corporations were able to exploit this circumstance that they were moved to conclude that 'Foucault himself could not have conjured a better example of the exercise of power through subtle and distributed disciplinary practices'.[123] The prospect of direction, or at least hierarchy, being established through legal regulation (whether of the hard or soft law variety) is therefore not only appealing, but necessary.

(eds.), *The New Corporate Accountability: Corporate Social Responsibility and the Law* (Cambridge: Cambridge University Press, 2007), p. 530.

121 *Ibid.* p. 531.

122 Phillip Rudolph, 'The Central Role of Lawyers in Managing, Minimizing, and Responding to Responsibility Risks – A US Perspective', in Mullerat, *Corporate Social Responsibility*, p. 318.

123 John Conley and Cynthia Williams, 'Engage, Embed, and Embellish: Theory versus Practice in the Corporate Social Responsibility Movement' (2005–6) 31 *Journal of Corporation Law* 1, at 34.

Hard law and soft law approaches

In fact, there is already plenty of law regarding the human rights obligations of corporations. As I have argued elsewhere,[124] domestic laws governing occupational health and safety, labour and workplace relations, anti-discrimination, privacy, environmental protection, property rights, freedom of expression, fair trial (complaints handling and disciplinary procedures) and criminal prohibitions (such as against physical abuse, fraud and corruption, and property offences) are typically found in the statute books of developed countries. Further, they are also, increasingly, to be found in developing countries, as the twin forces of global economic order and the rule of law propagate them, and the demands of regulatory certainty and fairness become ever more insistent.[125] Across and within nations, these laws are, of course, incomplete and imperfect, but the records of the state courts and tribunals that enforce them, such as they are, against corporations on a daily basis are testimony to the prevalence and importance of existing community expectations about corporate observance of human rights standards.

In all the debates about whether, or which, or how human rights obligations apply to corporations, it is important to remember that this array of legal regulation already exists. Too often the fact is overlooked by those blinded by their zeal to protect their position in the human rights and corporations debate. This, for example, was the effect of the barely disguised contempt with which some in the business world greeted the proposition that consideration be given to making TNCs in some way responsible for their human rights abuses at international law. In its lengthy submission to the OHCHR inquiry into the legal relationship between corporations and human rights (that was prompted by the 2003 UN Human Rights Norms for Corporations), the Confederation of British Industry achieved the astounding feat of not once acknowledging the breadth of domestic human rights and human rights related laws to which companies in the UK (and elsewhere) are already subject; an omission that it underlined by blandly stating that 'the principal, and practically

---

124 David Kinley, 'Human Rights as Legally Binding or Merely Relevant?', in David Kinley and Stephen Bottomley (eds.), *Commercial Law and Human Rights* (Aldershot: Ashgate Dartmouth, 2002), p. 25.

125 See David Trubek, 'The "Rule of Law" in Development Assistance: Past, Present and Future', in David Trubek and Alvaro Santos (eds.), *The New Law and Economic Development: A Critical Appraisal* (New York: Cambridge University Press, 2006), p. 74 at pp. 84–6.

the sole, source of human rights law is conventions in force', as if state legislatures (and a few hundred years of domestic jurisprudence) were simply non-existent.[126]

The regulatory questions that are to be addressed in this field are, therefore, concerned with how much further corporations should be made to wade into the waters of human rights, rather than with deliberations about whether they should get their feet wet in the first place. Peter Muchlinski, in his prodigious work on all aspects of the legal status of TNCs, correctly characterises the issue as arguments for and against the extension of corporations' human rights responsibilities.[127]

Domestic legislation, policies and practices regarding the requirements made of corporations to protect and promote human rights and the consequences of their breach must continue to be the most significant and effective vehicles to enunciate and enforce such responsibilities. This is all well and good, and while, evidently, not all states utilise their regulatory frameworks sufficiently and effectively in this regard, such limitations are due to variations in political will, administrative capacity and economic imperatives, *not* a lack of jurisdictional competence. What has been of vital importance to much of the debate about corporations and human rights since the late 1990s (and to my focus in this book on the global economy) is when the human rights actions of the corporations in questions are *trans*national: that is to say, when the corporation is legally incorporated in one (home) state, while it conducts its operations in another or other (host) states. The crux of this matter is when the human rights laws that apply to corporations differ significantly, in form and/or substance, between the home and host states. For such legal gaps in human rights protections lead, almost inevitably, to their neglect and abuse in practice. Though such gaps can appear between any two states, they are most obvious and potentially most damaging when the corporation's home state is a rich, liberal state in the West, and the host state is a poor, weakly governed state in the developing world.

---

126 Submission by letter (from John Cridland, Deputy Director-General, CBI) and annexures, headed 'Request from the Office of the UN Commissioner for Human Rights', 4 August 2004, at Annex B, para. 6; see www.ohchr.org/english/issues/ globalization/business/contributions.htm. This misunderstanding of such a basic point of international and constitutional law is made all the more remarkable by the fact that it relies on the advice of a senior English barrister briefed by the CBI.

127 Peter Muchlinski, *Multinational Enterprises and the Law*, 2nd edn (Oxford and New York: Oxford University Press, 2007), pp. 514–18.

Adopting the perspective of the victims (or potential victims) of abuse in these circumstances, there exist four possibilities by which legal regulation might possibly address corporate infractions and provide redress for the abused.

First, most directly, international and domestic pressure (from other states, international organisations, civil society and even corporations themselves) might be put on the states to plug the gaps in their own laws regarding corporate behaviour within their jurisdiction, by enactment of legislation where there is none or it is inadequate, or enforcing that which exists but is ignored or easily evaded. In situations of states with weak governance, however, this is of course to invest in hope more than expectation. By definition, weakly governed states lack capacity and probably political will, and many egregious breaches involving corporations are perpetrated jointly with (and often principally by) state organs themselves. In such cases this may be a pointless exercise – like 'throwing water at the sun', as I recall one Burmese activist putting it to me regarding efforts to raise the human rights consciousness of the ruling Junta there – and points of legal leverage will have to be sought elsewhere.

The second possibility is the extension of the extra-territorial reach of strong-state laws, effectively to make corporations liable at home (under home-state law) for their actions overseas (despite host-state laws). Extra-territoriality has many legal guises,[128] including, most directly, the criminalisation of acts taken by individuals or other legal persons, including corporations, offshore – relatively common examples of which include sex tourism, drug trafficking, terrorism activities and war crimes.[129] Tort liability is another example, in respect of offences against persons, negligence resulting in egregious harm such as severe environmental damage or, most notoriously, breaches of fundamental international legal norms, as with the US's revivified *Alien Torts Claims Act* (ATCA), provided that such norms are 'specific, obligatory and universal'.[130] In addition, other

---

128 Surya Deva, 'Acting Extraterritorially To Tame Multinational Corporations for Human Rights Violations: Who Should "Bell the Cat"?' (2004) 5 *Melbourne Journal of International Law* 37.

129 See Eric Engle, 'Extraterritorial Corporate Criminal Liability: A Remedy for Human Rights Violations?' (2006) 20 *St. John's Journal of Legal Commentary* 287, at 291.

130 As stipulated in the US Supreme Court's landmark decision in *Sosa v. Alvarez-Machain* 542 U.S. 692 (2004), at 732; see further Lucien Dhooge, 'Lohengrin Revealed: The Implications of *Sosa v. Alvarez-Machain* for Human Rights Litigation Pursuant to the Alien Tort Claims Act' (2006) 28 *Loyola of Los Angeles International and Comparative Law Review* 393. Also see Joanna Kyriakakis, 'Freeport in West Papua: Bringing Corporations

laws or legal techniques may have a facilitative extra-territorial capacity in this regard. Corporations laws, for example, regulate the nature and extent of legal liability of corporations for the actions of their overseas subsidiaries,[131] which can include actions that violate human rights, and there have been various attempts (so far unsuccessful) in Australia, the UK and the US to enact 'corporate code of conduct' legislation that would bind corporations, and/or their directors, in respect of their conduct overseas.[132] Use by corporations of *forum non conveniens* (FNC) to deflect litigation from home-state courts (which are normally far more rigorous, less tolerant and more punitively minded of corporate indiscretions than host-state courts) has also been watered down in certain common law courts in which it is applicable. As a result, this peculiar, but important, determinant of the jurisdictional competence (determining, that is, whether a home-state court has the power to hear a case regarding action taken in another state's jurisdiction, and if so, whether it should) has effectively extended the extra-territorial reach of home-state courts in cases where they are *not* 'seen as a clearly inappropriate forum'.[133] Such a broad interpretation of the doctrine allows considerable latitude to home-state courts as the onus is placed on the party claiming the defence of FNC to demonstrate that the home-state courts are indeed clearly inappropriate. Finally, the international legal facility of 'universal jurisdiction' – whereby states 'have jurisdiction to define and prescribe punishment for certain offenses recognized by the community of nations as of universal concern'[134] – has also been used by states to arrogate

---

to Account for the International Human Rights Abuses under Australian Criminal and Tort Law' (2005) 31 *Monash University Law Review* 95.

131   See *Lubbe and Others v. Cape Plc* [2000] 1 WLR 1545, in which the House of Lords, rejecting the defendant's argument of *forum non conveniens*, demolished attempts of a parent company to distance itself from the damage done by its asbestos mining subsidiary in South Africa.

132   Adam McBeth, 'A Look at Corporate Code of Conduct Legislation' (2004) 33 *Common Law World Review* 222.

133   This is the formulation that prevails in Australian courts as enunciated in *Oceanic Sun Line Special Shipping Company Inc v. Fay* [1988] HCA 32, per Deane J, at para. 18. In the UK, FNC was also similarly removed as an effective defence against removal of cases to home-state courts in *Connelly v. RTZ Corporation Plc and Others* [1998] AC 854. For a discussion of the much more limited inroads into the defensive use of *forum non conveniens* in the US, see Malcolm Rogge, 'Towards Transnational Corporate Accountability in the Global Economy: Challenging the Doctrine on *Forum Non Conveniens* in *In re*: Union Carbide, Alfaro, Sequihua, and Aguinda' (2001) 36 *Texas International Law Journal* 299.

134   These are the defining words used in the *Restatement (Third), The Foreign Relations Law of the United States (1987)*, section 404.

extra-territorial powers to their courts, which power might conceivably extend to corporations.[135]

All that said, such extra-territoriality in the specific respect of corporate behaviour that affects human rights is relatively rare, certainly as compared to normal, intra-territorial, law. It is a potentially highly charged, political issue. Extra-territorial laws emanate almost exclusively from Western states and are therefore seen by many developing states as, at best, presumptuous and somewhat patronising, and, at worst, imperialist challenges to their sovereignty.[136] In the home states themselves, the device can also be subject to intense political pressure – from those activists in favour, and, more significantly in terms of lobbying power, from the business community against such extended jurisdictional reach in respect of corporate activity. Indeed, the failures of the national corporate code of conduct bills mentioned above bear testimony to business's lobbying power,[137] and there can be no doubt that the ATCA would have met the same fate were it not for the fact that it was enacted more than two hundred years ago in 1789 (and with no intention that it would apply to corporations in the way pursued at least since the mid 1990s).

The benefit of extra-territorial legislation in this area for those whose human rights are abused is that it provides a potential alternative forum in which to pursue their claims against corporations. Sarah Joseph, in her meticulous review of corporations and transnational human rights litigation, asks us to consider whether 'it is unfair to TNCs for them to be subjected to forum-shopping in the law of their home state, or a state in

135 For an overview of the various forms of implementation of universal jurisdiction in the common law and civil law jurisdictions of Europe, see Human Rights Watch, *Universal Jurisdiction in Europe: The State of the Art* (June 2006), Vol. 18, No. 5(D). It should also be noted here that officers of corporations, as individuals, may be subject to the jurisdiction of the International Criminal Court for grave breaches of international law, including genocide, war crimes, crimes against humanity and the crime of aggression; *Rome Statute of the International Criminal Court 2000*, Articles 6–9.

136 In fact, sometimes developing countries actively support litigation in the courts of a corporation's home state rather than their own precisely in order to pursue higher damages claims. This was the position adopted by the Indian Government in the Bhopal case discussed at the beginning of this chapter.

137 Though, in Australia, it seems that this issue might be put to the test once again, following the Rudd Government's decision in June 2008 to support a Parliamentary motion to consider 'the development of measures to prevent the involvement or complicity of Australian companies in activities that may result in the abuse of human rights, including by fostering a corporate culture that is respectful of human rights in Australia and overseas', see Oxfam Australia media release, 23 June 2008, at www.reports-and-materials.org/Oxfam-Australia-on-parliament-motion-23-Jun-2008.doc.

which they do business, rather than the laws of the country in which they are operating'.[138] To which she answers, convincingly,

> TNCs themselves have shopped around for the best investment conditions, simultaneously promoting a 'race to the bottom' in developing countries, for example, in terms of environmental and labor standards. Forum shopping is the flipside of the jurisdiction-shopping of TNCs; should not both TNCs and their apparent victims be able to play the game of globalisation? The orthodoxy which promotes the unique freedom from regulation for TNCs, in that their various components which usually operate as a single economic entity are not regulated by the laws of any single state, enabling the apportionment of legal responsibility according to least risk without any concern for humanitarian consequences, is unsatisfactory. Economic globalisation, which confers huge benefits on TNCs, should be accompanied by the imposition of transnational responsibilities by a parallel globalisation of law. In this respect it is poignant to add that the putative forum-shoppers in the salient cases are innocent people who have been severely hurt by TNCs, and who are probably unable to receive appropriate recompense in the forum where the injury occurred. The 'intolerable double standard' that denies victims in the developing world but not the developed world relief from severe corporate maltreatment should not continue.[139]

Joseph's 'globalisation of law' in respect of the human rights obligations of corporations, however, has not been, and will not be, achieved on the back of extra-territorial laws alone. Even their most celebrated manifestation, the now much litigated ATCA, has so far yielded just one concluded trial (and then in favour of the corporation),[140] and one notable out of court settlement.[141] This is despite dozens of high-profile cases having

---

138 Sarah Joseph, *Corporations and Transnational Human Rights Litigation* (Oxford: Hart Publishing, 2004), p. 150.

139 *Ibid.* pp. 150–1.

140 On 26 July 2007, an Alabama jury found the coal corporation, Drummond, not to be guilty of complicity in the 2001 murder of three union leaders at one of its mines in Colombia; *In Re Juan Aguas Romero v. Drummond Company, Inc., et al.*, United States District Court for the Northern District of Alabama (Case No. 702-CV-00665). At the time of writing, the plaintiff had appealed to the Eleventh Circuit Court of Appeals.

141 Appeals pending in the *Unocal* litigation were dismissed by the Ninth Circuit Court of Appeals following the settlement of the case: see *John Doe I v. Unocal Corp.* 403 F.3d 708 (9th Cir. 2005). For a discussion of the settlement, see Rachel Chambers, 'The *Unocal* Settlement: Implications for the Developing Law on Corporate Complicity in Human Rights Abuses' (2005) 13(1) *Human Rights Brief* 14; and see EarthRights International, 'Historic Advance for Universal Human Rights: Unocal to Compensate Burmese Villagers', 2 April 2005, at www.earthrights.org/legalfeature/historic_advance_for_universal_human_rights_unocal_to_compensate_burmese_villagers.html.

been brought against some of the world's largest companies,[142] alleging human rights abuses including complicity in murder, forced and child labour, assault, rape, forced relocation and expropriation, and aiding and abetting apartheid. As a means to publicise the alleged bad deeds of corporations, the ATCA is a useful if somewhat quixotic instrument.[143] As a tool for effective and efficient legal regulation, it is quite another matter. With the insider knowledge of having represented a number of ATCA plaintiffs coupled with the big-picture perspective of a scholar, Harold Koh recognises the statute for what it really is: an extremely limited, highly conditional, litigable instrument of last resort.[144] To be sure, it is an important, indeed vital, backstop, but it does not and cannot serve as a central plank in any regulatory programme to address corporate abuses of human rights standards.

My third and fourth regulatory possibilities are both situated in the same transnational sphere and, though very different and controversial in their own ways, together offer the prospect of bolstering a more globalised perspective of the legal regulation of corporations in regard to human rights protections.

The third possible avenue relates to the human rights standards contained in transnational codes of conduct, developed by industry peak bodies, governments and NGOs or by TNCs themselves. Though soft law and, in the main, entirely voluntary initiatives, such codes nonetheless provide the foundations for harder legal regulation, not only because they constitute the policy firmament from which future domestic and international laws are likely to develop, but also because corporations, in their desire to stipulate standards and to proclaim their adherence to

---

142 Including Coca-Cola, Chevron, Chiquita, ExxonMobil, Nestlé, Shell, Texaco, Yahoo! and Wal-Mart. For an overview, see Beth Stephens *et al.*, *International Human Rights Litigation in US Courts* (Leiden: Martinus Nijhoff, 2008 (2nd edn)), pp. 309–33.

143 On which see the comments by Richard Herz, a lawyer from Earth Rights International which has been actively involved in a number of ATCA cases, including the Unocal case, regarding how the statute can be used as a powerful shaming tool: 'Holding Multinational Corporations Accountable for Human and Environmental Rights Abuses', in David Barnhizer (ed.), *Effective Strategies for Protecting Human Rights: Economic Sanctions, Use of National Courts and International Fora and Coercive Power* (Aldershot: Ashgate, 2001), p. 263.

144 Harold Koh, 'Separating Myth from Reality about Corporate Responsibility Litigation' (2004) 7 *Journal of International Economic Law* 263. Koh specifically notes that these conditions (as to forum and personal jurisdiction; compliance with the Statute of Limitations; nature of breaches of international law amounting to complicity in a state crime; and meeting the substantial burden of proof linking cause to effect) constitute 'very high multiple barriers to recovery' under the statute; at 269.

them, are in effect engaging in commercial speech – or, to put it more directly, in marketing.[145] All developed states, and many strictly so, have trade practices rules governing false advertising, and misleading or deceptive conduct such that a company is prevented from making any false or misleading claims in an effort to entreat you to purchase their products. In a landmark case brought against Nike in California, anti-corporate activist Marc Kasky claimed that he had been so entreated to buy a pair of Nike shoes on the basis of the company's self-declared good human rights business practice of not engaging sweat-shop labour in the manufacture of its products, only for him later to discover, he alleged, that the claims were false. The veracity of Kasky's allegations was never tested in court as the case was settled,[146] but the point was made that specific claims as to one's human rights practices can be just as strictly regulated as are those made in respect of the quality of one's stitching, or the curative effects of one's drugs, or the longevity of one's battery life. Rather curiously, there have been few repetitions of such litigation under similar trade practices and competition laws in other developed states, but the prospect of such litigation appears to have had the salutary effect of making corporations think more carefully about the justifications for their public pronouncements about their respect for or compliance with human rights standards. That is despite the somewhat dire and blinkered claims of both corporations and civil liberties organisations (like the American Civil Liberties Union),[147] that such commercial requirements infringe constitutional (that is First Amendment) free speech and have a chilling effect on corporate engagement in discussion of CSR and human rights concerns.[148]

---

145 Codes might also be framed and adopted in ways that make them contractually binding, such as when comprising part of a contractual agreement between a company and its suppliers.

146 Following controversy over working conditions in Nike's supply chain, Nike embarked on a public relations campaign claiming that it had improved conditions for overseas workers. In 1998, Marc Kasky filed a claim in California, alleging misleading advertising by Nike. The central legal issue was whether Nike's public statements were 'commercial speech' or 'political speech'– if the former, then Nike was subject to advertising and competition laws; if the latter, then Nike could rely on its First Amendment right to free speech. In 2002 the Supreme Court of California found in favour of Kasky (see *Kasky v. Nike, Inc.* 27 Cal. 4th 939 (2002)). Nike appealed to the US Supreme Court, which initially granted leave to appeal, but later determined not to decide the issue: *Nike, Inc. v. Kasky* 539 U.S. 654 (2003). In September 2003 the case was settled, with Nike agreeing to pay $1.5 million to the Fair Labor Association.

147 See its *amicus* brief in the *Nike v. Kasky* case, at www.aclu.org/FilesPDFs/nike.pdf.

148 See Ronald Collins and David Skover, 'The Landmark Free-Speech Case That Wasn't: The *Nike v. Kasky* Story' (2004) 54 *Case Western Reserve Law Review* 965.

The fourth possibility is perhaps the most ambitious as it entails pro-posals for the regulation of corporate entities regarding human rights under international law. There are in fact two dimensions to this possibil-ity. One is actively to encourage such international human rights bodies as the committees that oversee the implementation of the main UN human rights treaties, to make more use of their existing authority to press sig-natory states to do more within their respective jurisdictions to protect and promote human rights, *including* in respect of relevant acts of com-mission or omission by corporations. Some of these committees, through their consideration of periodic reports, hearings of individual commu-nications, and publication of General Comments, do already inquire of states what they are doing in this regard, make specific suggestions as to how they might do it better, and indicate more broadly how corporations might assist, or be required to assist, in the domestic protection of human rights. An SRSG survey of the position in respect of the UN's core human rights treaties concludes that 'an examination of the treaties and treaty bodies' commentary and jurisprudence . . . confirms that the duty to pro-tect includes preventing corporations – both national and transnational, publicly or privately owned – from breaching rights and taking steps to punish them and provide reparation to victims when they do so'.[149] In actual practice, however, moves to extend this duty to cover corporations are still in their infancy. Such moves also rely on the very entities that give us cause for concern about their competence to regulate effectively the errant activities of corporations – namely, states, and especially weakly governed states.

The other dimension is to seek to establish some form of international legal regime under which corporations might also be held *directly* liable for breaches of particular human rights standards, thereby, where needs be, avoiding the intermediary of state action. This is where the contro-versy begins. For while the first of these two international law options is unremarkable (if yet wanting in will and capacity), the second is more revolutionary because it promotes the as yet nascent idea that interna-tional law can apply to, and bind, non-state entities as well as states. As such, the notion has attracted both unprecedented levels of debate between all parties (not itself a bad thing, of course), and, as Rachel Chambers and I have remarked elsewhere, 'a potent mix of distrust and

---

149 SRSG, *State Responsibilities To Regulate and Adjudicate Corporate Activities under the United Nations Core Human Rights Treaties* (12 February 2007), para. 7, at www.humanrights.ch/home/upload/pdf/070410_ruggie_2.pdf.

suspicion, vested interests, politics and economics has given rise to a great deal of grand-standing and cant'.[150] The focus of so much of this debate and controversy has, at least since their 'publication' in 2003, been on the UN Human Rights Norms for Corporations.[151] It was in August that year that a UN body of experts – the Sub-Commission on the Protection and Promotion of Human Rights – endorsed the Norms and committed them for consideration the following year by the then Commission on Human Rights, comprising the state representatives.[152] There was nothing especially unusual in this process, and nor was the treaty format in which the Norms were drafted especially remarkable. In the main, the human rights included in the Norms were somewhat predictable[153] – non-discrimination, security of persons, workers' rights and children's rights.[154] The Norms, like so many UN human rights instruments before them, were, in effect, being submitted for consideration, debate, amendment, acceptance or rejection.[155] The ensuing furore, however, inside and outside the Commission, saw battle lines quickly drawn between states, human rights activists and corporate representatives that had the curious consequence of entrenching the existing contents and format of the Norms, as if they were already written in stone, rather than opening up the issue for broader discussion using the Norms as a starting point. Almost immediately, therefore, the debate became frustratingly narrow in focus – the arid terrain of lawyers (and quasi-lawyers) arguing over such drafting

---

150   David Kinley and Rachel Chambers, 'The UN Human Rights Norms for Corporations: The Private Implications of Public International Law' (2006) 6 *Human Rights Law Review* 447, at 447–8.

151   'Norms on the Responsibilities of Transnational Corporations and Other Business Enterprises with Regard to Human Rights', UN Doc. E/CN.4/Sub.2/2003/12/Rev.2 (26 August 2003).

152   Sub-Commission on the Promotion and Protection of Human Rights, Resolution 2003/16 of 13 August 2003, UN Doc. E/CN.4/Sub.2/RES/2003/16; and see Commission on Human Rights, Decision 2004/116 of 20 April 2004, UN Doc. E/CN.4/DEC/2004/116.

153   For further discussion of the reasons why these and other human rights are predictably applicable to corporations see David Kinley and Junko Tadaki, 'From Talk to Walk: The Emergence of Human Rights Responsibilities for Corporations at International Law' (2004) 44 *Virginia Journal of International Law* 931, at 960–93.

154   There was also the peculiar (but not irrational) inclusion of consumer protection and environmental protection as 'human rights', as well as the stipulation of a state's right – namely, as a sovereign entity – not to have its efforts to protect and promote human rights inhibited by corporate action.

155   See the article by David Weissbrodt (a member of the Sub-Commission and the primary architect of the Norms) and Muria Kruger, 'Norms on the Responsibilities of Transnational Corporations and Other Business Enterprises with Regard to Human Rights' (2003) 97 *American Journal of International Law* 901.

points as: if states are to be the 'primary' bearers of human rights responsibilities, what is the nature and extent of secondary responsibilities of corporations; and to that end, what is meant by 'sphere of influence' as it might apply to the legal obligations of corporations; and if international human rights obligations are to apply directly to corporations, how will their compliance be policed and enforced?

Let me be clear: I consider these to be important questions, but they were not the right – that is to say, the most important – questions to be asking at that time, or even now, and here I admit to tramping, with a number of colleagues, all over the terrain, albeit hunting oases.[156] To some degree, it was just this sort of need to stand back and put things in perspective that motivated the Human Rights Commission to recommend that the UN Secretary-General appoint a special representative, inter alia, to 'elaborate on the role of States in effectively regulating and adjudicating the role of transnational corporations and other business enterprises with regard to human rights, including through international cooperation'.[157] Professor John Ruggie, a political scientist from Harvard University with long experience working in and with the UN, was duly appointed in July 2005, and has since had his original two-year term extended twice, most recently for a further three years from June 2008.[158] Ruggie's tenure in the position has been marked by extraordinary energy; a commendable willingness to engage and openness to debate; a determination to find common ground and move off that which has been 'poisoned'; and a prodigious output of well-researched, succinct and readable reports and papers.[159] Through his work he has helped to broaden and broadcast the debate, and to harness some of the goodwill and better understanding generated by the very fact of so much debate (albeit some of it heated), and has managed to chart some way forward.

However, the SRSG has not been able to avoid getting bogged down in the trench warfare over the Norms. To be fair, he was explicit from

---

156 Kinley and Tadaki, 'From Talk to Walk'; Kinley and Chambers, 'The UN Human Rights Norms for Corporations'; David Kinley, Justine Nolan and Natalie Zerial, 'The Politics of Corporate Social Responsibility: Reflections on the United Nations Human Rights Norms for Corporations' (2007) 25 *Company and Securities Law Journal* 30; and David Kinley and Justine Nolan, 'Trading and Aiding Human Rights: Corporations in the Global Economy' (2007) 4 *Nordic Journal of Human Rights* 353.

157 Commission on Human Rights, Resolution 2005/69 of 15 April 2005, para. 1(b), UN Doc. E/CN.4/2005/L.87.

158 Human Rights Council, Resolution 8/7 of 18 June 2008, UN Doc. A/HRC/RES/8/7.

159 See SRSG's site on the Business and Human Rights website, at www.business-humanrights.org/Gettingstarted/UNSpecialRepresentative.

the outset that he felt compelled to wade into the debate in order to pull the two sides apart and try to bring the discussion back to first principles: how corporations relate to human rights at present; what regulations states already have in place currently; what the coverage of corporations is in international human rights law; what the practical as well conceptual obstacles are to strengthening regulation and enforcement of human rights laws against corporations. In part too, the terms of his mandate directed him into the technical debate over the meaning of 'spheres of influence' and 'complicity'.[160] But for some, he has been too quick to throw the human rights baby out with the bath-water of the Norms' procedural infelicities.[161] And his recent dismissal of the prospects of any international initiative to plug the gap (which he acknowledges is there and is serious) left by inadequate or non-existent state-based hard and soft law regulation, as impolitic and impractical because it would be 'unlikely to get off the ground' (and even if it did, likely to be counter-productive),[162] is seen by some as appealing too much to corporate sensibilities. The SRSG prefers instead reliance on the 'protect, respect and remedy' framework he outlined in his third report to the Human Rights Council in June 2008.

In and of itself, this framework is unobjectionable, rightly urging the following: states to 'protect', by taking more seriously and implementing more thoroughly their obligations under international human rights law regarding corporate activities in their jurisdiction (my first possibility above); corporations to 'respect' rights, by which Ruggie means, ultimately, that failure to do so 'can subject companies to the courts of public opinion – comprising employees, communities, civil society, as well as investors – and occasionally to charges in actual [domestic] courts';[163] and victims to have access to 'remedies' that 'could include

---

160 On which see the three-volume report of the International Commission of Jurists' Expert Legal Panel on Corporate Complicity in International Crimes, *Corporate Complicity and Legal Accountability* (Geneva: International Commission of Jurists, 2008). In Volume I, the Report outlines the basic conditions (causation, knowledge and proximity) necessary to establish corporate complicity in human rights abuses under international and domestic laws, at p. 8 *et seq.*

161 See Amnesty International, 'Submission to the Special Representative of the Secretary-General on the issue of Human Rights and Transnational Corporations and other Business Enterprises', July 2008, at www.reports-and-materials.org/Amnesty-submission-to-Ruggie-Jul-2008.doc.

162 John Ruggie, 'Business and Human Rights: Treaty Road Not Travelled', *Ethical Corporation*, 6 May 2008, at www.ethicalcorp.com/content.asp?contentid=5887.

163 Report of the Special Representative of the Secretary-General on the issue of human rights and transnational corporations and other business enterprises, John Ruggie,

compensation, restitution, guarantees of non-repetition, changes in relevant law, and public apologies'.[164] But this framework with these features does not address the problem set out at the start of this section, namely, situations in which states are so weak or unwilling to protect human rights, and corporations are so comparatively strong or conveniently transnational to evade human rights responsibilities. Moreover, Ruggie's reasons for not backing further negotiations on an international treaty are unconvincing.[165] If we were always to back away from the invariably tough challenges of establishing new international human rights regimes merely because 'treaty-making can be painfully slow' and 'serious questions remain about how [any treaty obligations] would be enforced', as he argues,[166] then few if any of the human rights instruments that populate the post-war international law landscape of today would have made it beyond the stage of high-minded rhetoric. His additional contention that even to start down (once again) the treaty path would be to risk 'undermining effective shorter-term measures to raise business standards on human rights',[167] is logically difficult to comprehend. For those corporations that implement and abide by such measures already have nothing to fear from discussions at the international treaty-making level and would, in fact, surely welcome the opportunity to participate, and hopefully level the playing field to their advantage by bringing other corporations up to their own standards. For those corporations that do not so implement or abide by these standards, or worse, are steadfastly opposed to any moves to make them do so, they should have something to fear, and rightly so. If, logic aside, the argument here is simply that, in reality, many corporations (and states)[168] will not generally welcome discussions that have the possibility of a treaty on the agenda, then that is surely to lack boldness, where boldness is called for. Ruggie, after all, has made it clear that

---

'Protect, Respect and Remedy: A Framework for Business and Human Rights', UN Doc. A/HRC/8/5 (7 April 2008), para. 54.

164 *Ibid.* para. 83.

165 Responding to this statement in correspondence with the author (7 September 2008), Ruggie defended his decision by arguing that on balance he did not see it as the right time to pursue the international option as it would probably set back 'pull-effect' of the efforts of vanguard corporations to advance corporate respect for human rights.

166 Ruggie, 'Business and Human Rights'.   167 *Ibid.*

168 Though that would not include Australia it would seem, following the Rudd Government's recently declared willingness to back the 'development at the international level of standards and mechanisms aimed at ensuring that transnational corporations and other business enterprises respect human rights'; Oxfam Australia media release, 23 June 2008.

he sees 'no inherent conceptual barriers to States deciding to hold corporations directly responsible [for violations of international law] . . . by
establishing some form of international jurisdiction'.[169]

There is no shortage of thoughtful and carefully constructed guides as
to how and why to start down the road from concept to practice. Steven
Ratner, for example, charts the various forms in which international
law has already imposed, or been read to impose, legal duties directly
on corporations – from the war crimes cases of Nazi-supporting industrial conglomerates after the Second World War, through duties to respect
labour rights under the ILO, environmental obligations mediated by 'pol-
luter pays' and related notions, and international prohibitions on bribery
and corruption, to UN sanctions that encompass corporations, and the
vast array of legal obligations to which European corporations are subject under the EU's *sui generis* regime of international law.[170] Ratner sees
these instances as, together, forming a sound basis upon which to construct a theory of international legal responsibility for corporations that
might encompass the responsibility not to infringe human rights, albeit,
crucially, of necessarily limited scope. The nature and extent of a corporation's association with the state, its proximity (spatially and legally)
to the affected populations, the precise form of the substantive rights at
issue, and the need to take into account the peculiarities of corporate
structure when seeking to attribute responsibility, must, in Ratner's view,
curtail the scope of any international human rights law duties imposed
on corporations.[171] Larry Catá Backer's work provides another intelligent
guide in respect of the particular matter of what forms these international
human rights law obligations might take. Backer, rightly, sees the Norms
as but the first, flawed attempt to travel down the road. Their value, he
believes, are as a harbinger of changes, already apparent, in the ways corporations are having to operate, and as symptomatic of 'rearrangements
in the relative power of systems of domestic, international, public and
private systems of governance', by making more visible private economic
orderings that were previously invisible.[172] Neither Ratner nor Backer is
providing a fully signposted roadmap – nor does either seek to do so –

169 John Ruggie, 'Interim Report of the Special Representative of the Secretary-General
  on the Issue of Human Rights and Transnational Corporations and Other Business
  Enterprises', UN Doc. E/CN.4/2006/97 (22 February 2006), para. 65.
170 Steven Ratner, 'Corporations and Human Rights: A Theory of Legal Responsibility'
  (2001) 111 *Yale Law Journal* 443, at 477–85.
171 *Ibid.* 497–522.
172 Larry Catá Backer, 'Multinational Corporations, Transnational Law: The United
  Nations' Norms on the Responsibilities of Transnational Corporations as a Harbinger

but their work and that of others does set down markers indicating ways to move forward down what will, inevitably, be a long road.

It may be that with another three years (from June 2008) added to the term of his mandate, and the extension of the mandate itself regarding, in particular, the provision of 'concrete and practical recommendations on ways to strengthen the fulfillment of the duty of the State to protect all human rights from abuses by or involving transnational corporations',[173] the SRSG will be able to develop a consensus for a bolder foray into the international field. Whatever the case, it must be said that the success of any mission will rely on constructive roles being played by all the main interested parties to the debate. Geoffrey Chandler makes a typically politically savvy point in this respect when he remarks that:

> [t]he fulfillment of the special representative's mandate is wholly depen-
> dent on the support of three stakeholders – NGOs, companies and gov-
> ernments. He has for the moment skillfully defused the opposition of
> the corporate world. But the human rights NGOs remain aloof, though
> the cause of human rights has everything to gain from the fulfillment of the
> mandate. They have dithered for the two or more years of the post-Norms
> period without a clear objective or a coherent strategy.[174]

The SRSG remains the most obvious and best-equipped instrument for advancing intelligent, engaged and committed investigation of how to fill the regulatory gaps that exist between domestic and international laws in respect of transnational human rights breaches by corporations, as the patent need, from the victims' points of view, for effective action remains as dire as ever.

Conclusion

In a submission to the UN HCHR inquiry into corporations and human rights in 2004, the US Council for International Business stated that '[t]here is much that business has done and can do to help promote respect for human rights'.[175] This is true and reflects the tenor of this

of Corporate Social Responsibility in International Law' (2006) 37 *Columbia Human Rights Law Review* 287, at 293, and further 356–88.

173 Human Rights Council, *Mandate of the Special Representative of the Secretary-General on the Issue of Human Rights and Transnational Corporations and Other Business Enterprises*, Resolution 8/7 (18 June 2008), para. 4(a).

174 Geoffrey Chandler, 'Business and Human Rights: One Step at a Time', *Ethical Corpora-tion*, 5 October 2007; at www.ethicalcorp.com/content.asp?ContentID=5420.

175 United States Council for International Business, Submission to the High Commissioner for Human Rights for the report on the 'Responsibilities of Transnational Corporations

chapter: namely, that business and its evident attributes and outputs benefit human rights. However, not only can it and should it do more, but its abuses of human rights – inadvertent, by neglect or design – must be curtailed. As a matter of principle, these are non-negotiable precepts; as a matter of practice, much more needs to be done. Geoffrey Chandler again, with his unique qualifications as both a former senior executive (with Shell) and a leading NGO activist (with Amnesty International) and commentator, is clear about where, ultimately, the burden to act must lie:

> I believe that leadership should come from within the corporate sector. There is indeed moral leadership within individual companies. But there is no collective leadership. Even the best companies, knowing themselves to be human and fallible, are reluctant to stand up and preach to others. And the corporate sector is ill-served on moral issues by its representative institutions such as the International Chamber of Commerce.[176]

Chandler then adds:

> [t]he NGO movement therefore has an opportunity as never before to shape the future. It has yet to seize that opportunity. But that is the challenge.[177]

To complete the picture, one must also stress the singular importance of the role of states in urging, facilitating and, if necessary, coercing corporations better to protect and promote human rights, starting by demonstrating greater vigilance themselves in these respects. The front line will be in corporate boardrooms and management mindsets. Lawrence Mitchell, an eminent corporate law scholar, has argued that CSR and the human rights guarantees it encompasses must be 'something central to the corporation's business, not something the corporation does in addition to business',[178] and as such, he maintains, 'corporate management that looks to the best interests of the business over the long term will largely, if not completely, fulfil many of the goals of CSR'.[179]

Corporate mindsets are changeable in this regard, and, as we have seen, there has been evidence to prove this in recent years, from the now

and Related Business Enterprises with Regard to Human Rights', September 2004 at www.reports-and-materials.org/USCIB-submission-to-UN.pdf.

176 Geoffrey Chandler, 'Business and Human Rights – A Personal Account from the Front Line', *Ethical Corporation*, 11 February 2008, at www.ethicalcorp.com/content. asp?ContentID=5695.

177 *Ibid.*

178 Lawrence Mitchell, 'The Board as a Path toward Corporate Social Responsibility', in McBarnet *et al.* (eds.), *The New Corporate Accountability*, p. 280.

179 *Ibid.* p. 181.

significant involvement of TNCs in embracing CSR and human rights principles at the level of business strategy, engagement with CSR and human rights experts and organisations, and implementation of lessons learned in policies and practices. Significantly, the centrality of CSR to the health and welfare of the global economy was stressed by G8 Heads of State in both their 2007 and 2008 meetings.[180] Such outcomes are preferable to all interested parties – corporate, activist, state, and above all those whose human rights might otherwise suffer. In the end, therefore, underpinning all the initiatives canvassed in this chapter, what will serve human rights best in the field will be if corporations 'pray not for lighter burdens but for stronger backs'.[181] And it will be up to states both to insist upon and assist in the quest.

---

180 See G8 Summit Declaration, *Growth and Responsibility in the World Economy* 2007; www.g-8.de/Content/EN/Artikel/_g8-summit/anlagen/2007-06-07-gipfeldokument-wirtschaft-eng,property=publicationFile.pdf, paras 21–9; and G8 Hokkaido Toyako Summit Leaders Declaration, 8 July 2008, www.g8summit.go.jp/eng/doc/doc080714_en.html.

181 Attributed to Theodore Roosevelt.

5

Civilising globalisation ahead

Introduction

> The Earth is one but the world is not. We all depend on one biosphere for
> sustaining our lives. Yet each community, each country, strives for survival
> and prosperity with little regard for its impact on others. Some consume
> the Earth's resources at a rate that would leave little for future generations.
> Others, many more in number, consume far too little and live with the
> prospect of hunger, squalor, disease, and early death.

These are the opening words of the Brundtland Commission's Report
published in 1987.[1] They remain as true today as they did then. Our
social as well as physical environments sustain us, and the state of their
upkeep and care directly determines our communal and individual health
and well-being. The Brundtland Report placed great importance on the
global economy – how it is managed, as well as what, and how much,
it produces; on global food security; on the political interdependency of
governance, security, environmental protection and economic and social
development; on the normative authority of human rights;[2] and on the
practicability of legal and institutional structures to help realise these
outcomes and objectives. Even though the Brundtland Commission's
perspective on these matters was primarily an environmental one, the
themes it traversed of the interdependency of economic and social imperatives, the mediation of politics and law, and the over-arching objectives
of fairness and sustainability, are echoed in this book with its avowedly
human rights perspective. The protection and promotion of universal
human rights, I maintain, must be recognised not only as a key strategic
objective of the global economy, but also as an important tool in civilising the global economy on its way towards the goal. On the other side

---

1 The World Commission on Environment and Development, *Our Common Future* (1987),
  Australian edition (Melbourne: Oxford University Press, 1990), p. 71.
2 Including the fundamental human right that 'all human beings have the fundamental
  right to an environment adequate for their health and well-being'; *ibid.* Annexe 1, p. 392.

of the equation, I have argued for recognition, indeed appreciation, of the global economy's role in pursuing the ends aspired to by these same human rights standards.

It is an exercise in the mitigation and balance of these global forces, which, if not delicate, is certainly challenging. It is a grand conceptual problem that has enormously important policy and practical consequences, whether done well or badly. Richard Falk notes how, if done badly, it

> presages a generally grim future for human society, including the tendency to make alternative orientations towards economic policy appear irrelevant; to the extent believed, this induces a climate of resignation and despair. To the extent that normative goals continue to be affirmed within political arenas, as is the case to varying degrees with human rights and environmental protection, their substantive claims on resources are treated either as an unfortunate, if necessary, burden on the grand objectives of growth and competitiveness or as a humanitarian luxury that is becoming less affordable and acceptable in an integrated market-driven world economy.[3]

In the book thus far, I have focused on how and why this balancing exercise has been conducted in the past and present, and with what successes and failures. The situation for human rights *in* the global economy is not yet freed from Falk's twin fates of inadequate balance – that is, viewed as either burdensome or profligate – but such views are now increasingly seen as narrow-minded and wrong-headed within trade, aid and commercial circles. Conceptually, it may seem somewhat incredible that there should have to be such a battle of views in the first place, given what we have seen to be the broad social objectives that sit alongside the economic goals of global trade and aid as conceived in the modern era, and the enduring fact that corporations are ultimately social licensees. And yet we have seen that, between concept and practice, there lies, of course, much scope for distortions effected by political expediency, legal friability, institutional inertia and native human selfishness and guile. In the midst of these somewhat predictable circumstances, we must not succumb to what the inimitable Roberto Unger refers to as the 'dictatorship of no alternatives that characterizes life and thought today'.[4] In the context of my quest in this book, this translates into the imperative that we not loosen our grip on the essential notion that the economy is, ultimately, in the service of

3 Richard Falk, *Predatory Globalization: A Critique* (Cambridge: Polity Press, 1999), p. 128.
4 Roberto Unger, *Free Trade Reimagined* (Princeton: Princeton University Press, 2007), Preface.

societal goals, including and especially the protection and promotion of human rights, and not *only* in the service of its own, autopoietic goals of efficiency, growth and consumption, or 'making, getting and spending', as the economic historian David Landes straightforwardly puts it.[5]

In this concluding chapter then, I want to coalesce and coordinate the observations and arguments made thus far as to how economic globalisation civilises, while at the same time itself needing to be civilised, and to project what more must be done to exploit effectively and fully its beneficial impact on human rights. I do so through three organising themes: (i) revisiting and reasserting the necessary interdependence of the global economy and human rights, (ii) assigning appropriate responsibilities for ensuring the global economy's protection and promotion of human rights, and finally (iii) assessing the wider, global security implications of success or failure in pursuing the prescriptions for civilising globalisation set out in the book.

Interdependence

Amartya Sen's starting premise for his highly influential thesis on the interdependency of economic development and political freedom is that he seeks neither to defend nor to chasten free market ideology.[6] Markets are necessary, he ventures, but their development gains are both contingent upon, and instrumental to, enhanced personal and civil freedoms: 'economic unfreedom can breed social unfreedom, just as social or political unfreedom can also foster economic unfreedom'.[7] The social advances that economic growth can deliver (and redeliver in the rolling circularity of this relationship) have been acknowledged by some economic theorists (among those, at any rate, who have not 'turned to the mathematical rendering of economics as a science of rational choice'),[8] as well as human rights advocates and scholars. In neither case, however, has much particular attention been paid to the precise nature and causes of these advances in human rights terms. This is perhaps explicable, if not excusable, in respect of economists. One looks in vain, for instance, in Joseph Stiglitz's recent work, for any appreciation, let alone analysis, of

---

5 David Landes, *The Wealth and Poverty of Nations* (New York and London: W. W. Norton & Co., 1998), p. xi.
6 Amartya Sen, *Development as Freedom* (Oxford: Oxford University Press, 1999), p. 7.
7 *Ibid.* p. 8.
8 As Peter Dougherty labels it, in *Who's Afraid of Adam Smith? How the Market Got Its Soul* (New York: J. Wiley, 2002), p. 67.

the human rights implications of globalisation, or the role they might play in his six-part formula for 'reforming globalization' to make it 'work not just for the rich and powerful but for all people, including those in the poorest countries'.[9] But the absenteeism of such analysis in human rights literature is both more difficult to comprehend and more reprehensible. Typically, for many human rights commentators, improved economic preconditions are assumed rather than articulated, reasoned and justified, as Philip Alston has noted, for example, in his assessment of the barely bridged gap between the Millennium Development Goals and human rights goals.[10] There is, further, in human rights circles, a more dangerous, naïve tendency to ignore, resist or dismiss economic solutions to social problems if they are not explicitly couched in human rights terms. In his critique of the 'right to development', David Kennedy sees this insistence not only as an unnecessary distraction from the ultimate goal of poverty alleviation, but quite possibly as a serious strategic mistake, as the abandonment of economic debate will cede the playing field to 'neo-liberal players who do not see development as a special problem'.[11]

Important and intricate

From the human rights perspective, therefore, there is a need better to understand, express, exploit and regulate this interdependency, which need this book seeks to address. It is important that both the critical (normally the focus of human rights commentators) and the facilitative (normally the focus of economic commentators) dimensions of the relationship be realised and built upon. I have sought to combine these dimensions in my preceding critiques of the human rights relationship with the trade, aid and commercial pillars of the global economy, and am now concerned to draw out their collective lessons.

As noted in the first chapter, Adam Smith not only accepted that the market ought not to sell its soul to the devil of unalloyed economic efficiency, but rather insisted it should not do so by compelling it to

---

9 Joseph Stiglitz, *Making Globalization Work* (London: Penguin, 2006), p. 292. His reformatory formula addresses poverty, aid and debt relief, fair trade, unchecked market liberalisation, environmental degradation and weak global governance; see his overview in *ibid.* pp. 13–19.

10 Philip Alston, 'Ships Passing in the Night: The Current State of the Human Rights and Development Debate as Seen through the Lens of the Millennium Development Goals' (2005) 27(3) *Human Rights Quarterly* 755, as discussed earlier, in chapter 3.

11 David Kennedy, 'The International Human Rights Movement: Part of the Problem?' (2002) 15 *Harvard Human Rights Journal* 101, at 109.

recognise and respect the social ends it exists to serve. Capitalism's creation of the 'wealth of nations', in Smith's trenchantly argued view, is conditional on the 'moral sentiments' that necessarily both guide and justify the enterprise.[12] Economic commentators such as Peter Dougherty and Diane Coyle have argued, separately, that despite this perspective of the intellectual progenitor of market capitalism, its soul has been forgotten,[13] if not asset-stripped and sold off. 'Few economists since Smith have been as intent as he was to specify the moral and social implications of capitalism', as Dougherty laments.[14]

The voices of those economists who have invested their efforts to such ends have tended to be drowned out by the noise of the more scientifically based analyses of economics that distrust, dislike or dismiss precepts anchored in moral philosophy as well as any serious considerations of the manifold non-economic consequences of economic enterprise, on account of the distortive immeasurability of such externalities. The voices are there; it is just that they often run counter to the fashion of the discipline, and the hungry politicians, policy-makers, industrialists, financiers and merchants that are economists' avid consumers have been somewhat tin-eared to the messages these voices deliver. And yet the lineage has some pedigree. John Maynard Keynes's all-consuming professional passion to address the socially ruinous effects of rampant unemployment led him to countenance interventionist government strategies to stimulate supply-side economic expansion.[15] In their own different ways, both J. K. Galbraith and Robert Heibroner warned against the consequences of untrammelled capitalism. Galbraith extolled the importance of the regulatory authority of the state over corporations being used to ensure their success in the promotion of economic growth, which he considered to be the paramount social goal.[16] More radically, Heibroner highlighted the vital need 'to remedy the malfunctions of the economic process'. He argued further that, 'as we depart, little by little, from a philosophy of

---

12 Drawing on the subjects and titles of his two great works: *The Theory of Moral Sentiments* (1759) and *The Wealth of Nations* (1776).

13 Diane Coyle argues that the malaise is due to neglectful communication on the part of economists and how they present their discipline in public debate; in *The Soulful Science* (Princeton: Princeton University Press, 2007), chapter 9.

14 Dougherty, *Who's Afraid of Adam Smith?*, p. 64.

15 Which is the central thesis of his monumental *The General Theory of Employment, Interest and Money* (London: Macmillan, 1936).

16 J. K. Galbraith, *The New Industrial State* (Boston: Houghton Mifflin, 3rd edn 1967), pp. 182–3. Of the goal of economic growth, he asks, rhetorically, 'what other goal *could* be socially so urgent?', *ibid.* p. 183.

laissez faire and espouse a philosophy of active guidance, the question of social responsibility is inescapably thrust upon us'.[17] Joseph Schumpeter also believed in the need to invoke the visible hand of the state to steady capitalism's inherently unstable nature of 'creative destruction' which through perpetual short-term innovation has the potential to respond to human needs, while at the same time destroying the means to continue to do so.[18] Even Paul Samuelson – the doyen of mathematical economics – accepted the need for intervention where the free market fails, albeit insisting that such a course is sub-optimal.[19]

In political, philosophical and even legal terms the venture to impose human rights imperatives on the operations of the global economy must draw on and build upon these broad, social (or at any rate non-core economic) considerations, conditions and caveats.

As we have seen, the specifics of the relationship between human rights and the global economy are complex – the extent of shared normative principles, the compatibility of policy goals, and the practicability of outcomes, especially regarding the linking of causes to effects. The dynamics of the relationship are neither as simple as correlating economic expansion with growth in human rights protection, nor the inverse, that human rights are degraded as the economy grows. In rightly dismissing these two linear explanations Jeffrey Dunoff constructs an interesting alternative picture of the relationship 'as analogous to a double helix':

> [t]hat is, while the two regimes started at the same time and with many common political commitments, they quickly assumed different trajectories. At times they moved promisingly in the same direction. At other times, they intersected at cross purposes. [It] ... is a story of historical and political contingency, of important but tentative gains and missed opportunities.[20]

17 Robert Heilbroner, *The Worldly Philosophers: The Lives, Times, and Ideas of the Great Economic Thinkers* (New York: Simon and Schuster, 4th edn 1974), p. 319.
18 Joseph Schumpeter, *Capitalism, Socialism and Democracy* (London: Allen & Unwin, 4th edn 1961), pp. 81–6.
19 While discussing responses to market failure – or as he puts it, when 'optimum conditions are *not* realized' – Samuelson states: 'another example to show that the failure of some conditions necessitates alteration of the rest is provided by the possibility of increasing welfare by deliberately selling below marginal costs to groups with a high marginal (social) utility of income. Given a faulty distribution of income, this can improve the situation, although it would be still better to have the full optimum conditions realized'; Paul Samuelson, *The Foundations of Economics Analysis* (Cambridge, MA: Harvard University Press, 1971), p. 253.
20 Jeffrey Dunoff, 'Does Globalization Advance Human Rights?' (1999) *Brooklyn Journal of International Law* 125, at 132.

This is a more subtle and accurate representation of the situation, but it is also one that can be supplemented. The nature of the relationship between these helixical axes is very largely determined by the 'contingencies' made, or 'balances' struck, within the three particular spheres of (1) the economy, (2) government and (3) jurisdiction. The onset of the current worldwide recession brought on by the dramatic failures in the global financial markets in late 2008 has muddied the waters still further. For while the crisis has prompted governments to inject enormous stimulus packages into the hardening arteries of their stricken economies, and to toy with notions of trade protectionism as the pace of international trade slows, the consequences for human rights domestically and globally have been lamentably ill-considered.[21]

(1) A central challenge to both understanding and channelling economic success is 'getting the balance right between government and the market',[22] as Joseph Stiglitz puts it, echoing the concerns expressed by each of the titanic economic intellectuals listed above. This challenge entails not only optimising the proclaimed benefits of the public and private sectors, separately and together, but also managing the failures of both. For a quarter of a century, policies promoting trade liberalisation, privitisation and financial services deregulation have been invoked to address perceived government failures in economic management and service delivery: policies that constitute the very stuff of economic globalisation. As a consequence, both human rights gains and losses have been registered, and many more argued over, in terms of what is and what might yet be. On the other hand, when the market fails, human rights concerns (among many others) accrue and regulatory responses are advocated at national or international level, or both. The lingeringly malignant global food crisis is seen by many to be a prime example of market failure that threatens protection of the right to food: that is, the immediate problem of Western agri-businesses swapping production from staple foods to biofuels,[23] as well as the longer-term threat to food supplies posed by

---

21 The substantial background document provided for the much-vaunted G20 London Summit in April 2009 on planning for global stability and recovery, for example, contained not one mention of human rights, and distressingly scant consideration of what the crisis means for the world's poorest countries; UK Government, *The Road to the London Summit: The Plan for Recovery* (London: UK Government, 2009).

22 Stiglitz, *Making Globalization Work*, p. xv.

23 The UN's Food and Agriculture Organisation (FAO) notes the estimates by both the World Bank and the IMF that biofuel production had been responsible for up to 65 per cent of recent global food price hikes; see *Soaring Food Prices: Fact, Perspectives, Impacts and Actions Required* (April 2008), para. 9; at www.fao.org/fileadmin/user_upload/foodclimate/HLCdocs/HLC08-inf-1-E.pdf.

biotech companies taking advantage of patenting rights over certain vital strains of staple foods that threatens food supplies in the longer term.[24] And yet, proving the point of the intricacy of the public/private mix, the food crisis is one unquestionably exacerbated by the recent 'beggar-thy-neighbour' protectionist responses of the governments of some of the countries worst affected,[25] as well as by the entrenched, agricultural protectionist measures pursued by the US and Europe.[26]

The process of trying to get the economic balance right is, in fact, determined as much by political, policy and legal factors as by economic ones. For combined reasons of jurisdiction, authority, function and responsibility, it is the states that undertake the task, whether domestically, or collectively in the international realm. These additional factors comprise my second and third spheres in which 'balance' is sought.

(2) National governments are invested with both myriad functions and the powers in order to fulfil them. They acquit themselves, to widely varying degrees of efficacy and success, by mediating a host of competing interests and concerns including social and human rights, as well as economic and commercial. This is a simple but important point. For while throughout the book I have been at pains to stress the importance of the economy, it is an importance born of the utility of the economy to achieve social and specifically human rights goals, not merely because of the economy's intrinsic importance. So, no matter how large the economy looms in the eyes of governments, they have other constituencies to serve. Within the world of commercial enterprise such a breadth of vision,

24 See Action Group on Erosion, Technology and Concentration, *Patenting the 'Climate Genes'... and Capturing the Climate Agenda*, Communiqué, Issue 99 (May/June 2008), which notes that: 'the world's largest seed and agrochemical corporations are stockpiling hundreds of monopoly patents on genes in plants that the companies will market as crops genetically engineered to withstand environmental stresses such as drought, heat, cold, floods, saline soils, and more. BASF, Monsanto, Bayer, Syngenta, Dupont and biotech partners have filed 532 patent documents (a total of 55 patent families) on so-called "climate ready" genes at patent offices around the world'; at www.etcgroup.org/en/materials/publications.html?pub_id=687.

25 As the UN Special Rapporteur on the Right to Food, Olivier de Schutter, reported in May 2008, many countries across the globe – both least developed and developing states – were indeed increasing export restrictions to stem the outflow of staple foods. However, many were also reducing import restrictions on staple foods to increase their inflow; see *Analysis of the World Food Crisis*, Background Note, 2 May 2008, pp. 10–11, at http://cridho.cpdr.ucl.ac.be/documents/ONU-UN/SRRTFnotefoodcrisis3.PDF.

26 To which there is a rather novel, possible market solution as proposed by Eskil Erlandsson, Sweden's Minister for Agriculture, who argues that if Europeans (for example) want to continue to promote the food produced in a certain way or in certain regions then 'let them label it and see if the market will pay for it!' As reported in *The Economist*, 'Let Them Eat Cake', 24 May 2008, p. 64.

alas, is too often dismissed as immaterial or simply ignored – even, for example, by those whose declared intention it is to equip the next generation of business leaders with the tools to 'predict industry change'. This, for example, is the object of the third of Clayton Christensen's trilogy of influential books on innovation in business. In *Seeing What's Next*, Christensen, from Harvard Business School, together with co-authors Scott Anthony and Erik Roth, recognises that governments have 'stated goals ... to promote social welfare', yet in the authors' consideration of these in the context of 'non-market factors that affect innovation',[27] no mention whatsoever is made of such obvious factors as the protection and promotion of environmental sustainability, human rights, and international peace and security. Further, they reduce the role of government to nothing more than facilitator of commercial innovation, 'to encourage disruptive innovators [their term for those whose innovation radically alters the status quo] to form a new value network that can ultimately change the seemingly unchangeable industry'.[28]

Invoking the same cry for innovation, but in a more broadly framed and directed way, Bill Gates called for more 'creative capitalism', in a speech at the World Economic Forum in Davos in 2008. This, he argued, would 'stretch the reach of market forces so that more people can make a profit, or gain recognition, doing work that eases the world's inequities'.[29] Such creativity is necessary and desirable, but it is neither sufficient on its own, nor automatically self-generating. As so vividly illustrated by government responses to the economic crises and contractions in 2008/9, the hand of government, no matter how compromised, will always be necessary as mediator and regulator of the economy, alongside all other dimensions of the state's functions and responsibilities. The trick is to identify which demands are most important and then to satisfy them as well as possible relative to each other pressing demand, for in the end, as Edmund Burke reminds us, 'all government ... is founded on compromise and barter'.[30]

(3) The question of jurisdictional balance refers to the relative roles of international and domestic authority and capacity in devising objectives, setting standards, formulating policies, imposing duties and policing

27 Clayton Christensen, Scott Anthony and Erik Roth, *Seeing What's Next: Using the Theories of Innovation To Predict Industry Change* (Boston: Harvard Business School Press, 2004), p. 73.
28 *Ibid.* p. 92.
29 'Prepared Remarks by Bill Gates', Speech at the World Economic Forum, Davos, Switzerland, 24 January 2008, available at www.gatesfoundation.org/MediaCenter/Speeches/Co-ChairSpeeches/BillgSpeeches/BGSpeechWEF-080124.htm.
30 Edmund Burke, *Speech on Conciliation with America* (1775), ed. Albert Cook (New York: Longmans, Green & Co., 1896), p. 67.

outcomes that relate to economic and human rights issues separately and together; the whole gamut of governance, in other words, viewed from the perspective of legal competence. In respect of human rights, there is a tension between the two levels. When states sign and ratify international human rights covenants they indicate not only their apparent belief in the importance of such standards for all individuals within their jurisdiction, but also their apparent preparedness to be bound by the obligations imposed on them by these covenants. In this 'age of rights', to use Louis Henkin's immortal phrase,[31] universalised human rights standards developed over the past sixty years or so constitute a valid normative and structural counterpoint to the orthodoxy of the sovereign state. 'This development', as David Held sees it,

> is a significant indicator of the distance that has been travelled from the classic, state-centric conception of sovereignty to what amounts to a new formulation for the delimitation of political power on a global basis. The regime of liberal international sovereignty entrenches powers and constraints, and rights and duties, in international law, which – albeit ultimately formulated by states – go beyond the traditional conception of the proper scope and boundaries of states, and can come into conflict, and sometimes contradiction, with national laws.[32]

The state, then, as both chief protector against, and perpetrator of, human rights abuses, finds itself in an almost perpetual state of compromise and conflict with international human rights laws and institutions. This, in itself, is not necessarily a bad thing; at best it can be viewed as a dialogue across the international and domestic divide. What is important is to recognise that such a tension is an inevitable complicating feature of human rights enforcement, made all the more complex when the human rights impact of the pursuit of economic imperatives at both the international and national levels, and by way of both public and private entities, is taken in to account.

What is central to all three of these spheres is that, in the main, it is by way of the medium of the law and legal institutions that balance is sought.

Laws and institutions

The prosecution of the global economy and the protection of human rights standards are both highly regulated realms of endeavour. Thus, the 'free market' is, in fact, only free within certain regulated limitations:

---

31 Louis Henkin, *The Age of Rights* (New York: Columbia University Press, 1990).
32 David Held, *Global Covenant: The Social Democratic Alternative to the Washington Consensus* (Cambridge: Polity Press, 2004), p. 131.

international trade is governed by a plethora of regional and global trade agreements; the commercial enterprise of corporations is subject to a host of national laws, both territorial and extra-territorial; and, of course, the manner in which development aid promotes the market economy (through privatisation programmes, trade-promoting initiatives and private/public partnerships) is closely governed by the rules, policies and operational standards of the development banks and bilateral aid agencies. And, as we have seen, increasingly included in these rules and regulations are provisions aimed at better securing human rights objectives.

In respect of human rights themselves, there can be no doubt that their modern era, as heralded by the adoption of the Universal Declaration of Human Rights in 1948, has been dominated by law and legal institutions. There are, to be sure, other non-law dimensions of human rights that must not be forgotten amid the law's dominion over the 'defining, interpreting and implementing of an ideal', as Başak Çalı and Saladin Meckled-García describe it,[33] but though these authors and others have stressed this danger, it should not be exaggerated. Led for many years now by such publications as the *Human Rights Quarterly*,[34] there is already a substantial body of literature dedicated to the interdisciplinary study and analysis of human rights, and certainly it is my experience within the practice of human rights education and training, in both developed and developing states, that the social, cultural, economic and above all political dimensions of human rights are registered as fundamental rather than as mere 'footnotes'.[35]

Most important of all, however, in respect of both the legal regulation of the economy and human rights, is the fact that laws and the institutions that make them and enforce them are not hermetically sealed

33 Başak Çalı and Saladin Meckled-García 'Introduction: Human Rights *Legalized* – Defining, Interpreting and Implementing an Ideal', in Saladin Meckled-García and Başak Çalı (eds.), *The Legalization of Human Rights* (London: Routledge, 2006), p. 1.
34 The journal's mandate declares that it offers 'scholars in the fields of law, philosophy and the social sciences an interdisciplinary forum in which to present comparative and international research on public policy within the scope of the Universal Declaration of Human Rights'. It was first published in 1979 (under the title *Universal Human Rights*), since when a number of other multidisciplinary human rights journals have joined the field.
35 This is a term used by Çalı and Meckled-García, in *The Legalization of Human Rights*, p. 2. Representing something of my own views on this necessary breadth of conception of human rights see: David Kinley, 'The Legal Dimension of Human Rights', in Kinley (ed.), *Human Rights in Australian Law* (Leichardt: Federation Press, 1998), p. 1; David Kinley and Trevor Wilson, 'Engaging a Pariah: Human Rights Training in Burma' (2007) 29(3) *Human Rights Quarterly* 368; and David Kinley, 'Human Rights Fundamentalisms' (2007) 29(4) *Sydney Law Review* 545.

from the forces that created them and that they in turn are designed to regulate. Law and legal institutions are themselves social phenomena that represent, respond to and reflect economic imperatives, community pressures, cultural mores and political interests. Law is at base more art than science; no matter its past pretensions to the latter. Even within the various legal communities themselves – legal practitioners, law-makers, courts and academics – this is now widely (if incompletely)[36] recognised as being the case in theory and practice.

As a process by which to facilitate better relations between the ways and means of the global economy and international human rights standards, and especially by articulating the ground rules for their engagement, mutual understanding and reasonable expectations, the law has great utility at a number of levels. Strategically, it promulgates normative principles against which the actions of the institutions of the global economy can be judged and justified. Substantively, it provides a set of agreed definitions (albeit necessarily imprecise), as to minimum standards for the treatment of individuals. Notably, as Jack Donnelly observes, 'claims of legal rights can accomplish things that cannot be done through claims even of substantively identical moral rights', such that 'human rights advocates and victims of violations often will prefer the agreed-upon legal definition'.[37] It is the legal format that gives human rights their character of obligation and capacity for enforcement, 'by the coercive power of the state',[38] including, crucially, against culpable arms of the state itself, which represents an essential feature of the notion of the rule of law. Law in this form, argues Anthony Woodiwiss, is 'a means of both constraining and facilitating political and especially state actions . . . [and] also a self-limiting activity in that it is rule-bound as well as rule-enforcing'.[39]

In their respective conceptual approaches to the rule of law, the globalising fields of the economy and human rights tend to subscribe more attentively to different features of the ideal: the former to the certainty and predictability of legal process; the latter to the fairness and equality of legal substance. I have previously argued that in practice the two diverge much less and that what is more important is that both fields

36 Some of the more detailed analyses of statutory interpretation and the application of precedent argued by counsel appearing before, and in the judgments of, common law superior courts might constitute exceptions to this rule in the eyes of many who have to read them.

37 Jack Donnelly, 'The Virtues of Legalization', in Çalı and Meckled-García (eds.), *The Legalization of Human Rights*, p. 69.

38 As Tom Campbell puts it; *Rights* (London: Routledge, 2006), p. 87.

39 Anthony Woodiwiss, 'The Law Cannot Be Enough', in Çalı and Meckled-García (eds.), *The Legalization of Human Rights*, p. 34.

not only accept but rely upon the regulatory forces exerted by the rule of law to achieve their ends.[40] This common ground not only provides further basis for building a 'mutually beneficial alliance' through law; it also, crucially, establishes the framework within which to ascribe responsibilities to ensure such an alliance works. This is a matter of pressing and gargantuan concern. The UN's Commission on Legal Empowerment of the Poor, for example, estimates that some 4 billion people worldwide live outside the rule of law, many of whom are already disadvantaged through poverty, discrimination or marginalisation. The consequences, it notes, of inadequate or non-existent legal systems are especially grave in both economic and human rights terms.[41]

Responsibilities

Having reviewed the importance of the interdependency of human rights and the global economy, I move now to extrapolating conclusions regarding the assignment of responsibilities specifically for making the economy work for rights. I do so, of course, by drawing directly on the analyses of the human rights relationship with the three dimensions of the global economy considered in the preceding chapters. Thus, at the broadest level of conception, it is maintained that the principal actors and agents of economic aid, trade and commerce are required to recognise the human rights implications of their actions, and expected, in certain significant respects, actively to protect and promote human rights standards. At the same time, the actors and agents of human rights advocacy have responsibilities both to recognise the necessity of the economic pretext to human rights protection, and to accept that there must be limits to human rights obligations that can be reasonably and efficaciously imposed on the institutions of the global economy.

If globalisation has promoted one aspect of modernity above all others, it is the sense and evidence of the dynamic interconnectedness of nearly all dimensions of public life. The neat post-war apportionment of institutional functions, powers and duties no longer (if it ever did) reflects practice on the ground. Danny Bradlow and Claudio Grossman, among the earliest and most perceptive writers in the area, noted in their seminal review of the problems that these jurisdictional pressures pose for international financial institutions (IFIs, specifically the World Bank and

---

40 David Kinley, 'Human Rights, Globalization and the Rule of Law: Friends, Foes or Family?' (2002–3) 7(2) *UCLA Journal of International Law and Foreign Affairs* 239.
41 Commission on Legal Empowerment of the Poor, *Making the Law Work for Everyone*, Vol. 1 (New York: UNDP, 2008), especially chapters 2 and 3.

the IMF) that '[t]his results in most international organizations seeking to solve the problems of the late twentieth and early twenty-first centuries with the institutional arrangements that were designed for a bygone era'.[42] The interconnectedness they rightly characterise as endemic means that

> the IFIs cannot address the problem of poverty or the monetary problems of developing countries without considering the issues of refugees, environmental degradation, the capacity of the state to effectively and equitably manage its resources, population policy, and human rights, including the status of women, indigenous people, and minorities. Environmentalists cannot seek resolution of environmental problems without addressing issues of refugees, information flows, population, and even security concerns. Trade organizations can no longer effectively regulate trade without seeking agreement on environmental issues, labor policy, investment matters, the regulation of intellectual property (which in itself raises important cultural rights issues), and regulation of trade in services (which also raises important monetary, financial and immigration policy questions). Human rights organizations cannot seek effective protection of human rights without considering the impact of poverty, foreign investment, trade and environmental degradation.[43]

All that said, however, it is a grave mistake to conclude that all these global institutions and organisations must transform themselves into polymath functionaries, striving to implement mandates of impossible breadth and often incompatible, if not contradictory, substance. There is already considerable 'goal congestion', as Michael Barnett and Martha Finnemore put it.[44] Trade organisations must remain focused on trade, aid agencies on development assistance, and corporations on commercial enterprise. But their individual impacts beyond their particular field of focus cannot simply be ignored, dismissed as irrelevant or dumped in the 'too hard' basket. Attribution of responsibility for the consequences that can be fairly said to be caused by their actions must be pursued, no matter the difficulties, political and/or legal. At this point in the book, I feel compelled to ask how it can be otherwise, given what I have sought to demonstrate and argue in the preceding chapters.

---

42 Daniel Bradlow and Claudio Grossman, 'Limited Mandates and Intertwined Problems: A New Challenge for the World Bank and the IMF' (1995) 17(3) *Human Rights Quarterly* 411, at 412.
43 *Ibid.* 414–15.
44 Michael Barnett and Martha Finnemore, *Rules for the World: Institutional Organizations in Global Politics* (Ithaca, NY: Cornell University Press, 2004), p. 64. The authors write: 'Conscientious bureaucrats quickly recognize that to accomplish a great many of the ambitious social tasks we set them, they need to reach outside the narrow compartments in which we place them. On the one hand, this is good. . . . On the other hand, this process can quickly come to resemble pulling on a loose thread.'

It is not as if such a proposition to ascribe responsibilities in this respect is unprecedented. We do not have to start completely afresh. The seeds of renewal were planted long ago in the form of the objectives and expectations that have been made of the global institutions and actors that are discussed in this book. A striking feature of the mandates of the global economic behemoths established at the conclusion of the Second World War,[45] as well as those, such as the WTO, set up since, is their respective levels of concern to achieve broad social goals by way of better economic management, including, directly or indirectly, human rights guarantees. The idea of a social licence to operate extended to corporations is also taking hold in corporate thinking. A recent report from a conference of the influential Caux group of global business leaders called on business for more long-term thinking about what contributions businesses can make to societies and referred grandly to the need 'to restore human rights as an absolute and intangible value for the whole of humanity'.[46] And states themselves are still publicly keen to commit themselves – as did so many in the Monterrey Consensus on Financing for Development in 2002 – to 'eradicate poverty, achieve sustained economic growth and promote sustainable development as we advance to a fully inclusive and equitable global economic system'.[47] Certainly, therefore, there is no shortage of profound statements articulating laudable aspirations and goals, but what yet remains to be seen is evidence of their sustained translation into practice. And for that to occur, responsibilities must be clearly assigned, acknowledged and acted upon.

Levels of responsibility

Throughout the book we have encountered, time and time again, three dichotomies of mooted responsibility.

---

45 And even before the war, as evidenced by the 1939 report of a Special Committee of the League of Nations on the Development of International Co-operation in Economic and Social Affairs (the 'Bruce Committee'), Doc. A/23/1939, which stressed the importance of economic and social interdependency on a global scale to the maintenance of peace, order, stability and freedom. The report's message was, with supreme irony, obliterated by the outbreak of the Second World War shortly after its publication, though it did form the basis for the establishment of the Economic and Social Council of the United Nations in 1945.

46 'Global Business Leaders Call for the Re-establishment of Trust', Press Release, 12 July 2008, at www.caux.ch/en/2008/news/6242.html.

47 Report of the International Conference on Financing for Development, Monterrey, Mexico, 18–22 March 2002 (A/CONF.198/11), para. 1. The report notes that 50 heads of state and more than 200 ministers took part in the conference.

The first and most basic of these has been the legal/non-legal binary. In fact, much of the debate about the nature of the responsibilities that institutions of the global economy hold, and should or could hold, in respect of human rights is expressed in non-legal terms. Allusions, usually somewhat vaguely articulated, are often made to the moral, ethical, political or even functional duties of IFIs, the WTO, and other similar bodies, as well as TNCs, in the midst of critiques of their individual actions. Certainly, as we have seen, detailed cases are also made out as to their specific legal duties, but it is noteworthy that these are nearly always couched within broader, rhetorical frameworks, reflecting the fact that in the arena that is the concern of this book, the battle is at least as much one of political hearts and minds as it is about defining legal mandates. Thus, for example, stock exchange regulations requiring listed corporations to make certain disclosures regarding their social and environmental policies evolved out of the surge in ethical investment;[48] the WTO's backing of the human rights conditionality of the preferential trade programmes that the EU and the US establish with poor states[49] grew out of the general discussions about how to accommodate exceptions to trade liberalisation for the sake of developing countries; and the increased incidence of aid programmes focusing on the protection and promotion of human rights reflects the impact of the burgeoning debate over human rights based approaches to development. The political and moral accompaniment to these regulatory arguments is also a reflection of the fact that, in respect of all three areas of the global economy, legal mandates as to human rights responsibilities are incomplete, imprecise or missing altogether. In so far as responsibilities are presented in legal terms, there are then two further dichotomies.

These two legal dichotomies are in fact closely intertwined. One represents the differences between hard and soft law responsibilities; that is, more particularly, the differences between duties couched explicitly in law (such as legislation, binding international instruments or judicial pronouncements), and duties which, though exerting some indirect or quasi-legal force of compliance by way of codification or standardisation of practice, nonetheless lack express, binding authority (such as

---

48 As the Conseil des Barreaux Européens – Council of Bars and Law Societies of Europe – notes: 'All French corporations listed on the Paris Stock Exchange are required to report on the sustainability of their social and environmental performance. There are also similar developments taking place in a number of other countries'; *Corporate Social Responsibility and the Role of the Legal Profession: A Guide for European Lawyers, Update No.2 (June 2008)*, p. 16 (footnote 17).
49 As discussed in chapter 2, pp. 85–9.

codes of practice, guiding principles or norms, and operational policies or standards). The other dichotomy focuses on the distinctions between obligations imposed by international or domestic law.

Soft law instruments exist at the levels of both domestic and international law. However, in the context of my present concern, it is in the international sphere that soft law has attracted particular attention. International law tends always to be much less 'hard' than domestic law. As the result, typically, of enormous cultural, political and economic compromise, international law is by nature more aspirational, less precise and conditionally enforceable (that is, generally speaking, only with the assent of the subject nation states themselves). The room for soft law is therefore correspondingly greater. The tension this situation gives rise to between hard and soft law is no more clearly demonstrated than by the highly charged debate surrounding whether, and if so how, international law can be used to regulate the activities of TNCs that affect human rights.

As charted in chapter 4, one of the key points of disagreement in this debate pits those who believe that international law can and must move away from its state-centric orthodoxy in order to impose human rights obligations directly on 'non-state international actors' such as TNCs, against those who reject such reasoning on grounds of international law jurisprudence and practicability. Both sides accept the need for soft law codes, norms, principles and guidelines. But the latter (mostly corporations) see these private and essentially voluntary initiatives as sufficient, while the former (mostly human rights advocates) insist that such voluntarism alone is inadequate and the solution lies, in part, in the crystallisation of soft laws into hard laws.[50] Normally, such codification of private agreements into public regulation occurs at the level of domestic law because that is where political pressure can be more effectively exerted and domestic regulation is also nearly always a more precise and powerful instrument than international law.[51] International law's inherent limitations in substance and process inhibit its capacity to portray

---

50 On which process, in respect of international law generally, see Martin Totaro, 'Legal Positivism, Constructivism and International Human Rights Law: The Case of Participatory Development' (2008) 48(4) *Virginia Journal of International Law* 720. Totaro makes the important point that 'the sociopolitical process of pushing toward the legalization of a moral norm can be a vibrant, robust procedure that need not make the mistake of improperly and prematurely according legal status to a norm still in the adolescent stage of rights formation under international law'; *ibid.* 720.

51 Though Muchlinski has convincingly argued that such a process can and is occurring in the international arena in respect of various corporate social responsibility standards; see Peter Muchlinski, 'The Development of Human Rights Responsibilities for MNEs', in Rory Sullivan (ed.), *Business and Human Rights* (Sheffield: Greenleaf Publishing, 2004), p. 33, at p. 51.

such classically 'hard law' features as enforceability. And as domestic law is typically loath to tread (extra-territorially) in the transnational arena, so, in terms of hard law at least, a legal gap is created. This is precisely the position that the debate over the human rights responsibilities of TNCs now finds itself in, in respect especially of what could and should be done with the UN's human rights norms for corporations.

At the level of the implementation of international human rights obligations, the balance between public and private responsibilities, is, in principle, straightforward. The orthodox position holds that international law directly binds the state (and all its public or even quasi-public emanations), and that domestic laws that transpose the international law into the national legal setting directly bind all relevant bodies, whether public or private, within its jurisdiction. The grey area between these black and white poles of direct responsibility comprises the instance and extent of *in*direct responsibility. Within international human rights law there has developed a significant line of jurisprudence that attributes to states responsibility for certain human rights abuses perpetrated by private, non-state entities, on the ground that such an indirect responsibility falls within the international obligation imposed on states to ensure the protection of human rights of all those within their jurisdiction. If a state fails to do so in circumstances where it would otherwise be reasonable to expect it to have acted in a way so as to prevent or prohibit the violation, then it has been made clear by such august tribunals as the European Court of Human Rights and the Inter-American Court of Human Rights that the state may be held to have transgressed its own direct duty to protect under international law.[52] Similarly, as states comprise the membership of inter-governmental organisations (IGOs) such as the UN, the WTO, the World Bank, the IMF and many others, their direct responsibilities under international human rights law affect, indirectly, the ambit of the IGOs especially in so far as the mandates of any of these bodies impact in practice on the protection and promotion of human rights. Even apparent setbacks in multilateral relations, such as the repeated collective failures of states to conclude the Doha Round of trade negotiations and the economic and social consequences that flow therefrom, underscore rather than undermine the continuing importance of the responsibilities of state actors.

---

52 See, respectively, the cases *Costello-Roberts v. UK* ECt.HR (1993), Ser. A, Vol. 247 (question of state responsibility for action of a private school) and *Velásquez Rodríguez v. Honduras*, Inter-Am.Ct.H.R. (1988) (Ser. C) No. 4 (question of state's responsibility for actions of vigilantes operating in its territory).

The centrality of the state

It is fashionable in the human rights and global economy milieu to focus on the responsibilities of the myriad non-state actors in the transnational field – especially international institutions, TNCs and international advocacy groups and NGOs. They are, relatively speaking, the new kids on the block; the expectations that are made of them in human rights terms are not yet fully understood, let alone precisely stated and regulated in law. The complexity of the situation is, as Andrew Clapham claims, due to a combination of the foundational difficulty encountered in trying to distinguish clearly non-state from state entities in terms of their status, functions and activities; the still evolving and ill-formed nature of the human rights obligations of non-state actors; and the variability of those obligations according to context.[53]

The attention, therefore, is not surprising, and indeed the matter of what their human rights responsibilities should be is manifestly important, as I have made clear throughout this book. However, not only does the state remain the key actor in the field, albeit alongside others; it constitutes the most appropriate, accessible and powerful forum within which to generate suitable regulatory responses. States have to be at the centre of any effort to impose human rights responsibilities on corporations (even if the impetus for such regulation is generated – as has in fact been largely the case – by debates within and between business, civil society, academics and certain international institutions), by way of domestic regulation. And equally, as states are the progenitors, bursars and final arbiters of the international bodies that populate this arena, so they have the authority, if not necessarily either the individual or collective will, to determine the nature and extent to which the protection of human rights ought to be a part of the objectives of the major international economic institutions. The state may be, as Friedrich Nietzsche put it, 'the coldest of all cold monsters',[54] but against his and others' fervent wishes it remains with us. What is more, we still appear very much to need it, as much, at least, as it needs us.

It is, I believe, in this symbiosis that there lies the scope for the state's essential guardianship of human rights within the context of the global economy. Working on the particular planes of the economic development

53 Andrew Clapham, *Human Rights Obligations of Non-State Actors* (Oxford: Oxford University Press, 2006), p. 561.
54 Friedrich Nietzsche, *Thus Spoke Zarathustra*, trans. R. J. Hollingdale (Harmondsworth: Penguin, 1969), p. 75.

of poor countries, and the governance problems of failed states, respectively, Dani Rodrik, and Asharf Ghani and Clare Lockhart see the vital role of the state in terms of gaps or failings in the way states work. Rodrik talks of an incipient crisis in the governance of the global economy – 'a no-man's world', he calls it – where jurisdictionally limited state institutions fail to support adequately globalised markets, at the same time as these very institutions are weakened 'by the desire [of] producers and investors to go global'. The first failure 'inhibits efficiency', while the second weakness 'inhibits equity and legitimacy', according to Rodrik.[55] Moreover, he adds that this dilemma is much more serious for developing countries, 'since they have weak institutions to begin with'.[56] Ghani and Lockhart, on the other hand, in their ambitious treatise *Fixing Failed States*, talk of a 'sovereignty gap' which, for seriously dysfunctional states, exists between international theory and domestic practice. This is a 'disjunction between the *de jure* assumption that all states are "sovereign" regardless of their performance in practice – and the de facto reality that many malfunctioning or collapsed states [are] incapable of providing their citizens with even the most basic services, and where the reciprocal set of rights and obligations are not a reality'.[57] The result, again, is one in which the very desperation of the present circumstances effectively throttles the institutional processes that one might expect to mount a revival.

Not only, then, is the global economy failing the least developed and the worst governed states, but, evidently, they are abjectly neglecting to protect their own peoples' human rights. All states – that is, those failing badly as well as those failing less badly, and those succeeding – are implicated here; all bear responsibilities to varying degrees for remedying human rights infringements and helping to protect them better in future. This, after all, was the broad object of what Henri Laugier in 1946 called the UN's 'very great enterprise' of establishing universal human rights standards,[58] and it is the practical essence of the philosophical argument of cosmopolitanism, which makes the legitimacy of statehood conditional

55 Dani Rodrik, *One Economics, Many Recipes* (Princeton: Princeton University Press, 2007), p. 196.
56 *Ibid.*
57 Asharf Ghani and Clare Lockhart, *Fixing Failed States* (New York: Oxford University Press, 2008), p. 21.
58 Summary Record of the First Meeting of the Commission on Human Rights, 29 April 1946, UN Doc. E/HR/6, at p. 1. Laugier was then the Assistant Secretary General for Social Affairs in the newly formed United Nations. I am indebted to John Pace for alerting me to this characterisation.

on, inter alia, respect for fundamental rights of the populace.[59] Human rights constitute the 'grammar of governance', as Upendra Baxi labels it,[60] providing both inhibitions to state power by demarking its legitimate boundaries, and facilitation of state power by underscoring its authority and responsibility to protect and promote the rights of the people the state represents.

By stressing the vital role of states in both the shouldering and assignment of responsibility for the protection of human rights within global economic relations, I want to bear out two fundamental points. One is that the states must take the cosmopolitan message of universal human rights standards seriously in their prosecution of government. The other is that while the state may necessarily be the final arbiter of what legal responsibilities ought to be borne by the other, non-state actors in the field, the latter are not somehow let off the hook. As we have seen in the previous chapters, they all already have certain legal human rights responsibilities albeit that, they are circumstantial and various, more than express and certain; they are increasingly subject to political, ethical and social expectations as to how they execute their specific mandates in trade, aid or commerce; and perhaps most importantly of all, some of their number already recognise these imperatives to some degree, and have taken steps accordingly.

Responsibility framework – principle, policy and practice

What all of this boils down to is a general framework of responsibility within the global economy: that is, a framework based on elemental demands made at the levels of principle, policy and practice, which apply, in different combinations, to all duty-holders, whether state or non-state, economic or human rights oriented.

---

59 Fulfilment of which gains you entry to the 'sovereignty club'. 'Membership in international society is conditional upon a State's professed respect for human rights', as Tony Evans puts it, in 'International Human Rights Law as Power/Knowledge' (2005) 27 *Human Rights Quarterly* 1046, at 1047. There are problems as well as possibilities with this approach, in terms of: international politics, as discussed by Evans at 1047 *et seq*; philosophy, as discussed by David Kinley, 'Human Rights Fundamentalisms', 567; and institutional legitimacy, as discussed by Philip Alston, 'Beyond "Them" and "Us": Putting Treaty Body Reform into Perspective', in Philip Alston and James Crawford (eds.), *The Future of UN Human Rights Treaty Monitoring* (Cambridge: Cambridge University Press, 2000), p. 501.

60 Upendra Baxi, *The Future of Human Rights* (New Delhi: Oxford University Press, 2002), p. 8.

In respect of 'principle' – there is the fundamental and abiding responsibility for all sides to the debate to understand each other's position. This does not entail, of course, wholesale or even substantial agreement on all matters, but it does mean that parties must sincerely engage with one another and seek common ground where at all possible. As I have already made clear, we are moving beyond the sterility of entrenchment where economic actors maintain that human rights are simply outside their remit and human rights advocates argue that the free market economy is essentially detrimental to their objects.[61] But strains of such untenable positions are still encountered in dialogue as well as (more often) in monologue, and there remains scepticism on both sides as to how the two disciplines can be more fully integrated to their mutual satisfaction. Mindsets must be addressed, and key actors encouraged to be more open and receptive. Few Chinese corporations, for example, even those forming part of supply chains linked to Western TNCs, have any clear understanding of what CSR entails and why it is important.[62] This is perhaps not surprising given the country's brief exposure to modern capitalism and its government's recalcitrant attitude towards such notions as transparency and accountability, as well as towards the protection of individual rights. But it is a problem of understanding and education for all corporations doing business in and with China.[63] Such disjunctures in understanding in situations where governments are either ineptly weak or repressively strong take time to repair. It is 'a slow evolution', as Jorge Daniel Taillant notes in his review of the impact of international development finance on human rights and development in Latin America, even in the region's post-dictatorship era. Both corporations and communities, he points out, have a hard time understanding precisely how human rights relate to their relationship when for so many decades they have associated the notion of

---

61 Which stances are worthy of the same put-down as Arthur C. Clarke's reputed, inimitable response to being asked what he thought of the many reports of UFOs – namely, that 'they tell us absolutely nothing about intelligence elsewhere in the universe, but they do prove how rare it is on earth'; as reported by *The Economist*, Obituary of Arthur C. Clarke, 29 March 2008.
62 It was noted in a 2005 *McKinsey Quarterly* survey of 4,238 global business executives, that in terms of countries/regions Chinese executives were the 'most lukewarm' towards notions of CSR; 25 per cent of them felt that the role of large corporations should focus solely on maximising investor returns, as compared to only 10 per cent of executives in India who believed this, and 16 per cent in the survey as a whole. See 'Global Survey of Business Executives', *McKinsey Quarterly*, January 2006, 5.
63 See Christine Bader, 'Business and Human Rights: Corporate Recognition and Responsibility', 2008 (1) *China Rights Forum* 7.

human rights with their egregious violation perpetrated by repressive dictators. Taillant maintains that '[t]o take the human rights discussion out of the civil and political rights realm relative to dictatorial regimes, and to break into grounds involving many economic, social and cultural rights, as well as civil and political rights, that corporations may be impacting or violating, will take significant evolution of the social mindset into more progressive understandings of what human rights are about'.[64]

The picture is varied, of course, within the commerce and human rights world, as well as throughout trade (where the requirement to understand is at a more basic philosophical level) and aid (in which context human rights are, at least, more familiar). But across the board, the principle of what the global economy can and should do for human rights together with an understanding of the in-built limitations of such expectations are essential first steps for all participants.

Regarding 'policy' – flowing directly from these responsibilities of principle are certain broad policy implications. The most important of all of these is the need to have human rights standards play a substantive role in the formulation of economic policy. The opportunity is there when one considers such oft-repeated statements as that made by Ben Bernanke, Chairman of the US Federal Reserve Bank, who, while extolling the enormous overall benefits yielded by globalisation, urged policy-makers 'to ensure that the benefits of global economic integration are sufficiently widely shared'.[65] Certainly, there is an onus on the types of economic actors highlighted in this book to entertain the prospect, but it is also incumbent on those advocating such a role to ensure that their arguments promote distinct policy options rather than merely restating in human rights terms what is already evident in social or even economic policy terms. Human rights arguments must add value to the policy debate. As Andrew Lang cleverly argues, they need not themselves spawn fully formed policy proposals, but when human rights are used as a basis for intervention in, for example, trade policy discussions they must, at least, 'provid[e] a trigger for policy learning and helping to create the conditions in which learning is more likely'; and must act, as he continues, 'as

64 Jorge Daniel Taillant, 'International Development Finance and Global Governance: Human Rights and Sustainable Development' (2007) p. 11; paper prepared for joint workshop on global administrative law issues in Latin America, University of San Andrés and New York University Institute for International Law and Justice, Buenos Aires, 9–10 March 2007; paper on file with author.
65 As reported in 'Economic Focus: On the Hiking Trail', The Economist, 2 September 2006, p. 62.

an impetus for the evolution of ideas about what is rational and desirable trade policy'.[66]

The added value that human rights might bring in this way to policy development would assist in addressing the problems of fragmentation of international law (and, necessarily, of the policies that inform it). The International Law Commission's Fragmentation Report identifies the tendency to fragment international law into regimes or clusters of speciality that are caused by and lead to zealous defences of territory – precisely the sort of segregation in respect of human rights and economic relations that this book argues is not just undesirable, but unsustainable. The need to be vigilant against over-specialisation in international law and to desegregate where necessary must be supported – indeed, even instigated – by the greater melding of international policy-making, in both multilateral and bilateral relations.[67]

Regarding 'practice' – the fundamental responsibility is to find ways to exploit in practice the permeability of the policy walls that separate the apparently discrete matters of human rights and the global economy, and between each of the main components of the latter. The burgeoning cross-fertilisation of language, approaches and even objectives is all well and good, but it comes to nought if the effects are not implemented on the ground. The key here is securely to link principle and policy to practice. As we have seen, there is in fact no shortage of practical initiatives that coalesce, or claim to coalesce, the two fields, from corporate codes of conduct, health and education programmes, to human rights conditionality in trade, and aid programmes promoting child welfare, women's rights or care for the disabled. But where these are ad hoc responses, born of some specific contingency or circumstance (corporate reputational damage or the political exigencies of government); or where, despite promoting a defined policy, the policy lacks consensus (for example, aid or trade conditionality); or perhaps worst of all, where the initiative is more spin than substance (such as that which motivates many of the nearly 4,500 corporations that have so far signed up to the Global Compact), then the efficacy of the programme is compromised.

---

66 Andrew Lang, 'Rethinking Human Rights and Trade' (2007) 15 *Tulane Journal of International and Comparative Law* 335, at 401.

67 *Fragmentation of International Law: Difficulties Arising from the Diversification and Expansion of International Law*, Report of the Study Group of the International Law Commission, finalised by Martti Koskenniemi, UN Doc. A/CN.4/L.682 (13 April 2006), see para. 24.

Thus, for example, the separation of issues into discrete policy portfolios that is so typical of domestic governmental bureaucracies can have a profound and lasting impact on the way such issues are advanced domestically and internationally. For when national privatisation programmes are drawn up, or international trade deals negotiated without adequate input on the social implications of such initiatives, *because* the responsible line-agencies are comprised, respectively, of competition and trade specialists, then naturally enough health, safety, educational, environmental, discrimination, and many other rights issues may not feature large, or at all, in the process. Western trade negotiators, as Joseph Stiglitz bluntly puts it, 'are trying to help producers, and their job is to get as much as they can. [They] have little incentive to think about the environment, health matters, or even the overall progress of science.'[68]

Another responsibility at the level of practice is to provide, to all actors and participants in debate over human rights and the global economy, the evidentiary means by which principles can be made clearer and policies can be better supported. And yet there is, as Michael Ignatieff and Kate Desmormeau have noted,[69] a dearth of instruments and initiatives that measure the effectiveness of human rights programmes in anything like the way in which economists measure (albeit still imperfectly)[70] the efficacy of their actions. The two fields are different, of course, but for the human rights lobby not to seek more assiduously to address this gap, while at the same time ceding ground to others (economists, development specialists, and governance analysts), is to undermine in practice a cause that is well made at the level of principle.

Freedom, development *and* security

There is a lot at stake in the fulfilment of these various responsibilities. The human rights implications, both positive and negative, of a widening

---

68 Stiglitz, *Making Globalization Work*, p. 131.

69 See Michael Ignatieff and Kate Desmormea, 'Introduction', in the Carr Centre Project Report, *Measurement and Human Rights: Tracking Progress, Assessing Impact*, Kennedy School of Government, Harvard University, Summer 2005; the authors ask: 'why have we [the human rights movement] been so slow to develop other indicators of progress based on actual human rights outcomes?', pp. 1–9, at www.hks.harvard.edu/cchrp/pdf/Measurement_2005Report.pdf.

70 As James Tobin remarked in his Banquet speech marking the occasion of his award of the Nobel Prize for Economics in 1981: 'We cannot make controlled experiments. We cannot be sure that the structure that generates our observations is constant in time and space. And as my great teacher, Joseph Schumpeter, said, a subject so close to politics and policy inevitably blends ideology and science'; 10 December 1991, at http://nobelprize.org/nobel_prizes/economics/laureates/1981/tobin-speech.html.

and deepening global economy are profound. They relate to just about every aspect of individual and collective social existence and effectively underpin our freedom, welfare, developmental prospects and security. The integrated role that the relationship between human rights and the global economy plays in the widest context of our security in the era of globalisation has long been recognised, touching most especially on 'security' in economic, environmental, and individual or personal terms, as well as in the more orthodox terms of state security. Former UN Secretary-General Kofi Annan famously remarked in his epochal *In Larger Freedom* Report in 2005, that 'we will not enjoy development without security, we will not enjoy security without development, and we will not enjoy either without respect for human rights. Unless all these causes are advanced, none will succeed.'[71] This was a self-conscious echo of the sentiments and intentions of the early days of the UN as expressed in the UN Charter and the Universal Declaration of Human Rights.[72]

It is in this broad context that I conclude this chapter, and the book, by underlining the wider implications of my argument to civilise globalisation by way of the twin objectives of harnessing globalisation's potential as a force for good, while constraining its potential as a force for bad. In this respect I am as concerned with what we stand to lose if the project fails, whether through mendacity, ignorance, arrogance or neglect, as with what we stand to gain if it succeeds.

Security – global, state and individual

Peace, order and security are desirable goals as well as means that themselves facilitate economic growth and prosperity and the enhancement of human rights standards. But today, security means much more than peaceful streets and secure borders. The current fixation with security is in respect of nearly all matters of political governance and social existence: economic, environmental, population and demography, individual or human, and of course national or state. As such, it provides a timely as well as vital spectrum through which to consider the implications of getting the balance right between human rights and the global economy. Security in all these aspects can be seen as striving to guarantee certain market fundamentals, to maintain domestic order and international

71 Kofi Annan, 'In Larger Freedom: Towards Development, Security and Human Rights for All', Report of the Secretary-General, UN Doc. A/59/2005, at para. 17; www.un.org/largerfreedom/contents.htm.

72 Part of the Preamble to the UN Charter declares that 'We the people of the United Nations determined . . . to promote social progress and better standards of life in larger freedom.'

comity, and to protect people's individual rights. There are also potentially enormous security consequences at all levels flowing from the economic, social and individual effects of climate change, and the projections of unprecedented growth in global population. The UNDP, for example, stresses how it is inevitable that the poor will suffer most from the developmental and human rights consequences of climate change and how, thereby, inequality between the rich and poor (countries and individuals) will be further entrenched.[73] Serving to emphasise such impact, both the UN Population Division and the US Census Bureau have, in recent years, revised upward their projections on population growth, having previously, for many years, consistently revised their projections downwards. Thus, as of 18 June 2008, the US Census Bureau estimated that by 2050 the world's population will have grown by more than 40 per cent of today's total – that is, from 6.7 billion to 9.5 billion.[74]

The importance of security so broadly conceived is evident when one considers the economic and social benefits that accrue to states that enjoy high levels of individual and collective security, in contrast to those that do not. Noteworthy in this respect is the success of the EU expanding hugely its jurisdictional cloak of security through shared interests and mutual dependency from its initial very particular economic concerns of coal and steel, to its grand concerns today of government en masse – trade, monetary policy, labour regulation, citizenship, environmental protection, human rights standards, legal and justice systems, and even security policy. Today, the practice of the EU pays very real homage to the prescriptions of Immanual Kant two centuries earlier, that durable peace could be built upon the tripod of representative democracy, international organisations and economic interdependence.[75]

The very fact of this mutual reliance, that can so profit the interests of human rights, economic prosperity and security, can, conversely, swing the pendulum in precisely the opposite direction should one or other of

---

73 See the UNDP, *Human Development Report 2007/08: Fighting Climate Change: Human Solidarity in a Divided World* (Basingstoke and New York: Palgrave Macmillan for the UNDP, 2007).

74 US Census Bureau, International Data Base, table: 'Total Midyear Population for the World: 1950–2050' (18 June 2008), available at www.census.gov/ipc/www/idb/worldpop.html. This is in fact a marked deceleration in growth, as compared to the massive increase in the fifty years between 1950 and 2000 when the world's population more than doubled from 2.5 billion to 6 billion; *ibid.*

75 Which are the words and imagery used by Douglas Irwin in his summary of the import of Kant's essay *Perpetual Peace* (1795); see Douglas Irwin, *Free Trade under Fire* (Princeton: Princeton University Press, 2002), p. 50.

the three supports weaken. John Prendergast of the International Crisis Group paints a lamentable picture of the downward spiral of despair that grips much of Sub-Saharan Africa as a consequence of lawless insecurity taking hold:

> the horrors continue to grab the headlines. With millions of Africans on the knife's edge of daily survival, vulnerability is extreme. Some countries are beset by war and organized criminal networks that control all the political power and economic opportunities. International and regional piranhas – including neighboring governments, rebel groups, multinational corporations and arms dealers – fund predatory militias to help them gain control over the production and distribution of diamonds, oil or other prized commodities. In the absence of effective governing institutions and in the face of a global economy stacked against them, conflict-ridden African countries are easily sucked into free-for-alls to determine who controls the few avenues for wealth creation.[76]

Empirical data back up both the plight of such failed or fragile states and the comparative success and solidity of thriving states. Nearly all democracies and emerging democracies enjoy economic prosperity (if not necessarily equitably distributed), relative security and good human rights records. With the exception of security and human rights related problems in Israel, these are all recognisable features of the top fifty states in the UNDP's Human Development Index 2007/08, which, in addition to per capita GDP, measures states' life expectancy rates, literacy rates, and levels of school and university enrolments.[77] In contrast, the bottom fifty states (with the possible exception of India which is a democracy, has a strong emerging economy and is relatively secure) are all severely hampered by various combinations of poverty, human rights abuses and either too much 'security' (in authoritarian regimes such as in Myanmar, Laos and Zimbabwe) or too little (where there is serious civil unrest such as in the Democratic Republic of Congo and Sudan).[78] There are, of course, exceptions to these rules in respect of the nations in between for many and various reasons, but the rules stand nonetheless as a good guide. Freedom House, a US based organisation that has been annually measuring political rights and civil liberties across the globe since 1971, has noted in one of its more recent reports that 'there is growing evidence

---

76 'Unraveling the African Tragedy', *Los Angeles Times*, 9 December 2004, available at www.crisisgroup.org/home/index.cfm?id=3158&l=2.

77 UNDP, *Human Development Report 2007/08*, table 1, 'Human Development Index', at pp. 229–32.

78 *Ibid.*

that most countries that have made measured and sustainable progress in long-term economic development are also states that respect democratic practices',[79] and, it can be added, have higher levels of respect for and protection of human security.

Fortune and freedom, it seems, favour those societies whose social, economic and political houses are in order. Yet, the fragile vitality of the interdependency of human rights and the global economy can be tested and torn when security breaks down, or indeed even when it is merely threatened. The obscenity of conspicuous wealth alongside abject poverty, for example, is not just shocking but destabilising, whether at the local level of slums abutting the walled compounds of the wealthy, or at the international level of tensions between neighbours North and South Korea, or South Africa and Zimbabwe. 'A cesspool of misery next to a world of growing prosperity is both terrible for those in the cesspool and dangerous for those who live next to it', as Paul Collier astutely remarks.[80] Though the threats to security are perhaps less obvious, gross inequalities in rich democracies can also sow seeds of discontent. The gargantuan vulgarity of the salary packages that some executives receive compared with those of their employees, or indeed of other professionals, has been a matter of simmering resentment at least since the day in 1994 when Cedric, a 280 lb pig, was paraded at the annual meeting of British Gas in London in protest over executive pay.[81] Recent US Congressional Committee hearings on executive compensation served both to illustrate the level of disquiet, and to expose the discomforting consequences of such pay deals, including, it must be said, the remarkable spectacle of executive representatives sincerely attempting to rationalise their circumstances.[82] Average real pay of workers in wealthy countries

79 Freedom House, *The Worst of the Worst: The World's Most Repressive Societies, 2008*, p. 2, at www.freedomhouse.org/uploads/special_report/62.pdf.

80 Paul Collier, *The Bottom Billion: Why the Poorest Countries Are Failing and What Can Be Done about It* (New York: Oxford University Press, 2007), p. 99.

81 Francesco Guerrera, 'Gentlemen, Please Empty Your Pockets', Corporate Finance, Special Report, *Financial Times*, 26 March 2008, p. 1.

82 See House of Representatives, Committee on Oversight and Government Reform, Hearing on 'CEO Pay and the Mortgage Crisis' (7 March 2008); the tone of the inquiry was apparent from the opening gambit of Harry Waxman, the Chair of the Committee, who pronounced that 'our subject is the compensation of executives who preside over billion-dollar losses. There seem to be two different economic realities operating in our country today, and the rules of compensation in one world are completely different from those in the other. Most Americans live in a world where economic security is precarious and there are real economic consequences of failure. But our Nation's top executives seem to live by a different set of rules'; transcript, p. 3, at

has, in fact, been stagnating or falling in recent years,[83] and for some states – most glaringly perhaps the US – the poor are actually growing in number. The US Census Bureau calculates that in 2006 more than 37 million people (12 per cent of the total population) were living beneath the official poverty line[84] (a figure that will surely have grown and will grow further with the current economic slump in the US economy), and according to the UNDP's latest Human Development Index, the US, of all Western countries, has the largest percentage of its population (17 per cent) living on less than 50 per cent of the nation's median income, and is therefore only marginally better than Russia (18.8 per cent).[85] Such statistics represent manifest encroachments on the economic and social rights of the poor living in rich states and as such ominously portend the fracture of the human rights/economy/security nexus in those states.

Where, however, security collapses altogether into armed conflict, the costs are both immediate and lasting. In human terms, the direct costs are manifest – the death, mutilation and mental scarring of combatants and civilians, and for the latter the appalling ripple effect that encompasses population displacement, sexual violence and exploitation, hunger and disease, and the conscription of child soldiers.[86] In economic terms, it is perhaps the consequent or indirect costs that are most damaging. In relation, particularly, to internal conflicts (which now predominate in figures on instances of conflict across the globe), the structure of economic enterprise is torn apart by the warring factions; children are deprived of education, individuals lose jobs, families are forcibly relocated, trade and businesses collapse; foreign and domestic investment dries up, and the organs of state warp and disintegrate.[87] The turmoil is quickly compounded on all fronts – economic, political and social – by the reactions of the global markets to situations of armed conflict, which is (by and large)

http://oversight.house.gov/documents/20080422110749.pdf. Global business leaders at a 'Caux – Initiatives for Change' conference in July 2008 called for a review of the runaway problem of executive compensation and 'the need to define a ratio of executive pay to that of the lowest paid'; 'Global Business Leaders Call for the Re-establishment of Trust', Press Release, 12 July 2008, at www.caux.ch/en/2008/news/6242.html.

83 'Economic Focus: On the Hiking Trail', *The Economist*, 2 September 2006, p. 62.
84 US Census Bureau, Current Population Reports, P60–235, *Income, Poverty, and Health Insurance Coverage in the United States: 2007* (2008), p. 12.
85 UNDP, *Human Development Report 2007/08*, table 4, 'Human and Income Poverty: OECD Countries, Central and Eastern Europe and the CIS', p. 241.
86 See Human Security Centre, *The Human Security Report 2005: War and Peace in the 21st Century* (New York and Oxford: Oxford University Press, 2005), Parts III and IV.
87 See, for example, Paul Collier, 'On the Economic Consequences of Civil War' (1999) 51 *Oxford Economic Papers* 168.

to by-pass the nation or nations involved. This is a serious problem, for as *The Economist* rightly remarks, 'whatever the problems of globalisation, they are dwarfed by the penalties of being untouched by it'.[88]

The illicit economy

Not all economic interests, however, desert conflict situations. Some are positively attracted to such circumstances, whether because of the nature of the conflict itself (as is the case with private security firms for example), or because of perceived opportunities flowing from the informalisation of the economy. In any event, the human rights consequences of such economic activity can be profoundly adverse. An excellent 2006 survey commissioned by the Norwegian Fafo Foundation of the links between commerce, crime and conflict in sixteen countries concluded that:

> [t]he evidence of recent years is conclusive: market-based economic activities – both licit and illicit – can sustain and benefit from conflict and human rights abuse, engender crippling levels of corruption, contribute to the loss of sovereign control over a nation's wealth and undermine social and economic development.[89]

Globally, illicit trade and commerce are huge and endemic, and though their adverse impact on human rights is apparent in many ways – consider the direct and indirect losses that people suffer through extortion, exploitation, corruption, theft, trafficking, enslavement, discrimination, political disenfranchisement, and physical abuse and death – it is almost impossible to quantify the full extent of the problem. The annual State of the Future Report in 2007 calculated, tentatively, that the total annual income of transnational organised crime 'could be well over $2 trillion, giving it more financial resources than all the military budgets worldwide'.[90] What drives such illicit trade is not 'low morals', as Moisés Naím astutely notes, but 'high profits'.[91] In their pursuit of profit, therefore, there is a natural inclination even for legally established entities to stray into the realms of illegality. This is reprehensible, of course, when

---

88 'Somewhere over the Rainbow', *The Economist*, 26 January 2008, p. 27.
89 Mark Taylor, 'Preface' to Anita Ramasastry and Robert Thompson, *Crime, Commerce and Conflict: Legal Remedies for Private Sector Liability for Grave Breaches of International Law*, Fafo Report 536 (Oslo: Fafo, 2006), p. 5.
90 Jerome Glenn and Theodore Gordon, *2007 State of the Future*, UN Millennium Project (New York: World Federation of UN Associations, 2007), p. 3 and fig. 12; at www.millennium-project.org/millennium/sof2007.html.
91 Moisés Naím, *Illicit* (London: Heinemann, 2005), p. 239.

the action is blatant, such as breaching trade sanctions as the Australian Wheat Board did in respect of the UN's Oil for Food Program for Iraq in the late 1990s and early 2000s,[92] an episode of skullduggery, incidentally, that comprised trade, aid and commercial interests. But it is, in fact, the more covertly illegal actions of corporations that are most damaging. According to Raymond Baker, no less than 60–65 per cent of all illicit global money transfers today comprise commercial tax evasion, which in broad terms operates consistently and prodigiously to the benefit of the rich (countries and people) at the expense of the poor.[93]

The private sector in public wars

The traditional roles of the public and private sector in conflict zones are being reconfigured – whether expanding, merging or exchanging. In particular the state's 'monopoly of the legitimate use of physical force', as Max Weber famously put it,[94] is increasingly being contracted out. For much of the duration of the war waged by the coalition forces in Iraq, the estimated number of employees engaged by private security contractors has been between 20,000 and 30,000,[95] representing 'a continuation of a trend', as a Congressional Research Service paper notes, 'that has seen the increasing growth – by many nations and organizations, including the United Nations – of the use of private contractors to provide security, as well as a variety of other functions in support of stabilization and reconstruction efforts'.[96] The dangers posed by the very nature of the work

92 Australian Government, *Report of the Inquiry into Certain Australian Companies in Relation to the UN Oil-for-Food Programme* (November 2006) (Cole Inquiry Report); www.offi.gov.au/agd/WWW/unoilforfoodinquiry.nsf/Page/Report.

93 'Illicit Money Transfers Deny Justice to the Poor', Media Release, Caux – Initiatives for Change, 12 July 2008, at www.caux.ch/en/2008/news/6243.html. Baker was reported as saying at a Caux conference that the conservative estimate of the total of such money transfers is in the range $1–1.6 trillion. Other 'criminal activities' (especially drug trafficking), he noted, made up the balance of such transfers – 30–35 per cent. Baker was here drawing upon and updating the research data contained in his highly acclaimed book *Capitalism's Achilles Heel: Global Illicit Financial Flows and How To Renew the Free-Market* (Hoboken, NJ: John Wiley and Sons, 2005).

94 Max Weber, *Politics as a Vocation* (1919), in Hans Gerth and C. Wright Mills (eds.), *From Max Weber: Essays in Sociology* (London: Kegan Paul, 1947), p. 78.

95 See Congressional Research Service, *Private Security Contractors in Iraq: Background, Legal Status, and Other Issues* (11 July 2007), p. 3. The report notes that these security personnel are part of the 182,000 individuals in Iraq now 'employed under U.S. government contracts to perform the spectrum of functions once carried out by U.S. military personnel', *ibid.*

96 *Ibid.* p. 2.

(which ranges from full combat missions, through guarding prisoners, to protective security for individuals and installations) are compounded by the lack of clear lines of responsibility. Not only have there been many cases of civilian deaths, injuries, assaults and intimidation due to the excessive or uncontrolled nature of actions taken by these private military corporations in conflict zones all over the world since the mid 1990s,[97] but many of their own employees have been killed. In Iraq, for example, the redoubtable advocacy organisation Human Rights First has estimated that around 1,000 private security personnel have lost their lives since 2003 (as compared to 4,000 deaths in the US military), and some 12,000 injured.[98] The same report repeats the growing concerns over how to control private security firms when traditional lines of accountability are so inadequate. For such firms are not considered to be public agencies, nor are they even quasi-public militias, and nor are they outlawed (under international law) as mercenaries. Rather, they are 'just' corporations under contract to the state.[99] Contract law, criminal laws (both international and domestic), military laws, possibly constitutional and administrative laws, and even human rights laws[100] may have some bearing on how the contractors operate and what responsibilities they bear, but the main problem is that there is a patent lack of political commitment to have this piecemeal approach bound into some more coherent and effective regulatory whole.[101]

At the same time, troops today are expected to act increasingly as peace-keepers, nation builders and even essential service providers, rather than as purely defensive or offensive combatants. The maintenance of strong military presences after the main 'theatre phase' of a conflict has ended, as in countries like Afghanistan and Iraq, obliges the military to play a

97 Oliver Jones, 'Implausible Deniability: State Responsibility for the Actions of Private Military Firms' (2007), unpublished paper (on file with author).

98 Human Rights First, *Private Security Contractors at War: Ending the Culture of Impunity* (New York: Human Rights First, 2008), p. 5, www.humanrightsfirst.org/us_law/pmc/pages.asp?country=us&id=10&misc1=exec-sum.

99 In respect of the problems encountered in trying to use international law to bring these entities to account, see *Report of Expert Meeting on Private Military Contractors: Status and State Responsibility for their Action*, convened by the University Centre for International Humanitarian Law, Geneva (August 2005), at www.adh-geneva.ch/events/pdf/expert-meetings/2005/2report_private_companies.pdf.

100 In the UK, for example, the House of Lords has recently ruled that the *Human Rights Act (1998)* applies extra-territorially in respect of military actions (and therefore possibly also those taken by private actors in the state's employ) undertaken overseas: *Al-Skeini and others v. Secretary of State for Defence* [2007] UKHL 26 (13 June 2007).

101 See, for example, the failures of the US Administration (and especially the Department of Justice) in respect of contractors operating in Iraq at present, Human Rights First, *Private Security Contractors at War*, pp. 23–31.

greater civilian role even while continuing combat actions in guerrilla warfare.[102] Expectation, indeed even reliance, on this post-conflict role of the modern military is problematic for civilian governments and their citizens, as well as for the military itself. The US Defence Secretary Robert Gates, for example, warns against the grave danger of having military action spearheading foreign policy in respect of fragile or failed states, when in fact such action should be subordinate to political and economic initiatives. 'We cannot kill or capture our way to victory', he announced in July 2008, underlining the point.[103]

The trade, aid and commercial arms of the global economy all have vital parts to play in post-conflict situations, even if they are difficult to define precisely and to coordinate on the ground, if the necessary political, social and legal institutions and practices are to be re-established and have any chance of operating successfully. But here, just as much as in situations where there was no preceding conflict, the economy's role has to be managed, its modus operandi defined (even if defined liberally) and regulated, and its outputs exploited effectively and fairly.[104]

'It's more than the economy – stupid!'

The channelling of the interdependency of human rights and the global economy to the best effect of the former relies very largely on the presence of earnest political will in both domestic and international forums. To be sure, the mediation of public power by government authorities is subject to all sorts of private influences and vested interests to act or not to act in certain ways, albeit that these differ between political structures and from country to country. Regarding the economy, trade liberalists, corporations and states themselves (individually or collectively) have many views, of course, as to which levers to pull, how, when and why. But whatever these opinions might be, no appeal can be legitimately made to the need to prefer the economy over human rights.

---

102 See Steven Bullimore, 'The Military's Role in Nation-Building: Peace and Stability Operations Redefined', Pentagon Report, No. A756844, 16 March 2006, at www.stormingmedia.us/75/7568/A756844.html.

103 Ann Scott Tyson, 'US Warning on Foreign Policy "Militarisation"', *Guardian Weekly*, 25 July 2008, p. 10.

104 For it is not just a question of curbing excesses; equally, as Peter Davis argues, it can be just as critical to ensure that the potential of (for example) the private sector in post-conflict renewal is not '*under*-utilised'; 'Post Conflict Development – Successful Companies Learn from Wider Debates', *Ethical Corporation*, 13 May 2008, at www.ethicalcorp.com/content.asp?ContentID=5908.

Throughout the book I have been adamant that the economy is a necessary ingredient in the human rights recipe, but not sufficient. John Stuart Mill and Adam Smith, the intellectual titans of liberalism who laid so much of the philosophical foundations of modern economic thought and practice, believed that the economy was but a means to greater ends. For Mill, 'the economical advantages of commerce are surpassed in importance by those of its effects which are intellectual and moral',[105] and Smith was adamant that while the benefits that commerce can bestow on individual freedom may be the 'least observed' advantage of commerce, they are 'by far the most important of all [its] effects'.[106] These are clarion calls that must be heard and heeded above the din of the market.

The protection and promotion of human rights are not optional extras in the political economy. Such tasks constitute the very fabric of what legitimises government and provides meaning and object for the nourishment of robust economic relations. Not economic myopia, nor political expediency, nor moral cowardice can ever excuse, let alone justify, treating human rights in any way less than as the principles upon which human beings are together bound, and individually respected. Since the dawn of the modern globalised age of human rights after the Second World War, not only has the presence and stature of human rights grown tremendously in the laws and relations within and between states, but their integration into the operations and even design of global economic intercourse has been made increasingly relevant and apparent. Certainly, there are debates, arguments and stand-offs between parties as to whether and how precisely the major global economic actors (including and especially states) should be made to acquit their responsibilities in this regard, more fully and fruitfully. But the idea that somehow global economic relations might be best quarantined from apparently non-economic concerns like human rights standards, and that, therefore, such debates are irrelevant or illegitimate, must now be seen for the sophistry it really is. 'The simple fact of the matter is', as Kofi Annan has remarked, 'if we cannot make globalization work for all, in the end it will work for none.'[107] The task

---

105 John Stuart Mill, *Principles of Political Economy* (1848), introduced by Sir John Lubbock (London: George Routledge and Sons, 1891) p. 394.

106 Adam Smith, *An Inquiry into the Nature and Causes of the Wealth of Nations* (1776) ed. R. H. Campbell, A. S. Skinner and W. B. Todd (Oxford: Clarendon Press, 1976), Volume I, p. 412.

107 Kofi Annan, 'Globalization Must Work for All', Address to the World Economic Forum, Davos, Switzerland, 30 January 2001.

before us is how to reconcile differences and create consensus, without resiling from the principle that respect for human rights is the ultimate foundation upon which rests the legitimacy of the actions of our governments, our international institutions, our corporations and business enterprises, our organs of civil society, and ourselves, presently and in future.

INDEX

economy, global (*cont.*)
  conditional dependency relationship
    with human rights 26–32
  conflict with human rights 23–36
  de-colonisation as factor in growth
    of 7
  economic interdependence as
    foundation for security 230
  economic policy, human rights role
    in forming 226–7
  future prospects for human rights
    emphasis 204–37
  growth of 14–18
    human rights implications of
      228–9
  historical factors in growth of 7–9
  historical role of trade and
    diplomacy 6
  human rights, and 1–36
  'humanisation' of, 'Geneva
    consensus' for 54
  illicit economy, effect of 234–5
  influence on states 19
  innovation, societal benefit from
    211–12
  interconnectedness resulting from
    globalisation 216–17
  interdependence with human rights
    204–5, 206–16
  international organisations as factor
    in growth of 7
  language in economic statements,
    importance of 32–6
  language of human rights,
    appropriation of 35–6
  liberalism as factor in growth of
    7–9
  mediatory role of states between
    human rights and 18–23
  moral dimension of 207–9
  necessity to human rights 238
  post-conflict situations, role in 237
  poverty 210–11
  priority of human rights over 237
  pro-globalisation arguments 24–5
  regulation of international
    organisations' promotion of
    29–32

  relationship to human rights 1–3
    complexity of 3–6, 207–13
    regulation of 213–16
  reliance on law 215–16
  right to globalisation, idea of 34–5
  service to societal goals, in 20–6
  social dimensions of, reports on
    29–30
  states' relationship to 223–4
  states' role in growth of 17–18
  technological advances as factor in
    growth of 7
Ecuador, pollution lawsuit against
  Chevron 161–2
'enabling environment' for human
  rights, TNCs' contribution to
  158–9
Enhanced Integrated Framework for
  trade/human rights dialogue
  60
environment
  Ecuador's pollution lawsuit against
    Chevron 161–2
  human rights issue, as 72–5
  language of human rights statements
    on 33–4
  legislation, effect of BIT stabilisation
    clauses 174–5
  mismanagement of, human rights
    and 20
  weak protection of, corporate abuse
    where 161–2
Equator Principles 102, 139, 171–3,
  181
ethical investment, role of 219
European Convention on Human
  Rights 1950 (ECHR) 11
European Union (EU)
  challenge to US ban on trade with
    Myanmar 80
  coalitions of countries in opposition
    to 66
  conditionality in preferential trade
    programmes 219
  expansion of security 230
  GSPs 85–90
  international constitutionalism of
    61

transnational corporations (*cont.*)
  human rights law relating to
    corporations law, use of
      189–90
    differences between home and
      host state laws, dealing with
      188–97
    extending extra-territoriality of
      189–93
    extent of 187–8
    forum non conveniens, use of 190
    'forum shopping' by victims of
      abuse 191–2
    international regulation,
      prospects and schemes for
      195–201
    pressure on states to improve
      189
    tort liability, use of 189
    transnational codes of conduct,
      use of 192–4
    universal jurisdiction, use of
      190–1
  image, importance of 167–8
  impact on human rights 148–9
  increase in human rights emphasis
    by 156–7
  influence on human rights, hard law
    and soft law approaches to
    regulation of 187–200
  international law applied directly to
    220–1
  Myanmar, remaining in 5
  NGO's role in influencing 202
  philanthropy of 185
  policy statements on human rights
    by 168–9
  political involvement of 167–8
  power of, extent of 163–6
  primary and secondary
    considerations of 166–8
  profit motive, restraint on 166–8
  progress towards greater human
    rights emphasis 201–2
  regulation of, strength of legal
    149
  regulation of relationship with
    human rights 177–9

  'reputation risk', importance of
    avoiding 156
  right under BITs to initiate
    arbitration proceedings against
    states 173–4
  role in trade 37
  size of 164
  social welfare concerns of 32
  society's responsibility to regulate
    behaviour of 159–60
  stabilising force, as 158–9
  states' motivation for intervention in
    activities of 160–3
  states' role in influencing 202–3
  subjection to human rights
    infringing policies of states
    162–3
  subjection to regulation 159–60
  UN Global Compact, corporate
    signatories to 168
  UN Human Rights Norms for 196–7
  UN Norms on human rights
    responsibilities of 181
  understanding positive and negative
    impacts on human rights of
    157–8
'triple bottom line' 183
Tuna/Dolphin cases 72–3

United Kingdom (UK)
  CBI, reference to domestic human
    rights law by 187–8
  'corporate code of conduct'
    legislation 190
  DFID's approach to HRBA 123
  Ethical Trading Initiative Base Code
    181
  official development assistance,
    levels of 113
  private giving from 100
United Nations (UN)
  Charter 11, 12
    human rights mandate 52–3
    power to impose sanctions under
      78
  Commission on Legal
    Empowerment of the Poor
    216